Canon® EOS 7D Mark II

FOR DUMMIES®

A Wiley Brand

by Doug Sahlin

Canon® EOS 7D Mark II For Dummies®

Published by: **John Wiley & Sons, Inc.,** 111 River Street, Hoboken, NJ 07030-5774, www.wiley.com

Copyright © 2015 by John Wiley & Sons, Inc., Hoboken, New Jersey

Published simultaneously in Canada

For general information on our other products and services, please contact our Customer Care Department within the U.S. at 877-762-2974, outside the U.S. at 317-572-3993, or fax 317-572-4002. For technical support, please visit www.wiley.com/techsupport.

Wiley publishes in a variety of print and electronic formats and by print-on-demand. Some material included with standard print versions of this book may not be included in e-books or in print-on-demand. If this book refers to media such as a CD or DVD that is not included in the version you purchased, you may download this material at http://booksupport.wiley.com. For more information about Wiley products, visit www.wiley.com.

Library of Congress Control Number: 2014957117

ISBN 978-1-118-72290-9 (pbk); ISBN 978-1-119-04958-6 (ebk); ISBN 978-1-119-04962-3 (ebk)

Manufactured in the United States of America

SKY10057443_101323

Contents at a Glance

Introduction 1

Part I: Getting to Know Your Canon EOS 7D Mark II 5
Chapter 1: Exploring the Canon EOS 7D Mark II 7
Chapter 2: Automatically Capturing Great Photographs.........................47
Chapter 3: Specifying Image Size and Quality 65
Chapter 4: Using the LCD Monitor...75
Chapter 5: Shooting Pictures and Movies with Live View.......................95

Part II: Going Beyond Point-and-Shoot Photography.... 115
Chapter 6: Getting the Most from Your Camera 117
Chapter 7: Using Advanced Camera Features.....................................147
Chapter 8: Mastering Your EOS 7D Mark II.......................................187

Part III: The Part of Tens 217
Chapter 9: Ten Tips and Tricks..219
Chapter 10: Ten More Tips and Tricks 237

Appendix A: Digital SLR Settings and Shortcuts 261

Appendix B: Photographing Landscapes 273

Index 291

Table of Contents

Introduction 1

About This Book 1
Foolish Assumptions... 1
Conventions Used in This Book.. 2
The Long and Winding Road Ahead.................................... 2
    Part I: Getting to Know Your Canon EOS 7D Mark II......................... 2
    Part II: Going Beyond Point-and-Shoot Photography 3
    Part III: The Part of Tens 3
Icons and Other Delights 4
Shoot Lots of Pictures and Enjoy!....................................... 4

Part I: Getting to Know Your Canon EOS 7D Mark II 5

Chapter 1: Exploring the Canon EOS 7D Mark II...................7

Getting to Know the Controls 8
    Exploring the top of your camera.................................... 8
    Exploring the back of your camera 10
    Exploring the front of your camera 13
    About the multi-function lock 15
Deciphering the LCD Panel.. 16
Decoding Viewfinder Information...................................... 19
Adjusting Viewfinder Clarity 22
Working with Lenses 22
    Attaching a lens... 22
    Removing a lens 23
    Using image stabilization lenses.................................. 24
    Using a zoom lens 25
    Using a lens hood... 26
Introducing the GPS Feature 26
Exploring Camera Connections 26
Modifying Basic Camera Settings 28
    Changing the date and time... 28
    Changing the auto power-off time 29
Working with Memory Cards 30
    Formatting a memory card... 31
    Removing a memory card... 33

Taking Care of Your Camera Battery 34
Charging Your Camera Battery.. 34
Cleaning the Sensor 35
Cleaning your sensor on command... 36
Cleaning your sensor manually... 37
Keeping your sensor clean 40
Accessorizing Your EOS 7D Mark II.. 40
Useful Canon accessories 41
Useful third-party accessories 42
Accessories for video 44
Keeping the Camera Body Clean 45

Chapter 2: Automatically Capturing Great Photographs 47
Ordering from Your Camera Menu.. 48
Taking Your First Picture 52
Understanding Exposure and Focal Length 54
Focusing On an Off-Center Subject.. 57
Focusing Manually... 58
Using the Flash in Full Auto Mode.. 59
Using red-eye reduction... 59
Shooting a red-eye–free portrait 60
Using the Self-Timer 61
Triggering the Shutter Remotely 62

Chapter 3: Specifying Image Size and Quality 65
Understanding Image Size and Quality... 66
Specifying Image Format, Size, and Quality 67
Comparing Image Formats and File Sizes... 69
Managing Image Files 71
Creating folders... 71
Selecting a folder... 72
Choosing a file-numbering method.. 73

Chapter 4: Using the LCD Monitor 75
Displaying Image Information 76
Using the Histogram... 77
Previewing Your Images 78
Magnifying images 79
Previewing images side by side 80
Modifying Image Review Time 81
Changing Monitor Brightness 81
Deleting Images.. 83
Rotating Images 87
Protecting Images... 88

Using the Quick Control Screen...89
Viewing Images as a Slide Show..90
Viewing Images on a TV Set 93

Chapter 5: Shooting Pictures and Movies with Live View.........95
Taking Pictures with Live View...96
  Displaying shooting information...97
  Focusing with Live View...98
  Using the Quick Control menu in Live View mode.....................100
  Displaying a grid in Live View mode 101
Exploring Other Useful Live View Options................................102
Making Movies with Your Camera...104
  Recording movies 105
  Displaying video shooting information...................................106
  Changing video dimensions and frame rate..............................107
  Taking a still picture while recording a movie..........................109
  Using the Quick Control menu while shooting movies.................109
  Changing audio recording options 110
Previewing Movies on the Camera LCD Monitor..........................111
About the Handy Pad 112
Tips for Movie Shooting...112

Part II: Going Beyond Point-and-Shoot Photography ... 115

Chapter 6: Getting the Most from Your Camera 117
Shooting with Two Cards 118
Understanding Metering..121
Taking Pictures with Creative Modes 121
  Understanding how exposure works in the camera....................122
  Using Programmed Auto Exposure mode.................................123
  Using Aperture Priority mode...124
  Using Shutter Priority mode..128
  Using Manual mode 130
  Shooting time exposures with Bulb mode...............................131
Modifying Camera Exposure 133
  Using exposure compensation...133
  Bracketing exposure..134
  Locking exposure..136
Locking Focus 137
Choosing a Drive Mode...138
Using Custom Functions 140
Clearing Custom Functions 141
Useful Menu Commands for Images..142

Enabling Long Exposure Noise Reduction...................................... 142
Enabling High ISO Speed Reduction... 143
Enabling Highlight Tone Priority 145

Chapter 7: Using Advanced Camera Features................... 147

Viewing Battery Information 147
Using the Auto Lighting Optimizer.. 149
Reducing Lens Flicker 150
Choosing a Metering Mode... 151
Displaying the Grid.. 152
Using the Electronic Level.. 153
Tailoring Autofocus to Your Shooting Style... 154
Choosing the autofocus mode 154
Choosing the autofocus point mode 155
Switching to a single autofocus point 156
Using zone autofocus 157
Modifying autofocus to suit shooting style 158
Choosing a Picture Style.. 160
Specifying the Color Space 162
Setting White Balance 164
Specifying Color Temperature 165
Creating a Custom White Balance 166
Using white balance compensation.. 168
Bracketing white balance... 170
Setting the ISO Speed 171
Extending the ISO Range... 172
Flash Photography and Your EOS 7D Mark II 173
Using the built-in flash.. 173
Changing the flash-sync speed in Av mode 175
Choosing second-curtain sync 176
Using auxiliary flash 178
Using flash compensation.. 179
Locking the flash exposure.. 180
Controlling External Speedlites from the Camera.............................. 180
Controlling a flash in the hot shoe 181
Going wireless 183

Chapter 8: Mastering Your EOS 7D Mark II 187

Choosing the Optimal Settings for Specific Situations 187
Photographing Action... 188
Photographing fast-moving subjects.. 188
Freezing action 190
Photographing slow-moving subjects... 193
Photographing Landscapes.. 194
Photographing the Sunset 196

Photographing People and Things 198
   Photographing people and pets 198
   Exploring selective focus 200
   Exploring macro photography 201
Photographing Wildlife 201
   Photographing animals at state parks 201
   Stabilizing the camera when using
      long telephoto lenses 203
   Photographing animals at the zoo 205
   Photographing birds 205
Enhancing Your Creativity 207
Composing Your Images 208
Seeing, Thinking, and Acting 211
   Being in the moment 211
   Practicing 'til your images are pixel-perfect 211
   Becoming a student of photography 212
   Never leaving home without a camera 213
   Waiting for the light 214
Defining Your Goals 214
   What's your center of interest? 214
   What's your best vantage point? 215
   What else is in the picture? 215
   The genius of digital photography 216

Part III: The Part of Tens .... _217_

Chapter 9: Ten Tips and Tricks 219
Creating a Custom Menu 219
Adding Copyright Information to the Camera 222
Adding Author Name to the Camera 224
Creating and Registering a Picture Style 226
Editing Movies in the Camera 228
Updating Your Camera's Firmware 230
Registering Camera User Settings 231
Restoring Your Camera Settings 232
Customizing Your Camera 233
Getting Help 235

Chapter 10: Ten More Tips and Tricks 237
Adding GPS Information to Images 237
Disabling the Autofocus Beep 241
Creating HDR Images 242
Creating Multiple Exposures In-Camera 246

Using the Interval Timer 250
Shooting Time Exposures with the Bulb Timer 252
Modifying the Rate button..255
Creating a Makeshift Tripod...256
Creating Abstract Images in the Camera...256
Working with Photoshop Lightroom...258

Appendix A: Digital SLR Settings and Shortcuts.......... 261

Capturing Sporting Events 261
Setting the camera 261
Taking the picture...262
Troubleshooting 264
Photographing Animals in the Wild 264
Setting the camera 265
Taking the picture...265
Troubleshooting 266
Photographing Horse Racing 267
Setting the camera 267
Taking the picture...267
Troubleshooting 269
Capturing a City Skyline...270
Setting the camera 270
Taking the picture...270
Troubleshooting 272

Appendix B: Photographing Landscapes 273

Photographing Grand Vistas..273
Setting the camera 274
Taking the picture...275
Troubleshooting 277
Photographing Mountains..278
Setting the camera 279
Taking the picture...280
Troubleshooting 281
Photographing Beach Sunsets 282
Setting the camera 282
Taking the picture...283
Troubleshooting 284
Photographing Reflections in Still Water..285
Setting the camera 286
Taking the picture...287
Troubleshooting 288

Index 291

Introduction

*Y*our Canon EOS 7D Mark II is the latest and greatest digital camera on the market — with a stunning 20.2-megapixel capture, Live View, high-definition video, and much more. But all this technology can be a bit daunting, especially if this is your first real digital single-lens reflex (SLR) camera. You no longer have modes like Portrait, Sport, Landscape, and so on. You've graduated to the big leagues. All you have to do is master the power you hold in your hands.

I've been using Canon digital SLRs since the EOS 10D, and I've learned a lot about the Canon brand of cameras since then. In addition to the EOS 7D Mark II I'm using to write this book, I also own an EOS 5D MKII and an EOS 7D, which has a lot of the features found on your EOS 7D Mark II. My goal is to show you how to become one with your camera. I don't get overly technical in this book, even though your camera is very technical. I also do my best to keep it lively. So if you want to master your EOS 7D Mark II, you have the right book in your hands.

About This Book

If you find the buttons and menus on your shiny new EOS 7D Mark II a tad intimidating, this book is for you. In the chapters of this book, I take you from novice point-and-shoot photographer to one who can utilize all the bells and whistles your camera offers. You'll find information about the camera menus and every button on your camera, as well as when to use them, and what settings to use for specific picture-taking situations. I also introduce you to a program you can use to edit your images to pixel perfection.

Foolish Assumptions

Ah, yes. *Assume.* When broken down to its lowest common denominator . . . Okay, I won't go there. But as an author, I have to make some assumptions about you, dear reader. First and foremost, you should now own, or have on order, a Canon EOS 7D Mark II. If you own one of those cute little point-and-shoot Canon cameras, good for you, but this book won't help you with that camera. You should also have a computer on which to download your images, and preferably a program with which to edit your images. A basic knowledge of photography is also helpful. I know, you probably meet all assumptions. But my editor assumes I'll put all the pre-requisites in this section in this part of the book.

Conventions Used in This Book

To make life easier, this book has several conventions that are used to identify pertinent information — stuff you should know. So to help you navigate this book easily, I use a few style conventions:

- ✓ Terms or words that you might be unfamiliar with in the context of photography, I have *italicized* — and I also define these.
- ✓ Numbered steps that you need to follow and characters you need to type are set in **bold.**
- ✓ Margin art is used to identify camera buttons. When you see one of these icons, it shows you what button to push or dial to rotate.
- ✓ The Canon EOS 7D Mark II menu has pretty little icons for each tab, of which there are many. Each tab has multiple menus. You'll find a table with tab names and menus in Chapter 2.

The Long and Winding Road Ahead

I divide this book into three parts, with each devoted to a specific aspect of your camera. The chapters flow logically from one subject to the next, to take you from shooting in Full Auto mode to becoming a seasoned photographer who knows which mode to choose and which settings to use for taking pictures of specific subjects. You can read the book from cover to cover — or, if you need quick information about a specific topic, peruse the Table of Contents or Index until you find the desired topic. Most of the sections in this book don't require reading additional material.

The following sections offer a brief overview of each part of the book.

Part I: Getting to Know Your Canon EOS 7D Mark II

Part I contains five chapters that help you get up and running with your EOS 7D Mark II:

- ✓ Chapter 1 introduces you to the camera and shows you how to do some basic tasks.

✔ Chapter 2 shows you how to take pictures using the Full Auto mode. I show you how to find your way through the maze of menus and much more.

✔ Chapter 3 shows you how to specify the image format. I show you how and when to choose JPEG and RAW format, discuss different sizes, and offer my recommendation for the ideal format.

✔ Chapter 4 shows you how to use the LCD monitor for a myriad of purposes. I show you how to review your images, use the histogram, and more.

✔ Chapter 5 shows you how to use Live View mode. I show you how to take pictures with Live View and change Live View autofocus modes. I also show you how to capture movies with Live View. So you're live in Chapter 5.

Part II: Going Beyond Point-and-Shoot Photography

In this part of the book, I cut to the chase and show you how to master the advanced features of your camera.

✔ Chapter 6 shows you how to use the creative shooting modes. In this chapter, I also show you how to modify camera exposure, bracket exposure, and use custom functions.

✔ Chapter 7 shows you how to use the advanced features of your camera. I show you how to set ISO, specify white balance mode, create a custom white balance, and much more. I also show you how to use your EOS 7D Mark II with Canon Speedlites.

✔ Chapter 8 shows you how to use your EOS 7D Mark II in specific shooting situations. I discuss sport photography, wildlife photography, landscape photography, and more.

Part III: The Part of Tens

The book concludes with two top ten lists, written by yours truly, who happens to have a gap between his teeth like David Letterman, who happens to be famous for his top ten lists. The lists are grouped according to subject matter, and a splendid time is guaranteed for all. And tonight Mr. Kite is topping the bill.

✔ Chapter 9 shows you how to create a custom menu and register your favorite settings. I also show you how to add copyright information to the camera, edit movies in the camera, and much more.

✔ Chapter 10 shows you how to create a makeshift tripod, create abstract images, create HDR images and multiple exposures in camera, and more.

Icons and Other Delights

For Dummies books have icons that indicate important bits of information. You can hopscotch from icon to icon and discover a lot. But when in doubt, read the text associated with the icon. In this book, you find the following icons:

- A Tip icon contains information designed to save you time and, in some instances, your very sanity.

- This icon warns you about something you should not do; something your fearless author has already done and decided it's not a good thing to do again.

- When you see this icon, it's the equivalent of a virtual piece of string tied around your finger. This is information you want to commit to memory.

- When you see this icon, it's for the geeks in the group who like to know all manner of technical stuff.

You'll also find icons in the margin that show you the controls and menu tabs on your camera.

Shoot Lots of Pictures and Enjoy!

Your EOS 7D Mark II is a digital photography powerhouse; use it and use it often. The old adage "practice makes perfect" really does apply. The only way to become a better photographer and master your equipment is to apply what you learn from what I show you, and shoot as many pictures as you can. While you're working your way through this book, keep your camera close at hand. When your significant other pokes his or her head into the room, grab your camera and start practicing your craft. Take one picture, then another, and another, and so on. With practice, you'll know your camera like the back of your hand. You'll also know which rules of photography and composition work for you — and you'll start to develop your own style. For that matter, you'll probably amaze yourself, too.

Part I

Getting to Know Your Canon EOS 7D Mark II

Visit www.dummies.com for great Dummies content online.

In this part . . .

- ✓ Get to know the lay of the land and become familiar with the controls of your EOS 7D Mark II.

- ✓ Find out how to take great pictures automatically as well as how to specify image size and format.

- ✓ Understand how to get around in the somewhat enigmatic camera menu.

- ✓ Learn to master the camera's LCD monitor.

- ✓ Visit www.dummies.com for additional Dummies content online.

Exploring the Canon EOS 7D Mark II

In This Chapter

- Getting familiar with camera controls
- Understanding the LCD panel
- Decoding and adjusting the viewfinder
- Attaching and removing lenses
- Using zoom and image stabilization lenses
- Changing basic camera settings
- Using memory cards
- Charging your battery
- Cleaning your sensor

The Canon EOS 7D Mark II, which evolved from the Canon EOS 7D that was introduced in late 2009, has all the latest bells and whistles Canon has to offer. It's a technological marvel that enables you to take great pictures and capture high-definition (HD) video. The camera has a new processor and an advanced, highly customizable 65-point autofocus system that gives you the ability to capture great images in low light and at a blindingly fast speed of up to 10 frames per second, which is ideal for action photography. You can also create HDR (high dynamic range) images and use the new interval timer to create time-lapse movies. And this camera features a viewfinder that shows you 100 percent of what the lens captures: What you see is what you get. A *dual-axis level* (the equivalent of a spirit level in a tripod) lets you capture pictures with horizon lines that are level. In addition, the camera has built-in GPS, which, when enabled, pinpoints the location where each image was captured and includes GPS data with the image meta-data. The camera also has a built-in flash system that can be used wirelessly to control external Canon Speedlites.

Getting familiar with all this new technology can seem daunting even to a sea-soned photographer. I was impressed, albeit a tad flummoxed, when I saw the first reviews for the all-singing, all-dancing EOS 7D Mark II. Even though I'm a seasoned Canon digital single-lens reflex (SLR) user — my first digital SLR was the EOS 10D — I still had a bit of a learning curve when I first had the camera in hand, chomping at the bit to create some pictures. But it's my job to get down to brass tacks with new technology and show you how to master it. The fact that you're reading this probably means that you want to know how to use all the bells and whistles Canon has built into the EOS 7D Mark II. In this chap-ter, I familiarize you with the controls, the camera lens, the camera settings, the battery, and the memory cards you use to capture images with the camera.

Getting to Know the Controls

If you're a longtime Canon user, you know that you can do an awful lot with the camera by using external controls, which saves you from poking around inside pesky menus. The camera controls are easy to reach and give you access to many powerful features. Although you may think it seems like a daunting task to know which button does what, after you use the camera for a while, you'll automatically know which control gives you your desired result and then reach for it instinctively, without taking your eye from the viewfinder. But first, you need to know what each control does. I explain the controls you find on the outside of the camera in the upcoming sections.

Exploring the top of your camera

The top of the camera, shown in Figure 1-1, is where you find the controls you use most when taking pictures. The top of the camera is where you change settings like ISO (International Organization for Standards) and shutter speed, choose a shooting mode, and press the shutter button to take a picture. You can do lots of other things from the top of the camera, which in my humble opinion, is the most important real estate on the camera, with the possible exception of the lens. I suggest you get to know the controls on the top of your camera inti-mately, like the back of your hand. Many photographers, including me, make it a point to memorize where the controls are and access them without taking an eye off the viewfinder. Here's what you find on the top of the camera:

- ✔ **Shutter button:** This button prefocuses the camera and takes a picture. (I discuss this button in greater detail in Chapter 2.)
- ✔ **Multi-Function button:** This button changes the function of a multi-purpose button, and is used extensively when specifying which autofocus

point or zone is used to achieve focus. I show you how and when to use this button when related to a specific task.

✏ **Main dial:** This dial changes a setting when you rotate it after pressing a button. For example, after you press the ISO speed button, you rotate this dial to change the ISO speed setting. I show you how to use this dial as it relates to a specific task.

✏ **LCD Panel Illumination button:** Press this button when you're in dim or dark conditions and you need to shed a little light on the LCD panel.

✏ **ISO Speed Setting/Flash Exposure Compensation button:** This button sets the ISO speed setting or the flash exposure compensation. (See Chapter 7 for more on the ISO speed setting and flash exposure compensation.)

✏ **Drive/AF button:** This button sets the autofocus mode. You can choose from three autofocus modes. You also use this button to change the drive mode from single shot to continuous shooting to auto-timer. (I give you the skinny on autofocus modes in Chapter 6.)

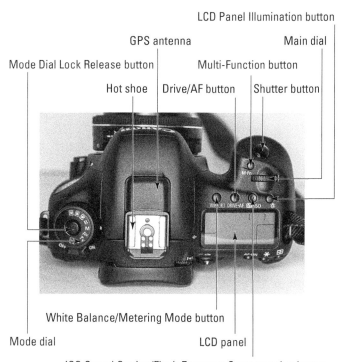

LCD Panel Illumination button

GPS antenna   Main dial

Mode Dial Lock Release button   Multi-Function button

Hot shoe   Drive/AF button   Shutter button

White Balance/Metering Mode button

Mode dial   LCD panel

ISO Speed Setting/Flash Exposure Compensation button

Figure 1-1: Get to know these controls like the back of your hand.

✔ **White Balance/Metering Mode button:** This button changes the white balance or metering mode. (See Chapter 6 for more on the metering mode and white balance.)

✔ **LCD panel:** This panel shows you all the current settings. I show you how to read the information in this panel in the section, "Deciphering the LCD Panel," later in this chapter.

✔ **Hot shoe:** Slide a compatible flash unit (a Canon flash unit is dubbed a *Speedlite*) that's compatible with the EOS 7D Mark II into this slot. The contacts in the hot shoe communicate between the camera and the flash unit. (I discuss flash photography in Chapter 7.)

✔ **GPS antenna:** The body of this camera is made of magnesium, which is wonderfully durable, but GPS signals have a hard time passing through it, which is why the wily engineers at Canon put the GPS antenna in a little bubble on top of the camera body. Looks kinda like a hood scope on a racing car. Way cool.

✔ **Mode Dial Lock Release button:** This welcome feature is a button that when pushed enables you to change from one shooting mode to another. When in the upright and locked position, it's not possible to accidentally change shooting modes in the heat of battle.

✔ **Mode dial:** You use this button to specify which shooting mode the camera uses to take the picture. (I show you how to use this dial to choose specific shooting modes in Chapter 6, and in Chapter 8, I show you how to choose optimal settings for specific picture-taking situations.)

Exploring the back of your camera

The back of the camera, shown in Figure 1-2, is also an important place. Here you find controls to power up your camera, access the camera menu, and much more. The following is what you find on the back of your EOS 7D Mark II:

✔ **AF Point Selection button:** This button enables you to change from multiple autofocus points to a single autofocus point (see Chapter 6).

✔ **AE Lock button:** This button enables you to lock exposure to a specific part of the frame (see Chapter 6).

✔ **AF-On button:** This button, in certain shooting modes, establishes focus (see Chapter 6).

✔ **Live View/Movie Shooting switch:** This switch enables you to shoot in Live View mode or to shoot movies, which I explain in detail in Chapter 5.

✔ **Start/Stop button:** Push this button to shoot in Live View mode. When you switch to movie shooting mode, this button starts and stops recording (see Chapter 5).

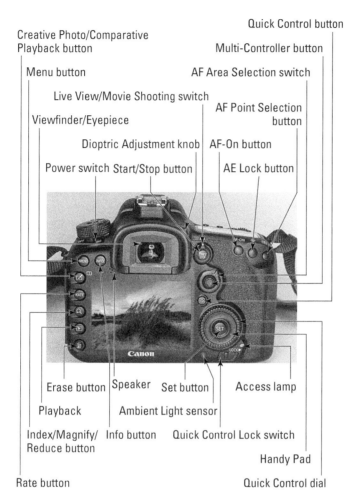

Creative Photo/Comparative Playback button
Menu button
Live View/Movie Shooting switch
Viewfinder/Eyepiece
Dioptric Adjustment knob
Power switch Start/Stop button

Quick Control button
Multi-Controller button
AF Area Selection switch
AF Point Selection button
AF-On button
AE Lock button

Erase button Speaker Set button Access lamp
Playback Ambient Light sensor
Index/Magnify/ Info button Quick Control Lock switch
Reduce button
Rate button Handy Pad
Quick Control dial

Figure 1-2: Buttons, buttons, and more buttons on the back of the camera.

✐ **Multi-Controller button:** Use this button for a myriad of tasks, such as changing the autofocus point, selecting an option when using the Quick Control menu instead of the camera menu, or switching from one camera menu to the next. (I explain this button in detail when it's associated with a specific task throughout this book.)

✐ **AF Area Selection switch:** This switch is used in conjunction with the AF Point Selection button to select the desired autofocus point or autofocus zone.

↙ **Quick Control button:** Press this button to display the Quick Control menu on the LCD monitor. (I show you how to use the Quick Control menu in Chapter 4.) It is also used in conjunction with the Menu button to quickly switch from one menu tab to another. (I show you how to use this button throughout this book as the need arises when selecting menu commands.)

↙ **Quick Control dial:** This dial selects a setting or highlights a menu item. This dial is used when performing various tasks, and I discuss it throughout this book as needed.

↙ **Handy Pad:** This convenient touch pad is used to change multiple settings when shooting movies in silent mode (see Chapter 5).

↙ **Set button:** Press this button to confirm a task, such as erasing an image from your card or setting a menu option. I show you how to use this button to perform a specific task throughout this book.

↙ **Ambient Light sensor:** Used to determine the brightness of the LCD monitor, unless you manually change the brightness. Be careful not to block this sensor when you choose the option to let the camera automatically determine LCD brightness based on the ambient lighting conditions (see Chapter 4).

↙ **Quick Control Lock switch:** This switch enables the Quick Control dial. Move the switch to the left to enable the Quick Control dial and to the right to lock the dial. Locking the Quick Control dial prevents you from accidentally changing a setting. You can use a menu command to modify which buttons are locked with this switch.

↙ **Access lamp:** Flashes when the camera writes data to the inserted memory card(s).

↙ **Dioptric Adjustment knob:** This control fine-tunes the viewfinder to your eyesight.

↙ **Viewfinder/Eyepiece:** Use the viewfinder to compose your pictures. Shooting information, battery status, and the amount of shots that can be stored on the memory card is displayed in the viewfinder. The eyepiece cushions your eye when you press it against the viewfinder and creates a seal that prevents ambient light from having an adverse effect on the exposure.

↙ **Speaker:** Plays audio when you play back movies.

↙ **Power switch:** Okay, this is a no-brainer. This switch powers the camera on and off.

↙ **LCD monitor:** Used to display images, movies, camera menus, and the Quick Control menu. (I tell you probably more than you ever wanted to know about the monitor in Chapter 4, and in Chapter 5, I show you how to use the monitor to compose pictures and movies while shooting in Live View mode.)

✏ **Info button:** Press this button to display shooting information on the LCD monitor. You can choose from many different information screens. (I inform you about the different screens in Chapter 4.) This button is also used in conjunction with certain menu commands, which I discuss throughout this book as the need arises.

✏ **Menu button:** Press this button to display the last used camera menu on the LCD monitor. (I introduce you to the camera menu in Chapter 2 and refer to the menu throughout this book.)

✏ **Creative Photo/Comparative Playback button:** This button is used to engage creative shooting modes such as HDR, or to select a picture style. You also use this button when reviewing images to display two images side by side. I discuss this button throughout this book as it relates to a specific task.

✏ **Rate button:** This button is used to rate images. This button can be modified through a menu command to protect images.

✏ **Index/Magnify/Reduce button:** When reviewing images, use this button in conjunction with the Main dial to view multiple thumbnails or to zoom out when viewing a single image (see Chapter 4).

✏ **Playback:** Used to review images (see Chapter 4).

✏ **Erase button:** This button deletes an image. (I show you how to delete images in Chapter 4.)

Exploring the front of your camera

The front of your camera (see Figure 1-3) has a couple controls you can use and other gizmos that the camera uses. Here you'll find a couple of buttons that you use every day and some that access features you rarely use. The following features are on the front of your camera:

✏ **Remote control sensor:** Senses the light from an RC-1, RC-5, or RC-6 remote (sold separately) to actuate the shutter.

✏ **DC coupler cord hole:** Plug the cord from the ACK-E6 power adapter (sold separately) into this hole to use the camera without a battery.

✏ **Depth-of-Field Preview button:** Press this button to preview the *depth of field* (the amount of the image in front of and behind your subject that's in apparent focus) at the current f-stop.

✏ **Body cap (not shown):** Use the body cap to protect the interior of the camera when a lens isn't attached.

✓ **EF index mount (not shown):** Align an EF lens with this mark when attaching it to the camera. (See the section, "Attaching a lens," later in this chapter for more information.)

✓ **EF-S index mount (not shown):** Align an EF-S lens with this mark when attaching it to the camera. (See the section, "Attaching a lens," later in this chapter for more information.) You can only use EF-S lenses with cameras equipped with an APS-C (Advanced Photo System Type-C) sensor like the one on your EOS 7D Mark II.

✓ **Flash button:** Press this button to pop up the built-in camera flash unit. (I show you how to use flash on your subjects in Chapter 7.)

✓ **Lens-Release button:** Press this button when releasing a lens from the camera. I show you how to attach and remove lenses in the section, "Working with Lenses" later in this chapter.

✓ **Microphone:** Records audio when recording movies.

Flash button

Remote control sensor

Microphone

DC coupler cord hole

Lens-Release button

Depth-of-Field Preview button

Figure 1-3: The front of your camera is an ergonomic wonder.

Finding the perfect camera bag

Your EOS 7D Mark II is a marvelous camera that you are probably going to want to take almost everywhere with you. Plus, Canon has more lenses than the law allows as well as Speedlites for flash photography, the stuff you use to clean your camera, filters, and so on. A good camera bag is a must to cart around all of your gear. Here are some tips for finding the perfect one:

- **Get a bag that's big enough for the gear you now own and any additional equipment you anticipate buying in the near future.**

- **Purchase a bag that's comfortable.** Make sure you try the bag on for size in the camera store. Place your camera in the bag and put it over your shoulder. If the bag isn't comfortable, try a different bag. Nothing is worse than a chafed neck after a daylong photography adventure.

- **Make sure the bag has enough pockets for your stuff.** The bag should have a place where you can pack extra memory cards, spare batteries, and other accessories.

- **Make sure the bag is sturdy enough to protect your gear.**

- **Make sure the bag is made so that you can get to your gear quickly.** Nothing is worse than fumbling for a piece of equipment while your digital Kodak moment disappears.

- **If you have a lot of gear, consider purchasing a hard-shell case that's big enough for all your equipment and a soft bag for day trips.**

- **Consider purchasing a customizable camera bag.** These bags come with removable partitions that are held in place with Velcro.

- **If it rains a lot where you live, purchase a water-resistant camera bag or one with a built-in rain cover.** Heavy rain and digital camera gear is a recipe for disaster.

- **Consider purchasing more than one bag.** I have one bag that has gobs of space for lots of equipment when I go on a hike in search of wildlife to photograph. The bag has outside pockets for water bottles and a place to park my tripod. I also have a bag that's big enough for two small lenses. I use this bag when I go on a photo walkabout in search of interesting things to photograph.

About the multi-function lock

The EOS 7D Mark II has lots of dials and buttons, and then more buttons and levers and switches, oh my. There are times when you don't want to inadvertently change a setting when shooting. All of the buttons on the body of this camera were discussed at the start of the chapter when I discussed the front, back, and top of the camera. Some of the buttons and sliders cannot be accidentally engaged, because you have to move a finger from the standard shooting position. The buttons that can be accessed easily are positioned so that you can quickly access them while shooting. However, there are times when you've got everything just the way you want it for the subject you're photographing and accidentally bumping a button and thereby changing a setting could have disastrous results, especially when you're photographing something that will never be repeated. Fortunately, the engineers at Canon considered this eventuality and added the multi-function lock to the camera.

The multi-function lock switch is located below the Quick Control dial, and is used to lock and unlock the Quick Control dial. Slide the switch to the right to lock the Quick Control dial. Slide the switch to the left to release the lock and return functionality to the Quick Control dial.

You can also use the multi-function lock switch to lock the Main dial, the multi-controller, and the AF Area Selection lever by navigating to the Custom Function C.Fn3, and choosing the controls you want to lock with the multi-function lock under the Multi-Function Lock menu item. (For more information on Custom Functions, see Chapter 6.)

Deciphering the LCD Panel

The LCD panel on the top of the camera displays a lot of information, such as the shutter speed, aperture, ISO speed setting, white balance, metering mode, and more. Figure 1-4 shows all the possible options that can appear on the LCD panel. However, you'll never see this much information when you take a picture. I show you the type of information you can expect to see on the LCD panel during specific picture-taking scenarios I discuss throughout this book. Here's a road map for the information you'll find on the LCD panel:

- **White Balance setting:** Displays the current white balance setting. You view the panel when choosing a white balance option. The icon for every possible white balance option is shown in Figure 1-4. (I discuss how to set white balance in Chapter 7.)

- **Shutter Speed:** Displays the shutter speed, as metered by the camera or set by you that will be used to shoot the next picture. If you're taking pictures with Shutter Priority mode or Manual mode (see Chapter 6), you can use the LCD panel to set the shutter speed.

- **Aperture:** Displays the f-stop that will be used to take the next picture. You can use this information to change the aperture when shooting in Manual mode or Aperture Priority mode (see Chapter 6).

- **Shots Remaining/Self-Timer Countdown:** This spot on the panel does double duty. When you're using the Self-Timer, the time remaining until the picture is taken displays here. Otherwise, the display shows the number of shots remaining that you can fit on the memory card you insert in the camera to capture your images. (A *memory card* is the digital equivalent of reusable film. But you probably already knew that, right?)

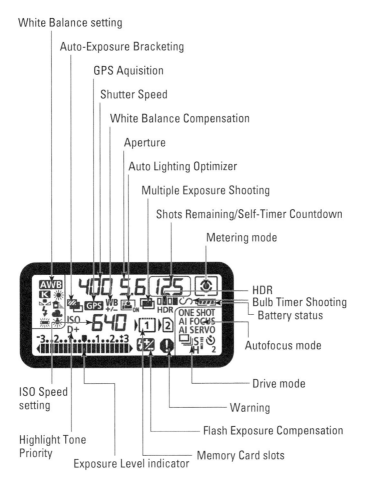

White Balance setting

Auto-Exposure Bracketing

GPS Aquisition

Shutter Speed

White Balance Compensation

Aperture

Auto Lighting Optimizer

Multiple Exposure Shooting

Shots Remaining/Self-Timer Countdown

Metering mode

HDR

Bulb Timer Shooting

Battery status

Autofocus mode

Drive mode

Warning

Flash Exposure Compensation

Memory Card slots

ISO Speed setting

Highlight Tone Priority

Exposure Level indicator

Figure 1-4: You find lots of useful information on the LCD panel.

- **Metering mode:** This icon displays the currently selected metering mode. I discuss metering modes in Chapter 6.
- **Auto-Exposure Bracketing:** This icon displays when you've enabled automatic exposure bracketing (see Chapter 6).
- **GPS Acquisition:** This icon flashes when a GPS signal is being acquired, and stops flashing when the signal has been acquired. (I discuss the EOS 7D Mark II's GPS feature later in this chapter.)
- **White Balance Compensation:** This icon displays when you bracket the white balance (see Chapter 6).

- ✔ **Auto Lighting Optimizer:** This icon displays when you enable the Auto Lighting Optimizer feature (see Chapter 7).

- ✔ **Multiple Exposure Shooting:** This icon displays when you use the Multiple Exposure feature (see Chapter 10).

- ✔ **HDR:** This icon displays when you use the HDR (high dynamic range) feature (see Chapter 10).

- ✔ **Bulb Timer Shooting:** This icon displays when you use the Bulb Timer (see Chapter 7).

- ✔ **Battery status:** This icon displays the amount of charge remaining in the battery.

- ✔ **Highlight Tone Priority:** This icon displays when you enable the Highlight Tone Priority feature (see Chapter 7).

- ✔ **ISO Speed setting:** The currently selected ISO speed setting displays here. You can also use this information when setting the ISO speed (see Chapter 7).

- ✔ **Memory Card slots:** Shows which memory card slots you are using.

- ✔ **Exposure Level indicator:** This feature is used when setting exposure compensation. After setting exposure compensation, an icon appears on the indicator that shows how much you've increased or decreased exposure. It also displays icons to indicate when you've bracketed exposure. (See Chapter 6 for information about exposure compensation and auto exposure bracketing.)

- ✔ **Flash Exposure Compensation:** This icon displays when you've enabled Flash Exposure Compensation (see Chapter 7).

- ✔ **Warning:** This icon displays when you choose the monochrome (black and white) picture style, when you correct white balance, when one-touch image quality is used, when you set high ISO or multi-shot noise reduction, or when you use spot metering. This is your camera's way of telling you that a mode not suited for every type of photography has been selected. It is a gentle reminder to deselect the option after you've shot the pictures for which these modes were selected.

- ✔ **Autofocus mode:** Displays the currently selected autofocus mode (see Chapter 7).

- ✔ **Drive mode:** Displays the icon for the currently selected Drive mode and whether the camera captures one image when you press the shutter button or multiple images. It also shows when you're shooting in high speed mode or engaging the self-timer (see Chapter 6).

You see examples of different scenarios on the LCD panel throughout this book as I discuss various picture-taking situations.

Decoding Viewfinder Information

The viewfinder, or *information central* as I like to call it, is another place you find a plethora of information. In the viewfinder, you see the image as it will be captured by your camera (see Figure 1-5). Your EOS 7D Mark II has a viewfinder that enables you to see 100 percent of what you'll capture, a feature that was introduced on this camera's predecessor, the EOS 7D. Use the viewfinder to compose your picture and view camera settings while you change them.

Figure 1-5 shows all the possible icons that can be displayed while taking a picture and displays all the autofocus points — you never see this much information displayed while taking a picture. (I show you different viewfinder scenarios when I discuss different picture-taking scenarios throughout the book.) When you peer into the viewfinder, you find the current shooting settings, icons for battery status, shots remaining, and much more. By default, all of the icons shown in Figure 1-5 are not visible until you use a menu command to display or hide information in the viewfinder. Here's the information displayed in your viewfinder (icons that can only be displayed by using a menu command are listed with an O for optional in parentheses):

- **Viewfinder level (O):** Displays the level in the viewfinder, enabling you to level the camera while looking through the viewfinder.

- **Autofocus points:** Figure 1-5 shows all of the autofocus points, plus the autofocus zones. You use these icons when selecting a single autofocus point, expanding an autofocus point, and selecting an autofocus zone.

- **Grid (O):** This icon appears when you enable a grid (see Chapter 7).

- **Exposure Level indicator:** This is used when manually setting exposure or metering flash.

- **Shooting mode (O):** This icon shows the currently used shooting mode (see Chapter 6).

- **White Balance (O):** This icon shows the white balance mode currently in use (see Chapter 7).

- **Drive mode (O):** This icon shows the drive mode currently being used (see Chapter 6).

- **Autofocus mode (O):** This icon shows the autofocus mode currently being used (see Chapter 7).

- **Metering mode (O):** This icon shows the metering mode currently being used (see Chapter 7).

- **Image format (O):** This icon shows the image format currently in use (see Chapter 3).

- **Warning:** This icon displays when the camera senses something you need to be warned about (see Chapter 7).

- **Flicker detection:** This icon displays when the camera senses that you should enable a menu command to reduce flicker (see Chapter 7).

- **AF Status indicator:** This icon appears when you press the shutter button halfway and the camera is achieving focus.

- **Battery status:** This icon shows you the amount of charge left in your battery.

- **AE Lock/AEB in Progress:** This icon indicates that you've locked the autoexposure to a specific point in the frame or that automatic exposure bracketing is being performed (see Chapter 6).

- **Flash ready:** This icon indicates that the flash has recycled to full power and is ready for use (see Chapter 7).

- **Flash Exposure Lock/FEB in Progress:** This icon indicates that you've locked the flash exposure to a specific point in the frame or that flash exposure bracketing is being performed (see Chapter 6).

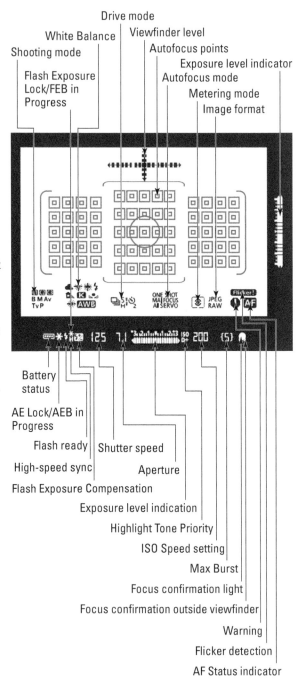

Figure 1-5: The viewfinder displays lots of useful information.

- **High-speed sync:** This icon indicates that you've changed the Flash mode to high-speed sync (see Chapter 7).

- **Flash Exposure Compensation:** This icon displays when you use flash exposure compensation (see Chapter 7).

- **Shutter speed:** Displays the shutter speed that will be used to take the next picture. You can also use this information to manually set the shutter speed when shooting in Shutter Priority mode or Manual mode (see Chapter 6).

- **Aperture:** Displays the f-stop that will be used to take the next picture. You can use this information to manually set the aperture when shooting in Aperture Priority mode or Manual mode (see Chapter 6).

- **Exposure level indicator:** This feature is used when setting exposure compensation. After setting exposure compensation, an icon appears on the indicator that shows how much you've increased or decreased exposure. It also displays icons to indicate when you've bracketed exposure. (See Chapter 6 for information about exposure compensation and automatic exposure bracketing.)

- **Highlight Tone Priority:** This icon displays when you enable Highlight Tone Priority (see Chapter 7).

- **ISO speed setting:** The currently selected ISO speed setting displays here. You can also use this information when setting the ISO speed (see Chapter 7).

- **Max burst:** Shows the maximum number of shots you can take when shooting in Continuous mode. If fewer shots are remaining on the card than the maximum burst, the shots remaining display.

- **Focus confirmation light:** Lights when you achieve focus.

- **Focus confirmation outside viewfinder:** This icon appears when you enable an autofocus command to display autofocus confirmation outside the field of view. When you enable autofocus confirmation outside the viewfinder, the AF icon does not appear.

In my estimation, the viewfinder is the place to compose your images. If you use the command to display optional information in the viewfinder, it's information overload, which diverts your attention from the task at hand, composing the image. The LCD monitor is the place to go when you need information such as the shooting mode, drive mode, and so on. If you'd like to experiment with the optional viewfinder displays, you can enable them using the Viewfinder Display command, which you find on the Set Up2 menu (part of the Set Up tab). For more information on using menu commands, see Chapter 2.

Adjusting Viewfinder Clarity

If you wear glasses, or if your vision's not perfect, you can adjust the viewfinder clarity, which makes it easier to compose your images and focus manually. After all, if what you see in the viewfinder isn't what you get, you won't be a happy camper. To adjust viewfinder clarity:

Dioptric Adjustment knob

1. **Attach a lens to the camera.**

2. **Look into the viewfinder and turn the dioptric adjustment knob (see Figure 1-6) left or right until the autofocus points look sharp and clear.**

Figure 1-6: A clear viewfinder. All the better to see you with, my dear.

If the knob is hard to turn, remove the eyepiece cup.

Working with Lenses

The beauty of photographing with a digital SLR is that you can change lenses to suit your creative need, or to suit the particular type of photograph you want to take. When you purchase lenses for your camera, make sure they are for the Canon EF mount. If this is your first digital SLR, read the following sections where I show you how to attach lenses, use image stabilization, remove lenses, and so on. If you already know this stuff, you can skip the following sections and do something interesting like use a macro lens to photograph dust bunnies.

Attaching a lens

The beauty of a digital SLR is that you can attach lenses with different focal lengths to achieve different effects. Your EOS 7D Mark II accepts a wide range of lens from super wide-angle lenses that capture a wide view angle, to long telephoto lenses that capture a narrow view angle and let you fill the frame with objects that are far away. Your camera can use EF lenses and EF-S lenses. The latter are specially made for cameras such as the EOS 7D Mark II that have a sensor smaller than the size of a frame of 35mm film. To attach a lens to your camera:

1. **Remove the body cap from the camera.**

   With the camera facing you, twist the cap counterclockwise to remove it. Alternatively, you'll remove the lens currently on the camera with the steps I outline in the upcoming "Removing a Lens" section.

2. **Remove the rear cap from the lens you're attaching to the camera.**

   Twist the cap clockwise to remove it.

3. **Align the dot on the lens with the mounting dot on the camera body (see Figure 1-7).**

   If you're using an EF lens, the dot on the lens is red and you align it with the red dot on the camera body. If you're using an EF-S lens, the dot on the lens is white and you align it with the white dot on the camera body.

4. **Twist the lens clockwise until it locks into place.**

   Don't force the lens. If the lens doesn't lock into place with a gentle twist, you may not have aligned it properly.

Removing a lens

When you want to use a different lens or store the camera body, remove the lens. Removing a lens and attaching another lens can be a bit of a juggling act. To remove a lens from your camera:

1. **Press the lens-release button.**

   This button unlocks the lens from the camera.

2. **With the camera pointed at you, twist the lens counterclockwise until it stops and then gently pull the lens out of the body (see Figure 1-8).**

EF Index mount

EF-S Index mount

Figure 1-7: Aligning the lens.

Rotate counterclockwise

Figure 1-8: Removing a lens from the camera.

To minimize the chance of dust getting on your sensor, always turn off the camera when changing lenses. If you leave the power on, the sensor has a slight charge that can attract dust floating in the air. Do not change lenses in a dusty environment because dust may inadvertently blow into your camera. I also find it's a good idea to point the camera body down when changing lenses. Dust on the sensor shows up as little black specks on your images, which is not a good thing.

Never store the camera without a lens or the body cap attached because pollutants may accidentally get into the camera, harming the delicate mechanical parts and possibly fouling the sensor.

Using image stabilization lenses

Many Canon and third-party lenses that fit your camera feature image stabilization. *Image stabilization* is a feature that enables you to shoot at a slower shutter speed than you'd normally be able to use and still get a blur-free image. The actual number of stops you can gain depends on how steady you are when handling the camera. To enable image stabilization:

1. **Locate the image stabilization switch on the side of your lens.**

   On Canon lenses, you'll find the switch on the left side of the lens when the camera is pointed toward your subject (see Figure 1-9). If you're using a third-party lens, look for a switch that reads IS, or refer to the lens manual.

2. **Push the switch to On to enable image stabilization.**

Figure 1-9: Slide this switch to enable image stabilization.

   Image stabilization uses the camera battery to compensate for operator movement. Therefore, a good idea is to shut off this feature when you need to conserve battery power and don't need image stabilization. Note that some lenses have two image stabilization switches: one that stabilizes the lens in a horizontal and vertical plane, and another switch that stabilizes the lens when you pan to follow a moving object.

When using a tripod to stabilize the camera, always turn image stabilization off, otherwise the feature may actually induce image blur when trying to compensate for non-existent camera motion.

Using a zoom lens

The kit lens that comes with the EOS 7D Mark II has a focal length range from 18mm (wide angle) to 135mm (telephoto). You can purchase additional Canon or third-party zoom lenses from your favorite camera supplier. Zoom lenses come in two flavors: twist to zoom, or push/pull to zoom in or out, respectively.

What's my focal length multiplier?

The sensor on your EOS 7D Mark II is smaller than the frame size of 35mm film. Therefore, the resulting image incorporates a smaller area than you'd capture with a 35mm film camera or a digital SLR with a sensor that's the same size as a frame of 35mm film — also known as a *full-frame sensor*. When you use a camera that has a sensor smaller than the 35mm film frame size, you can zoom in closer with a telephoto than would be possible with a camera with a full-frame sensor. Imagine looking through a window that's 4 feet × 6 feet. You see a large field of view including the sky. If the window is shrunk to 2 feet × 3 feet, you see less of the scene and sky, which is the same thing that happens when you use a camera with a sensor smaller than the 35mm film frame. Photographers who have previously shot film with 35mm cameras like to know how their lenses will behave on a camera without a full-frame sensor. They find out by multiplying their camera's focal length multiplier by the focal length of the lens. The focal length multiplier for your EOD 7D Mark II is 1.6. Therefore, a 50mm lens captures the same field of view as an 80mm (50mm × 1.6) lens does on a 35mm film camera or full-frame digital SLR. When I suggest a focal length, I refer to it as the *35mm equivalent*. For example, if I specify a telephoto focal length that is the 35mm equivalent of 80mm, this is a 50mm lens on the EOS 7D Mark II. The following image compares the difference between what a full frame camera captures and a crop frame camera captures (the area inside the red rectangle).

To use a zoom lens with a barrel that twists to change focal length:

1. **Grasp the lens barrel with your fingers.**
2. **Twist the barrel to zoom in or out.**

To use a push/pull zoom lens:

1. **Grasp the lens barrel with your fingers.**
2. **Push the barrel away from the camera to zoom in; pull the barrel toward the camera to zoom out.**

Using a lens hood

Unless you're pointing the camera directly at a strong light source, a lens hood prevents unwanted light from shining on the lens and causing lens flare. Most lens hoods are equipped with an index mark that you align with a mark on the end of the lens. Align the two marks and then rotate the lens hood counterclockwise until it locks into place. To remove a lens hood, rotate it counterclockwise. To store the lens and the lens hood in a camera case or camera bag, attach the lens hood in reverse.

Introducing the GPS Feature

The GPS (Global Positioning System) feature gives you the option of embedding the GPS coordinates of the location where you photograph an image as image metadata. This metadata can be used in applications that support GPS data such as Abode Photoshop Lightroom 5. In Adobe Photoshop Lightroom's Map module, images in your Library that have GPS data can be precisely positioned on the world map. The GPS feature also makes it possible for you to create a log of all the places you photographed images. I show you how to use GPS in more detail in Chapter 10.

If you're not using the GPS feature, disable it to conserve battery life.

Exploring Camera Connections

On the right side of the camera, you find two flaps that can be lifted. The flaps are weather-resistant to protect the connections under the flaps. Under the flaps you find a plethora of connections. This is where you connect various sundry connectors to your camera as shown in Figure 1-10. You have the following connections available on your camera:

- **Microphone port:**
  Connect an external
  microphone to this
  port to capture audio
  with your video.
  When you connect a
  microphone to this
  port, the onboard
  microphone is dis-
  abled. This port will
  capture stereo sound
  from a stereo micro-
  phone.

- **Headphone port:**
  Connect a head-
  phone to this port to
  monitor sound when
  recording movies.
  An external is also
  useful when setting
  audio levels (see
  Chapter 5).

- **PC port:** Connect a
  flash PC cord to this
  port when using flash
  units that are not
  compatible with the
  hot shoe on your camera.

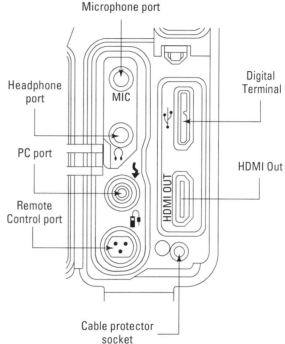

Figure 1-10: Connections from the camera to various sundry devices.

- **Remote Control port:** Connect an N3 type remote control device to this port and you can trigger the shutter remotely.

- **Digital terminal:** Connect the digital camera provided with the camera to a device with a USB port such as a printer to print on demand from the camera. This port can also be used to download images and movies directly from your camera to computer using the EOS Utilities.

- **HDMI Out:** Connect an HDMI (high-definition multimedia interface) cable from this port to an HDMI cable on your TV to watch high-definition video or view images on your TV that you captured on your camera.

- **Cable protector socket:** Insert the provided cable connector into this slot when connecting an interface cable to one of the ports. The cable protector provides support for the cable you are connecting to the camera.

Modifying Basic Camera Settings

Your camera ships with default settings for the country in which the camera was purchased. You also have default settings for the amount of time it takes the camera to power off when no picture taking or menu activity has occurred. You can modify these settings to suit your taste, as I show you in the upcoming sections.

Changing the date and time

Chances are your camera isn't set up for the right date and time when you get it. You can easily change this to the proper date and time by using a camera menu. Yes, consider this your baptism by fire if you've never worked with your camera menus before. To change the date and time:

1. **Press the Menu button.**

   The previously used menu appears on the LCD monitor.

2. **Use the Quick Control button to navigate to the Set Up tab, press the multi-controller button to navigate to the Set Up2 menu, and then use the Quick Control dial to select the Date/Time/Zone menu option.**

   The menu with the date and time options is displayed on your LCD monitor (see the left image in Figure 1-11).

3. **Press Set.**

   The month is highlighted.

4. **Rotate the Quick Control dial to change the number to the current month and then press Set.**

   The change is applied.

5. **Rotate the Quick Control dial to highlight the date.**

6. **Repeat Steps 4 and 5 to set the date.**

7. **Continue in this manner to change the year, hour, minute, and seconds to the current time.**

   You can also change the format in which the date is displayed by high-lighting the default option, pressing Set, choosing the desired option, and then pressing Set again to apply the change. For most users in Central and North America, the default is perfect.

8. **Rotate the Quick Control dial to highlight the Daylight Savings option, press Set, choose the desired option, and then press Set to apply the change.**

   With this option, you can enable the Daylight Savings option. If daylight savings is applicable where you live, enable the Daylight Savings option, and the camera will automatically set the time back or ahead according to your time zone.

9. **Rotate the Quick Control dial to highlight the Time Zone option, press Set, choose the time zone in which you live, and then press Set.**

   The right image in Figure 1-11 shows all of the options and is set for a photographer living in the Eastern time zone of the United States.

10. **Rotate the Quick Control dial to highlight OK and then press Set.**

    Your changes are applied. The date and time are added to the metadata of each picture you take.

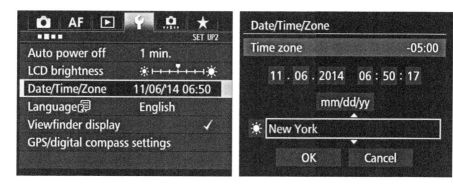

Figure 1-11: Changing the date and time.

Changing the auto power-off time

Your camera powers off automatically after a certain period of non-operation. You can specify a period of time from 1 minute to 30 minutes, or you can disable power-off. However, your camera will automatically power off after 30 minutes of non-activity even if you choose Off. If you choose a power-off time that's of a short duration, you'll conserve your battery. After your camera powers off, press the shutter button and the camera powers on again. To change the power-off time:

1. **Press the Menu button.**

   The previously used menu appears on the LCD monitor.

2. **Use the Quick Control button to navigate to the Set Up tab, press the multi-controller button to navigate to the Set Up2 menu, and then use the Quick Control dial to select the Auto Power Off option (see the left image in Figure 1-12).**

3. **Press the Set button.**

   The Auto Power Off options display (see the right image in Figure 1-12).

4. **Rotate the Quick Control dial to select the desired setting and then press Set.**

   The change is applied.

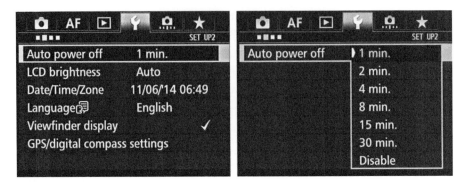

Figure 1-12: Changing the power-off time.

I recommend that you choose the shortest duration for auto power-off that you're comfortable with. This helps conserve battery power. As long as the power button is in the On position, your camera wakes almost instantaneously when you press the shutter button halfway.

To restore the camera to its default settings, press the Menu button and then use the Quick Control button to navigate to the Set Up tab. Next, use the multi-controller to navigate to the Set Up4 menu, choose Clear All Camera Settings, and press Set.

Working with Memory Cards

Your camera has slots for two memory cards: one for CF (CompactFlash) and one for SD (Secure Digital) cards to store the pictures you take. A *memory card* is a mechanical device similar to a hard drive. You insert a new card when you begin shooting and remove the card when it's full. With two cards you have many possibilities. For example, you can capture images in the RAW format on one card, and the same images in the JPEG format on the other card. This is a handy option if you shoot images that needed to be posted online quickly, but then processed to pixel-perfection at a later date.

To insert a memory card:

1. **Open the card cover on the right side of the camera as you look from the back.**

   To open the cover, slide it away from the camera until it stops, and then rotate it away from the camera. Note there are two slots. The big slot is for a CF card; the smaller slot is for an SD card.

2. **Insert the card in the slot.**

   As shown in Figure 1-13, the card label is facing you.

3. **Gently push the card into the slot.**

   Never force a card because you may damage the pins in the camera and the card. The card slides easily into the camera when aligned properly.

4. **If desired, insert a second card into the other slot.**

   Double your pleasure, double your fun.

5. **Close the card cover.**

   You're ready to shoot up a storm.

Figure 1-13: Inserting a memory card.

You may be tempted to pick up a 32GB or 64GB card, thinking you can store a gazillion images on one card and not worry about running out of room. But memory cards are mechanical devices that are subject to failure and will fail when you least expect it. If a large card fails, you lose lots of images. I carry a couple 16GB CF cards in my camera bag. Although I hate to lose any images, I'd rather lose 16GB worth of images than 32 or 64GB. I advise you to purchase smaller memory cards.

Even though newer memory cards are very reliable, they are subject to Murphy's Law and will fail at the least opportune time such as when you have hundreds of images on a card from your vacation. If your computer cannot read a card, you may be able to save it with a data recovery program, which you can search for online. Many companies let you download a trial version of their data recovery program. It will let you recover and view images, but not save them. If the application enables you to view images after recovery, purchase the full version and you'll be able to download your precious images to your computer. Unless the card is under warranty, throw it away after the data recovery application performs its magic.

Formatting a memory card

Remember back in the Jurassic era of photography when you had to remove film from a camera and send it off to be processed? I do. I know that dates me. But with a digital camera, after you download images to your computer and back them up, you format the card so you can use it again. A good idea is to format your cards before using them again, even if you didn't fill them. Doing this ensures you'll have a full card to work with and won't download duplicate images.

Your camera has two card slots: one for a CF (Compact Flash) card, and one for an SD (Secure Digital) card. In the following sections, I show you how to format each type.

Formatting a CF card

CF cards are big and solid. Photographers have actually driven over them by mistake and the cards survived to store images.

To format a CF card:

1. **Insert the card in the camera, as I outline in the preceding section.**

   The CF card goes in slot 1.

2. **Press the Menu button.**

   The previously used menu appears on the LCD monitor.

3. **Use the Quick Control button to navigate to the Set Up tab and then use the multi-controller button to navigate to the Set Up1 menu.**

4. **Rotate the Quick Control dial to select Format card and press Set.**

   The Format card option is selected (see the left image in Figure 1-14).

5. **Rotate the Quick Control dial to select Slot 1 and press the Set button.**

   The menu changes to show the amount of data on the card and displays a warning that all data will be lost (see the right image in Figure 1-14).

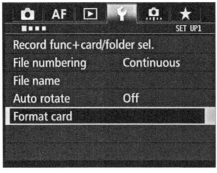

Figure 1-14: Formatting a CF card.

6. **Rotate the Quick Control dial to highlight OK and press Set.**

   The card is formatted. After formatting, you have a blank card that's ready to capture images from the camera. If you have two cards in the camera, repeat these steps and select the other card in Step 5. Note that when you format an SD card, you have different options, which are covered in the next section.

You can't undo formatting a card. Make sure you've downloaded all images to your computer before you format a card.

7. Press the shutter button halfway to exit the menu and resume taking pictures.

Formatting an SD card

SD cards are more fragile than CF cards. Canon hedged their bet by including an SD slot on this camera. They figured photographers upgrading to the EOS 7D Mark II may have previously owned cameras that use SD cards. You format SD cards exactly the same as mentioned in the previous section, except you choose Slot 2. The rest of the steps are identical except for the option to perform a Low Level Format.

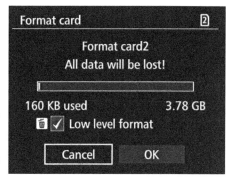

Figure 1-15: Enabling low level formatting on an SD card.

To enable Low Level formatting, press the Erase button, to select the Low level format checkbox (see Figure 1-15), and then rotate the Quick Control dial to highlight OK and press Set. Use Low Level formatting when the card has been used in another camera, the card is full of images, or a card error message is displayed.

Removing a memory card

When a card is full, remove it from the camera and insert a new one. To remove a memory card:

1. Open the memory card cover.

To open the cover, slide it away from the camera until it stops and then rotate it away from the camera.

2. Push the white button toward the rear of the CF card cover.

The CF card pops loose from the pins.

3. To remove an SD card, gently push it.

The card pops out of the slot.

4. Gently pull the card from the slot.

You're now ready to insert a new card and start shooting.

Taking Care of Your Camera Battery

The LP-E6N battery in your EOS 7D Mark II is a rechargeable lithium-ion battery that is engineered for a long life and enables you to capture about 800 images when you use the camera in warm weather. You'll also be glad to know that if you have LP-E6 Canon batteries, they are compatible with the EOS 7D Mark II. When you photograph in colder climates, the amount of images you can capture decreases. Here are some recommendations for getting the best performance from your camera battery:

- **After you charge a battery, replace the cover so you can see blue through the battery-shaped hole.** This signifies that you have a fully charged battery under the cover, useful information if you own more than one battery.

- **Remove the battery from the camera after you've finished shooting for the day.** The battery loses a bit of its charge if you store it in the camera.

- **When replacing the cover over a partially used or fully discharged battery, place the cover so that the blue does not show through the battery-shaped hole.** This is your indication that the battery is partially discharged.

- **In cold conditions, place the spare battery in your coat pocket.** This keeps it warm and extends the life of the battery charge.

- **Replace the battery immediately when you see the low battery warning.** If you deplete the battery power completely when your camera is writing data to the memory card, the card may be corrupted.

- **Never remove the battery when the data access light is blinking.** This indicates your camera is writing data to the card. Removing the battery prematurely can damage the memory card and cause loss of data.

- **Beware of third-party batteries that fit your EOS 7D Mark II.** They may not be compatible with your camera's battery information system, which means you won't know how much charge remains in the battery. If the battery runs out of charge while the camera is writing data to the memory card, you may damage the memory card, the battery, or both. Batteries that don't work with your camera typically come with their own charging units. Using a third-party battery may also void your camera warranty.

Charging Your Camera Battery

When you notice the battery status icon is red, it's time to charge the battery. Charge the battery using the charger supplied with the camera. You can recharge LP-E6N and LP-E6 batteries with this charger. To recharge your camera battery, follow these steps:

1. **Plug the battery charger into a wall outlet.**

   If you live in North America, your charger works in a 110-volt outlet. If you travel overseas with your camera, make sure you bring a converter. If you insert the charger into an outlet with the wrong voltage, you'll ruin it.

2. **Insert the battery (see Figure 1-16).**

   After you insert the battery, an orange light appears in the charger. If the light blinks once per second, the battery has 0 to 49 percent charge. When the light blinks twice per second, the battery has 50 to 74 percent charge. When the battery blinks three times per second, the battery has 75 percent or higher charge.

Figure 1-16: Charging the battery.

3. **Continue charging the battery until the light is green.**

   The battery has a 100 percent charge.

4. **Replace the protective cover over the battery (see Figure 1-17).**

Figure 1-17: Replacing the battery cover.

Cleaning the Sensor

When you power on your Canon EOS 7D Mark II, the sensor is automatically cleaned (see Figure 1-18). The camera accomplishes this by jiggling the sensor to dislodge any dust particles. This works well, but sometimes stubborn particles of dust don't fall off the sensor with the automatic cleaning.

You can, however, manually clean your sensor as outlined in the next section.

Cleaning your sensor on command

If you notice black specks in areas of your image that are one solid color, such as the sky, you have dust on your sensor. Your camera will automatically clean the sensor as outlined in the previous section. However, sometimes that's not enough. If you consistently see dust spots in the same area on several images, you'll be happy to know there's a menu command you can use to clean your sensor, whenever you feel the need, by following these steps:

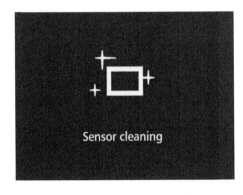

Figure 1-18: Shake it up baby, now. Shake it up baby. Clean me off.

1. **Press the Menu button.**

   The previously used menu appears on the LCD monitor.

2. **Use the Quick Control button to navigate to the Set Up tab and then use the multi-controller button to navigate to the Set Up3 menu.**

3. **Use the Quick Control dial to highlight Sensor Cleaning and then press Set (see the left image in Figure 1-19).**

   The Sensor Cleaning options are displayed.

4. **Use the Quick Control dial to highlight Clean Now (the right image in Figure 1-19) and then press Set.**

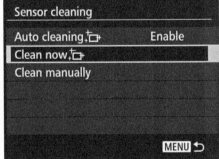

Figure 1-19: Cleaning the camera sensor.

5. **A dialog box appears, asking you whether you want to clean your sensor now.**

   OK is selected by default.

6. **Press Set.**

   Your camera performs a sensor cleaning cycle.

7. **Press the shutter button halfway to exit the camera menu.**

   You're now ready to start shooting with a squeaky-clean sensor.

After using the Clean Now menu command, put a lens on your camera, manually set the focus to the closest distance at which the lens will focus, and then take a picture of the clear blue sky. Open the image in your image-editing program and zoom in to 100 percent magnification. Sensor dust shows as dark spots. If you have stubborn specks of sensor dust on your camera, run the Clean Now menu command a couple of times. If the dust is still there, you can manually clean the sensor (as outlined in the next section).

Cleaning your sensor manually

Your camera has a self-cleaning sensor, and you can run a cleaning cycle whenever you want; however, you may inadvertently get a stubborn piece of dust that develops a magnetic attraction to your sensor and needs to be cleaned manually.

To determine whether you have dust on your sensor, follow these steps:

1. **Switch to Av (Aperture Priority) mode and choose your smallest aperture.**

   For further information on using Aperture Priority mode and manually setting your aperture, see Chapter 6.

2. **Switch the lens to manual focus and rack the focus to its nearest point.**

   That's right: You want the sky to be out of focus. That way the dust specks will show up as black dots.

3. **Take a picture of a clear blue sky, download the picture to your computer, and review it in your image-editing program at 100 percent magnification.**

   If you see black specks in the image, you have dust on your sensor.

The best way to clean dust off your sensor is to blow it off with a powerful bulb blower. Several blowers are on the market with generic names like Hurricane or Rocket. The Giottos Rocket Blaster is shown in Figure 1-20. A good blower is made of natural rubber and features a small opening at the tip that enables you to direct a strong current of air with pinpoint accuracy.

To clean the sensor manually:

1. **Switch to one of the Creative Zone modes and then take the lens off the camera.**

   The option to clean manually is not available in the Basic Zones.

2. **Press the Menu button.**

   The camera menu is displayed on the LCD monitor.

3. **Use the Quick Control button to navigate to the Set Up tab, and then use the multi-controller button to navigate to the Set Up3 menu.**

4. **Use the Quick Control dial to highlight Sensor Cleaning and then press Set.**

   The Sensor cleaning options are displayed.

5. **Use the Quick Control dial to highlight Clean Manually and then press Set.**

   A dialog box appears telling you the mirror will lock-up. OK is selected by default. When the mirror locks up, you have access to the camera sensor.

6. **Press Set.**

   The camera mirror opens and you have access to the camera sensor.

7. **Point the camera at the ground and place the air blower inside the sensor chamber, being careful not to touch the sensor.**

   When you point the camera at the ground, any dust you dislodge off the sensor falls to the ground. Gravity works. Be careful not to touch the sensor with the blower. I use a black felt tip marker to make a spot one-inch away from the tip of the blower. As long as the spot is visible, the blower won't touch the sensor.

8. **Squeeze the bulb repeatedly.**

   When you squeeze the bulb, move the blower around so the blast of air hits all areas of the sensor. This increases your chances of getting rid of all the dust.

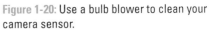

Figure 1-20: Use a bulb blower to clean your camera sensor.

9. **When you've finished blowing dust off the sensor, power off the camera.**

   When you flip the camera switch to off, the mirror closes. Make sure you put a lens on the camera or a body cap on the camera immediately. After thoroughly cleaning the sensor, you don't want dust getting back in the chamber.

Using sensor cleaning equipment

If you're a DIY (do-it-yourself) kind of photographer, you may want to consider cleaning your sensor with commercially available products. Lots of products — brushes, swabs, and chemicals — that you use to manually clean the camera sensor are on the market. Yes, that does mean you physically touch the sensor with a product. Therefore, the product you choose needs to be made from material that can't scratch the camera sensor. You must also have a very steady hand when using these products.

I've used sensor-cleaning products manufactured by VisibleDust (www.visibledust.com). VisibleDust manufactures a lighted sensor loupe that you place over the lens opening to examine the sensor for any visible dust — hence, the company name. The loupe is made of glass and makes it easy to see any specs of dust on your lens. VisibleDust also manufactures an Arctic Butterfly brush, which runs on two AAA batteries. To use this brush:

1. **Push a button to spin the brush.**

   This gives the brush a static electricity charge.

2. **Brush the sensor once with the charged brush.**

   Dust particles are attracted to the brush.

3. **Remove the brush from the camera body and then press the button to spin the brush again.**

   This discharges the particles into the air.

4. **Use the brush as needed to remove any dust that may have accumulated on the sensor.**

I've used both products with a good outcome on my cameras. For more information, visit www.visibledust.com or ask your favorite camera retailer for information about these products.

Never touch the sensor with the blower. Never use a blower with a CO_2 cartridge. CO_2 cartridges contain propellants that can foul your sensor.

Keeping your sensor clean

The best way to keep your sensor clean is to never change a lens. However, this defeats the purpose of a digital SLR. But if you are meticulous about changing lenses, and follow a bit of sage advice, you'll keep your sensor as squeaky-clean as possible. I first learned about sensor dust when I owned my first digital SLR, the Canon EOS 10D. I was on a business trip/vacation to California. When I was reviewing some images I shot of the Golden Gate Bridge, I noticed some horrible dust specks on the image. Since then I've learned that doing the following minimizes the chances of dust adhering to the sensor:

- **Power off the camera before changing lenses.** If you leave the power on, the sensor maintains a charge that can attract dust.

- **Never change lenses in a dusty environment.** If you're photographing in a dry, dusty environment, find a sheltered area in which to change lenses. When all else fails, the inside of your car is a better place to change lenses than in a dry, dusty area.

- **Never change lenses when it's windy.** In windy conditions, find a sheltered environment in which to change lenses.

- **Point the camera down when changing lenses.** This minimizes the chances of dust blowing into the sensor.

- **Have the other lens ready.** When I change lenses, it's a juggling act. I keep the lens I'm going to put on the camera in one hand with the rear cap off. I point the camera at the ground and grasp the lens I'm going to remove with one hand, and press the lens release button with a finger from the other hand. I then quickly remove one lens and replace it with the other. With practice, you can do this quickly and minimize the chance of dust fouling your sensor.

The sensor chamber of your camera is lubricated. Sometimes lubricant can get on the sensor and cause a spot to appear on your images. If conventional methods of cleaning the sensor don't work, send the camera to Canon for sensor cleaning, or to a local camera shop that offers this service.

Accessorizing Your EOS 7D Mark II

Your EOS 7D Mark II is a mechanical and technological masterpiece. But the camera comes with a nice cardboard box, which is great for shipping the camera, but not so great for storing the camera on a day-to-day basis. And the camera ships with this nice strap that tells the world you're shooting with a Canon EOS camera, but the strap is thin — and with a long telephoto lens, it will feel like you're carrying a brick around your neck. So, first and foremost, you need a decent camera case and you need a good strap. There are lots of other goodies you can invest in that will make using your camera more enjoyable.

Useful Canon accessories

Canon sells lots of goodies in its online store that may also be available from other sources such as your local camera retailer or your favorite online camera store. Here are a couple of items you may consider purchasing:

- **Extra LC-E6 battery pack:** If you shoot lots of pictures, having an extra fully-charged battery in your camera bag can save the day.

- **Car Battery Charger CBC-E6:** If you do a lot of remote shooting from your car, this accessory enables you to charge your camera battery from the car's 12-volt outlet, which was formerly known as the receptacle for the cigarette lighter.

- **BGE 16 battery grip:** This accessory is attached to the bottom of your camera and extends your shooting time. The battery grip houses one or two LP-E6N or EP-6 batteries or six AA batteries. The grip also features a variety of operating controls such as shutter button, Main dial, AF point selection button, AE lock/FE lock button, AF start button, multi-controller, and multi-function button. This is the ideal accessory if you're a high-volume shooter.

- **LC-5 wireless controller:** This accessory enables you to trigger the shutter of your EOS 7D Mark II wirelessly.

- **Dedicated Canon flash:** Your EOS 7D Mark II has an onboard pop-up flash unit. If you need a more powerful flash unit, Canon makes several flash units that are compatible with your camera. The beauty of using a dedicated flash is that the camera communicates with the flash unit when you place it in the hot shoe, and can also communicate wirelessly with one or multiple flash units as discussed in Chapter 7. The following flash units will work with your EOS 7D Mark II: 90 EX, 270EX, 320 EX, 430EXII, and 600EX-RT. I discuss flash photography with your EOS 7D Mark II in Chapter 7.

- **RS-80N remote switch:** This accessory plugs into the side of your EOS 7D Mark II and enables you to trigger the shutter by pushing a button. This accessory is ideal if you use your camera on a tripod. If you press the camera shutter button, vibration is transmitted to the camera, which may cause the image to be less than sharp. The remote switch prevents the vibration.

✒ **TC-80N3 timer remote controller:** This accessory also plugs into the side of your EOS 7D Mark II. You use it to trigger the camera remotely, but you can also program this accessory to capture multiple images over a period of time. You determine the amount of time between images. With the camera mounted on a tripod, you can create time-lapse photographs of an object or area and record the climate change, cloud movement, and such. You bring the captured images into a program like Photoshop and create a time-lapse movie. Your camera has a built-in interval timer, but some people prefer using devices instead of menus. If you fall into this group, the accessory may just be the bee's knees.

Useful third-party accessories

Canon makes great accessories for your camera, but there are other accessories you will need, such as tripods, camera cases, camera bags, and so on. Canon does offer some of these accessories, but your friendly author has been at this photography game for some time and offers the following list for you to consider:

✒ **Camera strap:** This is the first item I suggest you replace. In fact, I suggest you don't even use the strap that came with the camera. Leave it in pristine condition in its little plastic snuggie. Then, if you ever decide to sell the camera on eBay, you can offer it with an unused camera strap. I suggest you purchase a sling strap such as those offered by CarrySpeed (www.carryspeed.com) or Black Rapid (www.blackrapid.com). A sling strap distributes the weight of the camera and lens over your shoulder and places the camera at your hip. When you need to use your camera, you can quickly grab it from your side and bring it to your eye. The CarrySpeed strap features a mounting system that does not let the strap touch the camera, which could possibly mar the finish. Another great thing about the CarrySpeed strap is the actual strap; it's wide and has a neoprene backing which holds the strap in place. A sling strap comfortably distributes the weight of the camera and lens. If you shoot for long periods of time and with long lenses, a comfortable camera strap is a must-have accessory.

✒ **Camera case:** If you end up purchasing lots of accessories for your camera (such as additional lenses, additional batteries, and so on), you'll need a place for your stuff. A hard-shell camera case is the ideal place to store your gear when you're not using it. Pelican (www.pelicancase.com) makes a wide variety of cases that you can customize to fit your gear. Nanuk (www.nanukcase.com) also sells a line of customizable hard-shell cases. I own both and can vouch for the fact that they are quality products.

✒ **Camera bag:** A camera bag is a place to put your stuff when you're out on a photo shoot. If you don't own a lot of gear, you can get by with a small camera bag. However, if you do end up owning a lot of gear, plus the obligatory kitchen sink, you'll need a bag that can hold lots of stuff, or perhaps two bags: one that will hold most of your gear and accessories, and a smaller bag to use when you're going commando (shooting with just your camera, one or two lenses, and a minimum of accessories). My favorite bags are the Speed Freak Version 2 (shown at the top of Figure 1-21) and ChangeUp Version 2 (shown at the bottom of Figure 1-21), both made by Think Tank Photo (www.thinktankphoto.com). The bags are made of durable material, have bullet-proof zippers, and lots of hidey holes for your accessories. LowePro (www.lowepro.com) also makes a good camera bag. A rain hood is another good option to look for when purchasing a camera bag. Rain and digital equipment are like oil and water; they don't mix.

Figure 1-21: A comfortable camera bag is a must for any serious photographer.

- **Tripod:** If you shoot landscapes, HDR (high dynamic range), or shoot in low light, a tripod is a useful accessory. A tripod steadies your camera when you shoot at low shutter speeds. When you shoot with a tripod, it's advisable to have a remote-control device to trigger the shutter (as mentioned in the previous section). When you purchase a tripod, buy a device that will support the weight of your camera body plus the heaviest lens you anticipate purchasing or using. Add 50 percent to that figure. If you purchase a tripod that will only handle the weight of your camera and its heaviest lens, you'll run into an issue known as *tripod creep*. This is when the tripod slowly sinks. You also need a sturdy tripod when photographing in windy conditions. Most tripods have a hook underneath the tripod head to which you can attach a sand bag, which helps steady the tripod in windy conditions. You also have to consider the weight of the tripod. If you use your car as a base of operations, or photograph in studio conditions, tripod weight is not that much of a factor. However, if you photograph wildlife and nature and do a lot of hiking, lugging a heavy tripod will quickly wear you out. If this is the case, consider purchasing an aluminum or carbon-fiber tripod. I purchased a carbon-fiber tripod as a gift for my wife and she loves it. The tripod will support her camera plus a 400-mm lens. The light weight makes it possible for her to hike several miles with the tripod and a camera bag in absolute comfort. Another useful option for a tripod is a built-in spirit level. Even though your camera has a built in dual-axis level, sometimes it's easier to take a quick look at the tripod. A good tripod head is also a must. If you can afford a lightweight tripod with a ball head, you'll have everything you need to capture blur-free photos with ease.

- **Hot-shoe level:** This is yet another way of making sure your camera is straight. Sometimes I like to get a low vantage point, but don't feel like being prone on the ground. When I run into this scenario, I use a small dual-axis bubble level that slides into the camera's hot shoe.

  Even though your camera has a built-in dual-axis level, it will be hard to use in scenarios like this.

- **Extra memory cards:** Memory cards are cheap. Buy a couple of extra CF and SD cards so you have a fresh card when you're photographing your favorite place, or a place you've never been to before.

- **Lens-cleaning kit:** Purchase a micro-fiber cloth that is designed to clean optical equipment. You can also purchase lens-cleaning fluid to use in conjunction with your micro-fiber cloth.

- **LCD protector:** Your LCD monitor is a vulnerable part of your camera. It can be chipped or otherwise damaged. Consider purchasing a screen to protect your LCD monitor from damage. Zagg (www.zagg.com) makes a shield that is transparent and scratch-resistant. As of this writing, a shield is not available for your EOS 7D Mark II, but the EOS 7D shield will cover the monitor nicely.

Accessories for video

Video is a whole different kettle of fish. Digital SLRs were not designed to capture video, so they're not user-friendly for videographers, but on the other hand, digital SLRs can capture incredible video that rivals conventional video recorders. Here are a few options to consider if you're going to create video with your Canon EOS 7D Mark II:

- **Tripod:** Review the information about tripods in the previous section. You can use the same tripod for still images and video. The only difference will be that you'll need to purchase a fluid ball head like the Manfrotto 504 HD Fluid Video Head. When you purchase a video head, make sure it will support the weight of your camera body, plus the heaviest lens you anticipate using for shooting video, plus 50 percent.

- **Video shoulder rig:** In addition to shooting from a tripod, you can shoot video using a rig that mounts the camera on your shoulder, or you can purchase a device that will hold the camera steady while you move. There are lots of rigs available in all different price ranges. My advice is to get one you can afford and one that will hold your camera steady. This may involve considerable research. I don't personally own a video rig, so I'm not in a position to make a recommendation. However, if you visit an online camera store like B&H Photo (www.bhphotovideo.com)

or Adorama (www.adorama.com), look at the various models that are available. If there are reviews posted by users, read them as well. When you've narrowed it down to a couple of devices, call the camera store and ask them for their opinions.

✏ **Video viewfinder:** When you shoot video with your EOS 7D Mark II, the LCD monitor is your viewfinder. However, the LCD monitor can be difficult to view in bright light. Therefore, a video viewfinder is a useful accessory. Hoodman (www.hoodmanusa.com) makes an affordable video viewfinder called the Hoodloupe. You can combine this with an item called Hoodstrap that will mount the Hoodloupe to your camera to create a fairly inexpensive video viewfinder.

✏ **High-speed memory card:** When you capture video with your EOS 7D Mark II, your camera is capturing video at the rate of 24 to 60 frames per second. A standard memory card may not be able to keep up with the fast frame rate. For video, it's recommended that you use a card with a data-transfer rate of 90 Mbps. Sandisk (www.sandisk.com) offers a memory card series called Extreme Pro that is ideal for capturing video.

Keeping the Camera Body Clean

You've invested a considerable amount of money in your EOS 7D Mark II and accessories. To maintain your investment, and to keep the camera in top operating condition, you need to take care of your purchase. As mentioned previously, you can clean your lenses with a lens-cleaning fluid and microfiber cloth. However, you should never use a solvent on your camera body. When you want to clean your camera body, wet a soft cloth and then wring it almost dry. Gently rub the cloth over the camera body to remove any residue from skin oil or airborne pollutants. Some areas of your camera (such as the Quick Control dial) have ridges that are traps for dirt and debris from your skin. You can clean these areas with a soft toothbrush. It is also recommended that you clean your camera body with a soft, almost-dry cloth whenever you're photographing near the ocean when there's a salty mist in the air.

2

Automatically Capturing Great Photographs

In This Chapter

- Looking at the camera menu
- Understanding exposure and focal length
- Focusing your camera
- Working with flash in Full Auto mode
- Starting the self-timer
- Triggering the shutter remotely

Your EOS 7D Mark II can do some pretty amazing things. You have lots of control over the camera to get ideal pictures. But if all the control seems a bit daunting when you're getting to know your new toy, you can let the camera make most of the decisions for you. If you're thinking point and shoot, yup, that's what you get when you let the camera take the reins. However, you can still get some great pictures with your EOS 7D Mark II when you take pictures using the Full Auto mode.

If you're an experienced photographer, breeze through this chapter and you can show someone else how to get great pictures with your high-tech camera — that is, if you can part company with it long enough for someone else to use it. In this chapter, I show you how to get the most out of your camera's auto mode. I also show you how to use the self-timer in case you want to take a self-portrait, and I show you how to use the on-camera flash automatically.

One of the exciting features of the EOS 7D Mark II is *Live View mode,* which lets you compose your image with the LCD monitor. In this chapter, I deal exclusively with taking pictures through the viewfinder. If you're chomping at the bit to find out how to shoot with Live View, fast-forward to Chapter 5.

Ordering from Your Camera Menu

Some of your picture-taking tasks involve using the camera menu. For example, when you format a memory card, you use the menu. You also use the menu to specify image size and quality as well as set the parameters for tasks, such as automatic exposure bracketing. I give you a brief introduction to the camera menu in Chapter 1 when I show you how to format a memory card and change the date and time. In this section, I give you a brief overview of the menu system. Throughout this book, I show you how to use the menu to perform a specific task. To access the camera menu:

1. **Push the Mode Dial lock and then rotate the Mode dial to P (see Figure 2-1).**

   P on the Mode dial stands for *Programmed Auto Exposure mode.* When you access the menu in one of the creative shooting modes (P, Tv, Av, M, or B), you have access to all the menu items.

Figure 2-1: You have access to all menu options when you shoot in Programmed Auto Exposure mode.

2. **Press the Menu button and then press the Quick Control button to navigate to the Shoot tab on the left (see the left image in Figure 2-2).**

   The first menu on the Shoot tab is called Shoot1, which is your first set of shooting options. In Table 2-1 after these steps, I list each tab and the accompanying menus for easy reference. Certain menu options, such as changing image format, aren't available when taking pictures with the Full Auto mode (A+ on the Mode dial).

   When you access a menu, the first option is selected by default. In this case, Image quality is selected.

3. **Press the Set button.**

   Your menu display changes to reveal the image quality options (see the right image in Figure 2-2). Notice the icon to the right of the RAW options. This signifies that you use the Main dial to specify this setting.

Notice the icon to the right of the JPEG settings. This signifies that you use the Quick Control dial to specify this setting.

4. **After changing a menu option, press Set.**

   This commits the change and returns you to the previous menu.

5. **To highlight another option in the current menu, rotate the Quick Control dial to the desired item.**

   This highlights the menu option.

6. **To access the menu option, press Set.**

   You can now change the menu option. Sometimes you use a combination of the multi-controller button, the Quick Control dial, and the Main dial to make a setting. In most instances, you commit the change by pressing Set, although the Menu and Info buttons are used on some occasions. An icon appears on each menu, indicating the button to press to apply the change.

7. **Press the multi-controller button to the right.**

   This displays the Shoot2 menu. The amount of menus with the tab you select depends on the mode in which you're shooting. If you followed my instructions in Step 2, you see six tabs, and each tab has associated menus. For example, the Shoot tab has six Shoot menus. Throughout the rest of the book, I show you how to use options in these tabs to perform various tasks.

8. **Press the Menu button or press the shutter button halfway to exit the menu.**

   Either operation returns you to shooting mode. I prefer pressing the shutter button halfway.

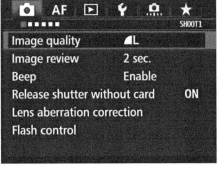
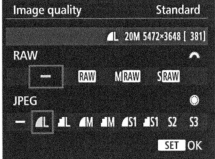

Figure 2-2: This menu has shooting options.

Table 2-1		The Camera Menu Tabs
Tab Icon	*Menu Name*	*Description*
[camera icon]	Shoot1	The first menu from the Shoot tab is used to specify image format, review time, flash control, and similar options.
[camera icon]	Shoot2	The second menu from the Shoot tab is used to set exposure compensation, ISO speed, color space, and similar options.
[camera icon]	Shoot3	The third menu from the Shoot tab is used to specify picture style, highlight tone priority, dust delete data, and a plethora of other options.
[camera icon]	Shoot4	The fourth menu from the Shoot tab is used to enable red-eye reduction, the interval timer, and similar options. This menu has different commands when you shoot movies.
[camera icon]	Shoot5	The fifth menu from the Shoot tab is used to enable Live View shooting, choose the auto focus method, display the grid, and so on. This menu has different commands when you shoot movies.
[camera icon]	Shoot6	The sixth menu from the Shoot tab is used to specify Live View Silent shooting mode and set the Metering Timer. This menu has different commands when you shoot movies.
AF	AF1	The first menu from the AF tab is used to specify autofocus options for specific shooting scenarios.
AF	AF2	The second menu from the AF tab is used to set Auto Focus Image Priority.
AF	AF3	The third menu from the AF tab is used to enable features such as autofocus assist beam firing.
AF	AF4	The fourth menu from the AF tab is used to specify how autofocus selection is achieved, whether the lens will continue to attempt focusing during difficult or impossible focusing situations, and so on.
AF	AF5	The fifth menu from the AF tab is used to fine tune manual autofocus point selection, specify how autofocus points are displayed during focus, and so on.

Tab Icon	Menu Name	Description
	Play1	The first menu on the Play tab is used to protect images, erase images, and similar options.
	Play2	The second menu on the Play tab is used to resize and rate images, set up slide shows, and so on.
	Play3	The third menu on the Play tab is used to enable Highlight Alert, display the playback grid, set histogram options, and so on.
	Set Up1	The first menu on the Set Up tab is used to choose the file numbering method, change the default file name, format a card, and so on.
	Set Up2	The second menu on the Set Up tab is used to choose LCD brightness option, set date and time, and similar options.
	Set Up3	The third menu on the Set Up tab is used to display battery information, clean the sensor, specify the video system, and a partridge in a pear tree.
	Set Up4	The fourth menu on the Set Up tab is used to assign a custom shooting mode to the camera Mode dial, clear camera settings, add photographer's copyright information to each image, and similar options.
	C.FN1	The first menu from the C.FN (Custom Function) tab is used to set custom exposure settings.
	C.FN2	The second menu from the C.FN (Custom Function) tab is used to set custom exposure and drive settings.
	C.FN3	The third menu from the C.FN (Custom Function) tab is used to set custom display and operation settings.
	C.FN4	The fourth menu from the C.FN (Custom Function) tab is used to add cropping information to the viewfinder and specify the default erase option.
	C.FN5	The fifth menu from the C.FN (Custom Function) tab is the Hail Mary menu with only one command that enables you to clear all custom settings.
	My Menu1	This menu is to create custom tabs to keep your most frequently used menu commands in one place.

Where did all the cute icons go?

If you've upgraded from an earlier Canon camera, such as the EOS 50D, and have explored your EOS 7D Mark II's Mode dial, you may wonder where all the cute little icons are. You may be thinking that the icon with the mountain, the girl with the floppy hat, and so on, are present on every Canon camera. Not so. You graduated into the big leagues when you bought this camera; it has professional features, and pros don't use cameras with funny icons that designate shooting modes that, er, rank amateurs use. Having said that, your EOS 7D Mark II has a Full Auto mode, which enables you, or someone who doesn't have a lot of photography experience, to still get good photos automatically.

Taking Your First Picture

You can easily get great results with your EOS 7D Mark II automatically. In Full Auto mode, all you have to do is compose the picture, achieve focus, and press the shutter button. The camera literally takes care of everything. You don't have to mess with choosing the shutter speed, aperture, ISO setting, or anything else for that matter. The camera meters the amount of light coming to the camera and makes all the heavy decisions for you.

When you're shooting in Full Auto mode, the camera chooses the actual shutter speed, aperture, and ISO used, which is determined by the amount of available light. The camera chooses a shutter speed and aperture to ensure a properly exposed image (see "Understanding Exposure and Focal Length" later in this chapter). When you're taking pictures in dim lighting or at night, the camera will attempt to choose a shutter speed that ensures a blur-free image (see the sidebar "Shutter speed and image sharpness" later in this chapter) and the flash may pop up as well. If the shutter speed is too slow, you need to mount the camera on a tripod to ensure a blur-free image.

Depending on the lighting conditions, the camera may have to increase the ISO setting, which makes the camera more sensitive to light. An ISO setting above 800 may result in digital noise in the darker areas of the image. When you shoot in Full Auto mode, the camera also determines the aperture, which combined with the focal length of the lens you're using and determines how much of the image is in apparent focus from front to back.

When you unpacked your camera and started exploring the controls, you probably noticed the Mode dial on the top-left side of the camera as you look at it from behind — the same position from which you take pictures. The default setting for this dial is *A+*, which of course, means *Automatic.* These instructions are generic and don't assume you've bought the camera with the kit lens. To take a photograph automatically, follow these steps:

1. **Insert a memory card in the camera (see Chapter 1), power on the camera, format the card, and then attach the desired lens to the camera.**

   If you're not familiar with formatting a card or attaching a lens to the camera, check out Chapter 1.

2. **If you're using a lens with image stabilization, move the switch to IS.**

   If you bought the camera kit with the 18–135mm lens, you'll find this switch on the left side of the lens with the camera in front of you.

3. **Make sure the lens is set to AF (autofocus).**

   If you're using a Canon lens, you'll find a switch labeled AF on the left side of the lens when the camera is pointed toward your subject.

4. **Press the Mode Lock button and then rotate the Mode dial to the A+ (Full Auto) setting.**

   It's the first setting, the green rectangle on the Mode dial (see Figure 2-3).

5. **Look through the viewfinder and compose your scene.**

   When you look through the viewfinder, you'll have a clear uncluttered view, unless you muck about in the camera menu and change the viewfinder display options.

6. **Press and hold the shutter button halfway.**

Figure 2-3: Shooting pictures in Full Auto mode.

   The camera achieves focus and a bunch of black dots appear in the viewfinder. These are the points the camera uses to focus based on the information the camera gathers through the lens. In essence, the camera looks for objects with well-defined edges. You can customize the way the autofocus system works to suit your style of photography when shooting in one of the creative modes, something I show you in Chapter 6.

   Make sure your subject is under one of the autofocus squares. If you're photographing a person, you can compose the image so that the person is or isn't centered in the frame. If you decide to get artsy-fartsy and place your subject on the left or right side of the frame, I show you how to do that in "Focusing On an Off-Center Subject" later in this chapter. When your camera achieves focus, a green dot appears on the right side of the viewfinder, and the camera beeps. With the default viewfinder option, you also see AF on the right side of the viewfinder. If the camera can't achieve focus, the dot flashes, which is a rare occurrence with 65 — oil your abacus — count 'em, *65* autofocus points. If this occurs, switch to manual focus (see "Focusing Manually" later in this chapter). The autofocus points that the camera uses to focus your subject are also illuminated (see Figure 2-4).

If your subject is moving, after the camera achieves focus, it automatically switches to another focus mode (AI Servo, which I cover in Chapter 7) and keeps your subject in focus. On the LCD panel on top of the camera and in the viewfinder, you see the shutter speed, aperture, and ISO setting the camera uses for the picture. If the shutter speed flashes, the speed is too slow to ensure a blur-free image while handholding the camera. If this is the case, mount your camera on a tripod.

Figure 2-4: Taking your first picture.

7. **Press the shutter button fully.**

The camera takes the picture.

When the camera records data to the memory card, the red light below the Quick Control dial illuminates. Do not turn off your camera while the light is on. If you do, the image isn't recorded to the memory card. Powering off the camera while the light is illuminated may also damage the memory card, the camera, or both.

8. **Review the image on the LCD monitor.**

You can view other information regarding the image on your LCD monitor. You can view exposure information, a histogram, and much more. I show you how to display image information on the LCD monitor in Chapter 4.

In most situations, you get a beautifully exposed image with Full Auto mode. If, however, you're photographing a scene with tricky lighting conditions or photographing a fast-moving object, the image may not be to your liking. Or maybe now that this brief tutorial has given you a taste of the camera's brilliance, you want to move on and get the most out of your camera. If this is the case, fast-forward to Chapters 6 and 7.

Understanding Exposure and Focal Length

When you take a picture in Full Auto mode, the camera determines the shutter speed and aperture (see Figure 2-5). The *shutter speed* is the amount of time the shutter remains open. When you use a fast shutter speed, the shutter is open for a short amount of time, which stops action. A slow shutter speed keeps the shutter open for a long time and is needed when you don't have a lot of available light. The *aperture* determines how much light enters the camera. Each aperture equates to an f-stop number.

The *f-stop number* is a value. A small f-stop number, such as f/2.8, designates a large aperture, which lets a lot of light into the camera. A large f-stop number, such as f/16, is a small aperture that lets a small amount of light into the camera. I know. It's counter-intuitive, but don't shoot me, I'm only the messenger. Figure 2-6 shows a comparison of apertures and the amount of light each setting sends to the camera.

The f-stop determines another important factor: the depth of field. The *depth of field* is the amount of the image that's in apparent focus in front of and behind your subject:

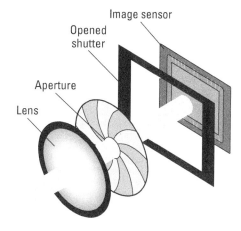

Figure 2-5: The shutter speed and aperture determine the exposure.

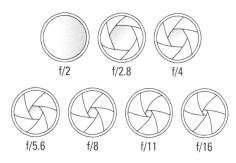

Figure 2-6: The aperture opening determines how much light enters the camera.

- **Small depth of field:** A large aperture (small f-stop number) gives you a shallow depth of field, especially when you're shooting the image with a telephoto lens, which gets you closer to your subject and results in an even shallower depth of field. Telephoto focal lenses are the 35mm equivalent of 70mm and greater. Large apertures and telephoto lenses are ideal for portrait photography.

- **Large depth of field:** On the other hand, a small aperture (large f-stop number) gives you a very large depth of field, especially when you're using a wide-angle focal length. A wide-angle focal length has a large angle of view. Wide-angle focal lengths have a range that is the 35mm equivalent of 18mm to 35mm.

As you can see, a large number of factors determine what your image will look like.

The following list explains what action the camera takes when you take pictures in various modes:

- **Full Auto mode:** The camera determines the shutter speed and f-stop.

- **Creative modes:** These include P (Programmed Auto Exposure), Av (Aperture Priority), Tv (Shutter Priority), M (Manual), or B (Bulb). Choosing a creative mode enables you to take complete control by manually setting aperture and/or shutter speed.

- **Aperture Priority mode:** You supply the aperture (f-stop value), and the camera calculates the shutter speed needed for a properly exposed image.

- **Shutter Priority mode:** You supply the shutter speed, and the camera provides the aperture (f-stop value) to create a properly exposed image.

The decisions the camera makes regarding shutter speed and aperture are determined by lighting conditions. If you're taking pictures in low-light situations or at night, the camera may choose a shutter speed that's too slow to ensure a blur-free picture (see the upcoming sidebar, "Shutter speed and image sharpness"). If this is the case, you have to mount the camera on a tripod to ensure a blur-free picture. But if you want complete control over

Shutter speed and image sharpness

When you take a picture with the camera cradled in your hands, a certain amount of motion is transmitted to the camera, which is caused by movement made by the camera operator. When you take pictures with a high shutter speed, the shutter isn't open long enough for any operator movement to affect the sharpness of the image. However, when you shoot at a slow shutter speed, the shutter is open long enough for operator movement to be apparent in the image, which shows up as an image that isn't tack sharp. The clarity of your images depends on how steadily you hold the camera and the shutter speed used to capture the image.

The rule of thumb for handheld photography is to shoot with a shutter speed that's the reciprocal of the 35mm equivalent of the lens focal length. For example, if you're using a lens with a focal length that measures 50mm, the 35mm equivalent for your EOS 7D Mark II is 80mm.

Therefore, you should use a shutter speed of 1/100 of a second or faster to get a blur-free image. If the camera chooses a slower shutter speed, you need to steady the camera with a tripod. If you use a lens with image stabilization, you can shoot at a slower shutter speed than normal. Even without image stabilization, if you hold the camera very steady, you may be able to shoot at a slower shutter speed than the rule of thumb listed here. The best way to find out how steady you are is to experiment with different shutter speeds on each lens you own. Due to the narrow angle of view, you'll find that operator movement is very apparent when you take pictures with telephoto lenses. Remember that if you shoot for an extended period of time, your arms will get tired and you won't be as steady as you were at the start of the shoot. That is of course unless you work out four hours a day.

the exposure, use one of the creative modes: Programmed Auto Exposure, Aperture Priority, Shutter Priority, Manual, or Bulb, which I outline in detail in Chapter 6.

When I got my first SLR — yup, I started taking pictures before the digital era — I had a hard time wrapping my head around how the f-stop value I chose would affect the resulting image. I remembered it like this: Small f-stop value equates to a shallow depth of field, and a large f-stop value equates to a large depth of field.

Focusing On an Off-Center Subject

There are lots of rules for composing photographs, and many of them can be broken. However, one useful rule says that when you're photographing a person, she shouldn't be in the center of the frame. A photograph with your subject to the right or left of center is more interesting than one where she's smack-dab in the center of the frame. You can easily focus on an off-center subject by following these steps:

1. **Compose your scene through the viewfinder.**

   Move the camera until you achieve the desired composition.

2. **Move the camera until the center autofocus point is positioned in the middle of your subject.**

   The only exception to this is when your subject is a person or animal. If you're shooting a close-up, position the center autofocus point over the subject's eye that is closest to the camera. After all, the eyes are the windows to the soul. If you're photographing a group of people, place the autofocus point over the most important person in the scene, which, in the case of a family group picture is the patriarch, or in the case of a group shot of the people you work with, your boss.

3. **Press the shutter button halfway.**

   When the camera achieves focus, the green dot on the right side of the viewfinder appears and the camera beeps. If the dot is flashing, the camera hasn't focused on your subject.

4. **With the shutter button held down halfway, move the camera to recompose your picture.**

   By holding down the shutter button halfway, the focus locks on your subject, even as you move the camera.

5. **Press the shutter button fully.**

   The camera records the image.

Focusing Manually

You can have the greatest camera and lens in the world, but if your images aren't in focus, nobody — including you — will care to look at your pictures. Your EOS 7D Mark II has a sophisticated multi-point focus system. In Chapter 6, I show you how to modify the autofocus system to suit specific shooting scenarios, and in Chapter 7, I show you how to modify the autofocus system to suit particular photography situations.

When you shoot images with the lens set to autofocus mode (AF on Canon lenses), the camera looks for areas of changing contrast *(edges)* or objects that are under autofocus points, and then uses these areas to focus the scene. However, in low light or when you're taking a picture of a scene with lots of detail in the foreground and background, the camera may not be able to achieve focus. The green focus indicator light in the viewfinder is solid when you achieve focus, and you see an AF in the viewfinder. You may notice the autofocus motor on the lens is quite active as the camera tries to achieve focus. One the rare occasion when the camera can't achieve focus, or you want to manually focus the lens to creatively blur your subject while keeping other areas of the image sharp, you have no choice but to manually focus the lens. Canon lenses and most third-party lenses give you the option of switching to manual focus.

To manually focus the lens, follow these steps:

1. **Move the Focus switch to MF, as shown in Figure 2-7.**

   On most lenses, you'll find this switch on the left side when the camera is facing your subject.

2. **Press the viewfinder to your eye and twist the lens focus ring until your subject is in clear focus.**

   Concentrate on areas with contrast or sharp lines. This makes it easier for you to see when your subject is in focus. Remember to focus on the center of interest in your scene. If you're photographing a person, focus on his eyes, or if your subject has his head turned, focus on the eye nearest the camera. The curve of your subject's eyelid should be in focus in the resulting image; it's also an easy area to focus on.

Figure 2-7: Focusing manually.

3. **Take the picture.**

   Switch the lens back to autofocus (AF) when lighting conditions permit the camera to focus automatically.

Using the Flash in Full Auto Mode

Your camera features a built-in flash unit, but it's no ordinary built-in flash unit. This one has the power to command other Canon flash units that are compatible with your camera, which enables you to shed lots of light on your subject. However, when you shoot pictures using one of the auto modes, you don't have access to those bells and whistles, which by the way, I cover in Chapter 7.

When you take pictures in Full Auto mode, the flash automatically pops up when the camera senses there's not enough light to properly expose the picture. Don't expect miracles from the on-camera flash, though; it's effective only for a distance of about 16 feet at f/3.5 with an ISO setting of 200. After that the on-camera flash falls off so much, it's not usable. Other issues you'll find with on-camera flash is red-eye when you're photographing people. The camera does have a built in red-eye reduction system, however.

Using red-eye reduction

When you enable red-eye reduction, the camera fires a pre-flash that causes your subject's pupils to constrict, thereby reducing red-eye. The effectiveness of red-eye reduction varies from subject to subject. The alternative is using an auxiliary flash that can bounce the flash off a large surface, such as a wall, which diffuses the light and doesn't beam it directly into your subject's eyes. Note that you will not be able to use red-eye reduction while shooting in Full Auto mode. To enable red-eye reduction:

1. **Press the Menu button.**

   The previously used menu appears on the LCD monitor.

2. **Press the Quick Control button to navigate to the Shoot tab, press the multi-controller button to navigate to the Shoot4 menu, and then use the Quick Control dial to highlight Red-Eye Reduc, as shown in the left image in Figure 2-8.**

   Oh my. It's like digital Visine.

3. **Press Set.**

   The Red-Eye Reduc menu displays, as shown in the right image in Figure 2-8.

4. **Turn the Quick Control dial to highlight Enable and then press Set.**

   Red-eye reduction is enabled.

5. **Press the shutter button halfway.**

   You're ready to take a picture with no red-eye.

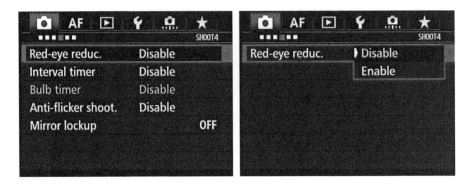

Figure 2-8: Specifying red-eye options.

Shooting a red-eye–free portrait

When you shoot a portrait under dodgy (dim) lighting conditions, the flash pops up automatically when you shoot in Full Auto mode. If you're shooting a portrait of your significant other, or photographing a group of friends, red-eye reduction is the order of the day. In the following steps I show you how to shoot a red-eye–free picture of people. Note that this technique doesn't work well when you take flash pictures of dogs or cats.

To take a picture when red-eye reduction is enabled:

1. **Enable red-eye reduction, as I outline in the preceding steps.**

2. **Press the Flash button.**

   The flash unit pops up.

3. **Compose your image in the viewfinder.**

   You'll get your best results if your subject looks directly at the red-eye reduction lamp on the front of the camera (see Figure 2-9).

4. **Press the shutter button halfway.**

   The red-eye reduction lamp lights. When the green light on the right side of the viewfinder appears, your subject is in focus.

Red-eye reduction lamp

Figure 2-9: The red-eye reduction lamp.

5. **Wait until the exposure compensation display at the bottom of the viewfinder disappears.**

   This is your signal that the red-eye reduction lamp is functioning optimally. The compensation display disappears on the LCD panel as well. When the display disappears completely, the red-eye reduction lamp has done its thing.

6. **After the display disappears, press the shutter button.**

   In a flash, the image displays on the LCD monitor. Review the image to make sure no red-eye is visible. If necessary, take the picture again.

Using the Self-Timer

Your camera has a built-in self-timer that you use whenever you want to delay the opening of the shutter. This option is useful when you want to take a self-portrait or you want to be in a picture with other people. the self-timer is also handy when you're taking pictures on a tripod, especially when the shot requires a long exposure. The countdown allows time for any camera shake that was caused by pressing the shutter to subside. The EOS 7D Mark II self-timer counts down from 2 seconds and one that counts down from 10 seconds. To enable the self-timer:

1. **If you're not already in shooting mode, press the shutter button halfway and then press the Drive-AF button.**

2. **Look at the LCD panel and then turn the Quick Control dial to select either the 2-Second or 10-Second Timer.**

   The image on the left in Figure 2-10 shows the LCD panel with the 2-Second Timer selected, and the image on the right shows the 10-Second Timer selected.

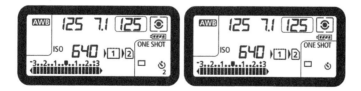

Figure 2-10: Selecting one of the Self-Timer modes.

3. **Compose your scene in the viewfinder.**

   If you're shooting a self-portrait or will be in the picture, mount your camera on a tripod. If you're not looking through the viewfinder when you used the self-timer, you'll also have to remove the eyecup and place the eyepiece cover over the viewfinder. This little piece slides into the same slots as the eyecup. The eyepiece cover is on the camera strap that shipped with the camera. The eyepiece cover prevents stray light from changing the exposure. If you're using a third-party camera strap, remove the eyepiece cover from the camera strap and store it in your camera bag so you'll have it on hand when using the self-timer. Alternatively you can drape a dark cloth such as a black microfiber lens cleaning cloth over the eyepiece.

4. Press the shutter button halfway to achieve focus.

The green light on the right side of the viewfinder shines when focus has been achieved.

5. Press the shutter button.

The camera begins to count down. As the camera counts down, you hear a beeping sound and a light on the front of the camera flashes. Two seconds before the end of the countdown, the light stays on and the beeping sounds faster. If you're taking a self-portrait, say "cheese" when the red light is solid.

Triggering the Shutter Remotely

You can trigger the camera shutter remotely using the RC-1 or RC-5 remote control, which is sold separately. You use the remote controllers in conjunction with the timer. This option is handy when you're creating still-life photos. Instead of walking between the camera and your subject, you can make subtle changes to the composition and then trigger the camera remotely. To trigger your camera remotely:

1. Mount the camera on a tripod.

2. Switch the lens to manual focus and focus on your subject.

For more information on manually focusing the camera, see "Focusing Manually" earlier in this chapter.

3. Press the Drive-AF button.

4. While looking at the LCD panel, rotate the Quick Control dial to select the desired remote mode.

You can trigger the camera remotely and have it count down from 10 or 2 seconds. The left image in Figure 2-11 shows the LCD panel with a 2-second remote, and the right side of the panel shows a 10-second remote.

5. Compose your scene through the viewfinder and then focus on your subject.

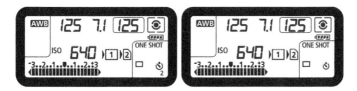

Figure 2-11: Taking a picture with a remote control device.

6. **Point the remote controller at the camera's remote sensor and then press the remote's trigger button.**

   The remote sensor is located near the handgrip on the left side of the camera as you look at it.

   The self-timer counts down, the shutter actuates, and the picture is taken.

3

Specifying Image Size and Quality

In This Chapter

- Determining image size, format, and quality
- Comparing image formats and file sizes
- Creating folders and a file-numbering method

*Y*our camera captures images with a resolution of 20.2 megapixels, which is humongous, ginormous, or any other adjective you prefer to indicate something that's really, really big. The good news: This gives you a tremendous amount of flexibility. You can print images as large as 23.9 x 15.2 inches. Thinking of the possibilities of decorating your house with your photographs? The bad news: The large size takes up lots of room on your memory cards and lots of room on your hard drive. Fortunately, you can specify different sizes by using camera menu options if you have memory cards and hard drives with small capacities.

In addition to concerning yourself with image size, you also have the file format you choose to worry about. Your camera can capture images in the RAW or JPEG format. When you capture images in the RAW format, you must process them. Think digital darkroom, and you get the idea. The RAW format gives you a tremendous amount of flexibility. After you download RAW images to your computer, you process the images with software included with your camera or with third-party software, such as Adobe Photoshop or Adobe Photoshop Lightroom.

If you capture images in the JPEG format, the camera does the processing for you. Think of this as the digital equivalent of a Polaroid image. You get instant gratification, but can't do much with the image except crop it and perform minimal image editing. If you capture images in the JPEG format, you also have to think about image quality. The setting you choose determines the image quality and the file size.

If you're new to digital photography, file format, image size, and quality may seem a tad overwhelming. But hey, don't worry — be happy. I show you how to specify image size, quality, and a whole lot more in this chapter.

Understanding Image Size and Quality

Your camera can capture large images. The default option captures images at a size that most photographers — except professionals — won't ever need or use. But before you specify sizes, you need to understand the relationship between the image size and the resolution. The default image size your camera can capture measures 5472 x 3648 pixels. If you do the math:

$5472 \times 3648 = 19,961,856$ pixels

$19,961,856 \div 1,000,000 = 19.96$

Round up to get 20 megapixels

The default resolution for your camera is 240 pixels per inch (ppi). If you do a little more math, the default image size and resolution equate to an image size of 23.9 x 15.2 inches:

$5724 \div 240 = 23.9$ inches

$3648 \div 240 = 15.2$ inches

Please don't try this math at home unless you own a well-lubricated abacus.

Another factor to consider is the final destination of the images. If you're going to edit the images with Canon or third-party software and then print them, you need to factor this into the choices you make when specifying image size and quality. You can get high-quality prints with the 240 ppi default resolution. However, some printers prefer 300 ppi. If you're capturing images that will be displayed on a web site only, you can get by with a much smaller image and a resolution of 72 or 96 ppi. When you use images on the web or in a blog post, you'll rarely need one that's wider than 640 pixels. You can resample images to a higher resolution with third-party software, such as Photoshop, Photoshop Elements, or Photoshop Lightroom.

The default image size is great if you're printing images and have gobs of space on your hard drive and a pocket full of 16GB memory cards. However, if your storage capacity is at a premium or you're running out of room on your last memory card with no computer readily available to download to, it's important to know how to change image size and quality, a task I show you how to do in the upcoming sections.

Specifying Image Format, Size, and Quality

Your EOS 7D Mark II has many options that determine the dimensions, image format, quality, and file size. You can choose from two image formats: JPEG and RAW. You have three different sizes for each the RAW image format and five different sizes for the JPEG image format. If you capture images with the JPEG format, you can also specify image quality. You can capture both formats when you shoot an image, or choose either format. If you're shooting with two cards in the camera, you have different options, which I discuss in Chapter 6.

Your decisions regarding format, image size, and quality determine the crispness of the resulting images, the file size, and the amount of flexibility you have when editing your images. To give you an idea of the difference in file sizes, you'll end up with a file size of 6.6MB when you capture the largest size image using the JPEG format with Fine quality compared to a file size of approximately 24MB when you capture the same size image using the RAW format. I explain the differences between the two formats in an upcoming "JPEG or RAW? Which is right for you?" sidebar. I also give you my take on which options you should choose in the "My recommendations" sidebar later in this chapter. The following sections show you how to choose options from the camera menus.

One of the first decisions you make regarding your images is the file format. You can capture JPEG or RAW images. When you choose the file format, you also specify the image size. If you choose the JPEG format, you specify the quality as well. You even have an option to capture both formats simultaneously, and have other options if you shoot with two card as I show you in Chapter 6. If you're curious about the difference between the formats, check out the "JPEG or RAW? Which is right for you?" sidebar in this chapter. To specify the image format:

1. **Press the Menu button.**

   The previously used menu appears on the LCD monitor.

2. **Press the Quick Control button to navigate to the Shoot tab and then use the multi-controller button to navigate to the Shoot1 menu.**

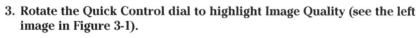

3. **Rotate the Quick Control dial to highlight Image Quality (see the left image in Figure 3-1).**

4. **Press the Set button.**

   Your image format, size, and quality options display (see the right image in Figure 3-1).

5. **Rotate the Main dial to specify a RAW setting.**

   Choose this option to capture RAW images, or perform this step with Step 6 to capture JPEG images simultaneously when you press the shutter button. Your options are RAW (5472 x 3648 pixels), MRAW (4104 x 2736 pixels), or SRAW (2736 x 1824 pixels). When you select an option, the file size, image dimensions in pixels, and the number of images that can be captured on your memory card in the camera display in the upper-right corner of the Quality menu.

6. Rotate the Quick Control dial to specify a JPEG setting.

Choose this option to capture JPEG images, or perform this step with Step 5 to capture RAW images simultaneously when you press the shutter button. Your options are Large with Fine, Large with Normal, Medium with Fine, Medium with Normal, Small (S1) with Fine, or Small (S1) with Normal. The dimensions, respectively, are 5472 x 3648 pixels, 4104 x 2736 pixels, or 2736 x 1824 pixels. There is also an S2 and S3 option. These images are very small and suitable for the Internet only.

7. Press Set to apply the change.

The selected image information displays next to Image Quality on the Shoot1 menu.

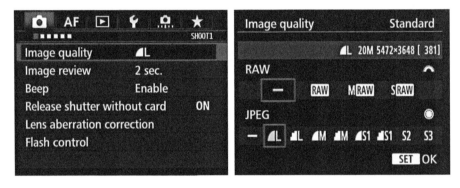

Figure 3-1: Setting image format, size, and quality options.

JPEG or RAW? Which is right for you?

The answer to those questions depends on how serious you are about your photography. Before you decide, let me point out the differences between the two formats. When you capture an image in the JPEG format, the camera processes the image. The camera also compresses the image based on the quality option you specify in the camera menu. You can store more images on a card when you specify a smaller image size and quality. However, you'll notice the difference when you print your images.

When you choose the RAW format, you have the ultimate in flexibility. The camera sensor transmits the RAW data to your memory card. Yup. What the sensor captures is what you get. You do have to process RAW images with either the Canon software provided with your camera or with third-party software such as Photoshop Elements, Photoshop, or Photoshop Lightroom. The software lets you fine-tune virtually everything about the photo.

Comparing Image Formats and File Sizes

When you capture images with a higher resolution, the file size is bigger and they take up more room on your memory card. The image format also enters into the equation, and if you choose to capture images with the JPEG format, the image quality is a factor. Photographers also like to know the maximum number of images they can capture simultaneously when shooting in Continuous (Burst) mode. The number of images depends on the image dimensions and quality, which equates to the file size. When you capture smaller images in the JPEG format that have been compressed, the file size is smaller; therefore, the maximum number of images you can capture before the card is filled is greater. Table 3-1 shows you how many images you can fit on an 8GB card for each available format and quality option. The information is based on capturing images with an ISO speed setting of 100. This table is only for reference. Your results will differ based on the subject and ISO speed setting.

Table 3-1	How Many Images Fit on a Card?			
Image Format and Quality	*Megapixels Recorded*	*File Size*	*Number of Shots*	*Maximum Burst*
JPEG Large Fine	20	6.6MB	1,090	130
JPEG Large Normal	20	3.5MB	2,060	2,060
JPEG Medium Fine	8.9	3.6MB	2,000	2,000
JPEG Medium Normal	8.9	1.8MB	3,030	3,060
JPEG Small (S1) Fine	5	2.3MB	3,060	3,060
JPEG Small (S2) Normal	5	1.2MB	5,800	4,800
JPEG S2 Fine	2.5	1.3MB	5,240	5,240
JPEG S3 Fine	0.3	0.3MB	20,330	20,330
RAW	20	24.0MB	290	24
MRAW	11	19.3MB	350	28
SRAW	5	13.3MB	510	35

If you prefer to capture your images in the JPEG format, the quality you choose determines what the final image looks like. If you compare the Normal quality to the Fine quality, you'll notice a difference when you print the image at the largest size possible. The Normal quality image won't be as crisp and sharp as the Fine quality image. On the left side of Figure 3-2 is an enlargement of an image captured with the JPEG Fine quality. The image on the right side of Figure 3-2 was captured with the JPEG Normal quality. The images have been magnified so you can more clearly see the difference in sharpness and detail.

 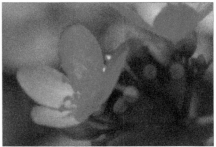

Figure 3-2: Comparing the JPEG Normal and Fine qualities.

My recommendations

When I take a photograph, I think of all possible uses. My first option is to post an image I like to my blog. Eventually I'll make prints of my best images. Some of those prints may be 4 x 6 inches for a small album, or I may have the image printed on a 30 x 20–inch canvas to decorate my home. I may also select images for a photo book, which range in size from 3 x 5 inches to 11 x 13 inches. Therefore, I always capture images with the RAW option. This enables me to do anything I want with the image. Yes, they take up a lot of room, but memory cards and hard drives are fairly inexpensive. The hard drive on my computer is 2TB (terabyte), and I store my images in a special folder and back them up religiously in case of hard drive failure.

Sometimes I photograph events that require me to produce images quickly, yet I still want to edit them to perfection at some point in time. When I run into a scenario like this, I capture RAW and JPEG images simultaneously. If the images that need to be turned around quickly are for the Web, I use the Small JPEG option with Normal quality in addition to the large RAW setting.

If the images will be printed, say for example in a local newspaper or magazine, I use the Large JPEG option with Fine quality and capture large RAW images simultaneously. Both options enable me to give the client a JPEG image almost immediately and then edit RAW images for other outputs at a later date.

If you photograph an event, such as a wedding, you have other considerations. In this case, I recommend that you use the RAW format for all the standard wedding images, such as exchanging vows and rings, marching down the aisle, and so on. I also recommend you use RAW when shooting the formal shots of the family members with the bride and groom. However, when you're photographing the reception, use RAW for the first dances, and then switch to MRAW or SRAW for the candid shots of the couples at tables and the guests dancing. These photographs are generally ordered as 4 x 6–inch images. Therefore, you don't need a full 18-megapixel capture for a high-quality-print. Switching to SRAW or MRAW for the less important shots conserves room on your card.

Managing Image Files

By default, your images are numbered continuously until 9999 and then the file number is reset to 0001. Your images are also stored in a single folder on your memory card. You can, however, create folders in which to store your images and then change the file-numbering method. I show you how in the following sections.

Creating folders

By default, your camera creates the 100EOS7D folder on your memory card where images are stored. You can, however, create as many folders as you want. A folder can hold a maximum of 9,999 images. When you exceed the maximum allowable images in a folder, a new one is created automatically. You can have a maximum of 999 folders on a card. Organizing your work in folders is a good idea if you work with large memory cards and want to store images from multiple shoots in separate folders. To create a folder:

1. **Press the Menu button.**

   The previously used menu appears on the LCD monitor.

2. **Press the Quick Control button to navigate to the Set Up tab, press the multi-controller button to navigate to the Set Up1 menu, and then Rotate the Quick Control dial to highlight the Record Func+Card/Folder Sel option (see the left image in Figure 3-3).**

   The Record Func+Card/Folder Sel menu options display (see the right image in Figure 3-3).

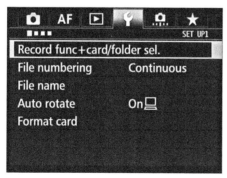
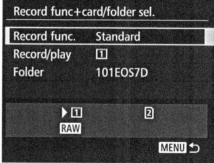

Figure 3-3: Time to set up a new folder.

3. **Rotate the Quick Control dial to highlight Folder and then press the Set button.**

   The Select Folder menu appears showing you the current folders on the card and the number of photos in each folder (see Figure 3-4).

4. **Rotate the Quick Control dial to highlight Create Folder and press Set.**

   The menu refreshes the a dialog appears asking you to confirm creation of the folder.

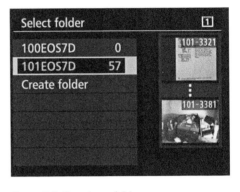

Figure 3-4: Creating a folder.

5. **Rotate the Quick Control dial to highlight OK and then press Set.**

   The new folder is created.

Selecting a folder

Folders are convenient when you want to separate images from different photo shoots. When you have more than one folder, you can choose the folder to store your images. To select a folder:

1. **Press the Menu button.**

   The previously used menu appears on the LCD monitor.

2. **Press the Quick Control button to navigate to the Set Up tab, press the multi-controller button to navigate to the Set Up1 menu, and then Rotate the Quick Control dial to highlight the Record Func+Card/ Folder Sel option (see the left image in Figure 3-5).**

   The Record Func+Card/Folder Sel menu options display.

3. **Rotate the Quick Control dial to highlight Select Folder and then press the Set button.**

   The folders you've created display (see the right image in Figure 3-5).

4. **Rotate the Quick Control dial again to highlight the desired folder and then press Set.**

   The next images you shoot will be stored in that folder.

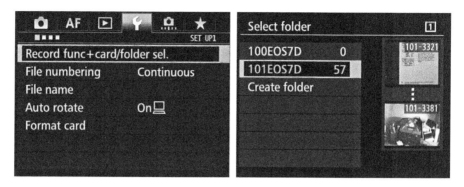

Figure 3-5: Selecting a folder.

Choosing a file-numbering method

Your camera automatically names and numbers each image you take. The name isn't all that descriptive, and the numbers are consecutive. Some photographers stay with the default numbering system because it helps keep track of the number of shutter actuations. But your EOS 7D Mark II is rated for 200,000 shutter actuations so that's a moot point. To change the file-numbering system:

1. **Press the Menu button.**

   The previously used menu appears on the LCD monitor.

2. **Press the Quick Control button to navigate to the Set Up tab, press the multi-controller button to navigate to the Set Up1 menu, rotate the Quick Control dial to highlight File Numbering (see the left image in Figure 3-6), and then press the Set button.**

   A menu appears with your file-numbering options (see the right image in Figure 3-6).

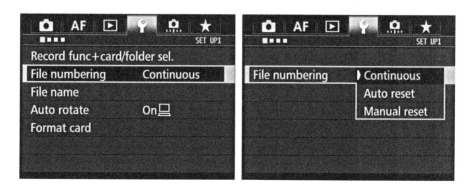

Figure 3-6: Selecting a file-numbering option.

3. **Rotate the Quick Control dial to highlight one of the following options:**

  • **Continuous:** Numbers files in sequence, even when you insert a new card or store images in a different folder. Images are numbered to 9999 and then start over at 0001. When you use this option, start with a newly formatted card each time. If you use multiple cards that already have images on them, you may run into problems with duplicate filenames because file numbering may continue from the last image captured on the card. Duplicate filenames isn't a good thing if you're storing all your images in the same folder.

  • **Auto reset:** Numbers the first image with 0001 each time you insert the card in the camera or when images are stored in a new folder. This option works well if you store images from each shoot in their own folder when you download them to your computer, or as I strongly suggest, rename the images when you download them to your computer.

  • **Manual reset:** Creates a new folder and resets the numbering to 0001 after you press the Set button. After manually resetting file numbering, the numbering system reverts to the last option you specified, Continuous or Auto Reset.

4. **After highlighting the desired option, press Set to commit the change.**

  The file-numbering option remains in effect until you change it with this menu command.

Using the LCD Monitor

In This Chapter

Displaying your image's information

Working with the histogram

Previewing, erasing, rotating, and protecting images

Modifying image review time and monitor brightness

Using Quick Control

Viewing images as a slide show and on a TV set

igital photography is all about instant gratification. You snap a picture, and it appears on your LCD monitor almost instantaneously. This gives you a chance to see whether you captured the image you envisioned, or something not quite to your liking, also know as a *dud*. But your LCD monitor can do much more than just display your images. You can get all sorts of useful information, such as the shutter speed, aperture, and other pertinent information about the image. You can even display a spiffy graph known as a *histogram* that shows the distribution of pixels from shadows to highlights.

The information you can display on the camera LCD monitor gives you the opportunity to examine each image and make sure you got it right in the camera. Photographers should always do their best to get it right in the camera and rely as little as possible on programs such as Adobe Photoshop or Lightroom to correct exposure problems and other issues that could have been avoided when taking the picture. After all, *Photoshop* is a noun, not a verb. So instead of taking the picture and saying you'll "Photoshop it," rely on the information your camera supplies to determine whether you got the exposure right. Programs like Photoshop and Lightroom are designed to enhance images, not fix them.

In this chapter, I show you how to use the EOS 7D Mark II's LCD monitor to review images, display image information, and much more. I also show you how to erase, rotate, and protect your images from accidental deletion.

Displaying Image Information

When you take a picture, you see it almost immediately on your LCD monitor. When you want the big picture, you view the image with the exposure information. The large image lets you evaluate things like composition and image sharpness, which enables you to decide whether the image is worth keeping. However, if you can deal with a smaller image, you can view all sorts of information about the image that can tell you whether you nailed the shot. If you're shooting in Full Auto mode (A+ on the mode dial), examining this information helps you become a better photographer.

Getting camera information on the camera LCD monitor is easy. All you need to do is press the Info button. Each time you press the button, the display changes to reveal different information. The image size changes depending on the information shown.

 Each time you press the Info button, a different set of information appears, as shown in Figure 4-1. You can view the image only (the upper-left corner of Figure 4-1), with shooting information only (in the upper-right corner of Figure 4-1), with a histogram showing brightness (the lower-left corner of Figure 4-1), or detailed information with a brightness histogram and a histogram for each color channel (the lower-right corner of Figure 4-1). The information displays that show a histogram display more information than can fit on the LCD monitor. Use the multi-controller button to scroll down and view additional information.

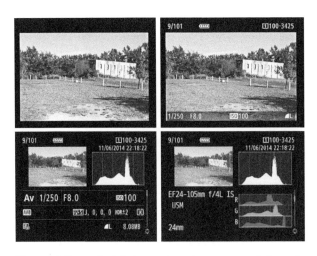

Figure 4-1: Press the Info button to review exposure information.

Using the Histogram

Even though your EOS 7D Mark II is a very capable camera, it can get it wrong when you're shooting under difficult lighting conditions. That's why your camera lets you display a histogram alongside the image on your camera's LCD monitor (see Figure 4-2). A *histogram* is a wonderful thing: It's a graph — well actually it looks more like a mountain — that shows the distribution of pixels from shadows to highlights. Study the histogram to decide whether the camera — or you, if you manually exposed the image — properly exposed the image. The histogram can tell you whether the image was underexposed or overexposed. If you notice the sharp spike on the right side of the histogram, this indicates that all detail has been lost in some of the highlights. Your camera can display a single histogram and display a histogram for the red, green, and blue channels, as shown in Figure 4-3.

A peak in the histogram shows a lot of pixels for a brightness level. A valley, however, shows fewer pixels at that brightness range. Where the graph hits the floor of the histogram, you have no data for that brightness range.

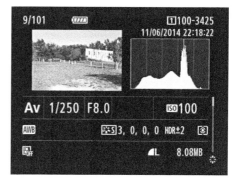

Figure 4-2: Deciphering a histogram.

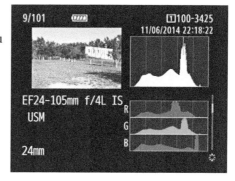

Figure 4-3: Displaying a histogram for each color channel.

When analyzing a histogram, look for sharp peaks at either end of the scale. If you have a sharp peak on the shadow (or left) side of the histogram, the image is underexposed. Also, if the graph is on the floor of the histogram in the highlight (or right) side, the image is underexposed. However, if a large spike is right up against the highlight (right) side of the histogram, the image is overexposed and a lot of the details in the image highlights have been blown out to pure white. You can correct for overexposure and underexposure to a degree in your image-editing program, but it's always best to get it right in the camera. If you analyze a histogram and notice that the image is overexposed or underexposed, you can use your camera's exposure compensation feature to rectify the problem. For more information on exposure compensation, see Chapter 6.

The histogram is a tool. Use it wisely. When you're analyzing a scene that doesn't have any bright highlights, you may end up with a histogram that's relatively flat on the right side. When that happens, judge whether the image on the camera LCD monitor looks like the actual scene. If you rely on the histogram when you see a flat area in the highlights and add exposure compensation, you may make the image brighter than the scene actually was.

Previewing Your Images

In addition to displaying information with your images, you can display multiple images on the monitor, zoom in to study the image in greater detail, or zoom out. This flexibility makes it easier for you to select a single image from thumbnails, to study the image up close to make sure the camera focused properly, and to ensure that you have a blur-free image. To preview images on the camera LCD monitor:

 1. **Click the Playback button to preview an image.**

   The last image photographed or reviewed displays on the monitor (see Figure 4-4). You can change the information displayed with the image or video by pressing the Info button, as I outline in "Displaying Image Information" earlier in this chapter. A movie is designated by an old-fashioned movie camera icon with the duration of the movie shown above the icon. For more information about movies, refer to Chapter 5.

Figure 4-4: Displaying a single image.

  2. **Click the Index/Magnify/Reduce button and rotate the Main dial counterclockwise.**

   Four thumbnails appear on the LCD monitor (see the left image in Figure 4-5). A filmstrip icon appears around a movie when it's shown in thumbnail view.

3. **Rotate the Main dial counterclockwise again.**

   Nine thumbnails appear on the camera LCD monitor (see the right image in Figure 4-5). Each time you rotate the Main dial counterclockwise, more images are displayed on the LCD monitor. You can view a maximum of 99 thumbnails on the monitor, but if you view that many images, you won't be able to see much detail.

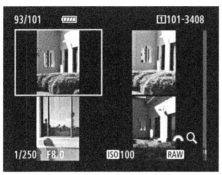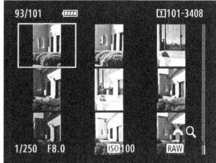

Figure 4-5: Displaying multiple images as thumbnails.

4. Rotate the Quick Control dial to navigate between images.

5. Press the Set button to fill the monitor with the selected image.

If the image was shot with the camera held vertically, the image doesn't fill the screen unless you enable the menu option to rotate images (see the section, "Rotating Images," later in this chapter).

Magnifying images

When you preview an image you get a good view thanks to your camera's three-inch monitor. However, there are times when you want a closer look at details to make sure you nailed the shot. This is especially important when you create someone's portrait. You can zoom in to make sure the eyes are in focus and any other important details. To zoom in on an image:

1. Click the Playback button to preview an image.

The last image photographed or reviewed displays on the monitor.

2. Press the Index/Magnify/ Reduce button and rotate the Main dial clockwise.

The image is magnified. Each time you rotate the Main dial clockwise, the image zooms to the next highest magnification. A white rectangle indicates the part of the image to which you've zoomed (see Figure 4-6).

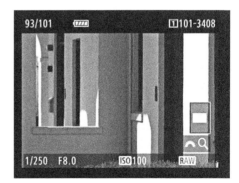

Figure 4-6: Zooming in on an image.

3. **Press the multi-controller button to pan to different parts of the image.**

   With this button, you can move left, right, up, or down.

4. **Rotate the Main dial counterclockwise to zoom out.**

   Each time you rotate the dial counterclockwise, you zoom out to the next lowest level of magnification. Eventually you can zoom out until the image fills the monitor. If you rotate the Main dial counterclockwise again, you display thumbnails as outlined previously in this section.

Previewing images side by side

When you take several pictures of a subject, sometimes it's hard to separate the wheat from the chaff. You can delete images that are obviously duds, but you can also preview images side by side. To preview images side by side:

1. **Press the Creative Photo/ Comparative Display button.**

   Two images are displayed on your LCD monitor. The last displayed image, or last photographed image is highlighted with an orange frame (see Figure 4-7).

Figure 4-7: Comparing images side by side.

2. **Press Set to highlight the other image.**

   You can now select an image to compare with the currently selected image.

3. **Rotate the Quick Control dial to display another image.**

   When you rotate the dial, the image with the orange frame changes. This makes it possible for you to compare one image to another. You can zoom in on the currently selected image to view details.

4. **If you zoom in on the currently selected image, press the Quick Control button.**

   This displays both images at the same magnification.

5. **Press the Playback button to display the highlighted image as a single image.**

6. **Press the Creative Photo/Comparative Display button to return to side-by-side display.**

Modifying Image Review Time

You can modify the amount of time the image displays on the LCD monitor after the camera writes it to your memory card. You can set the preview time from 2 to 8 seconds or display the image until you turn off the camera or return to shooting mode. To modify the image review time:

1. **Press the Menu button.**

2. **Press the Quick Control button to navigate to the Shoot tab and then use the multi-controller button to navigate to the Shoot1 menu.**

3. **Rotate the Quick Control dial to highlight Image Review (see the left image in Figure 4-8).**

4. **Press the Set button.**

The Review Time menu appears showing the options for image review (see the right image in Figure 4-8). The Hold option displays the image until you press the shutter button halfway, navigate to another image, or power off the camera.

When you increase image review time, you decrease battery life.

5. **Highlight the desired option and then press Set.**

The new review options take effect the next time you take a picture.

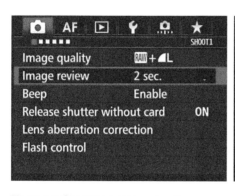

Figure 4-8: Changing image review time.

Changing Monitor Brightness

Camera LCD monitors have come a long way, baby. The monitor on your EOS 7D Mark II offers a brilliant display with lots of pixels; the better to see images with, my dear reader. However, at times, the monitor isn't bright enough, for example, when the setting sun is shining brightly waiting for "Sister Moon" (thank you, Sting). You can get some help by shading the monitor with your hand or the brim of a baseball cap. You can also get some assistance from the camera by changing the monitor brightness. You can increase or decrease the default brightness of your monitor in Auto mode. This option is handy when the monitor is too dark or too bright for your taste. You can also adjust the brightness manually.

To change the default LCD monitor brightness in Auto mode:

1. **Press the Menu button, use the Quick Control button to navigate to the Set Up tab, and then use the multi-controller button to navigate to the Set Up2 menu (see the left image in Figure 4-9).**

2. **Rotate the Quick Control dial to highlight LCD Brightness and then press the Set button.**

   The LCD Brightness menu displays (see the right image in Figure 4-9). In most instances, Auto is perfect, and it's the default selection. You can, however, increase or decrease the relative brightness of your monitor to suit your vision and taste.

3. **Rotate the Quick Control dial to increase or decrease brightness.**

   Use this option if the default brightness of the LCD display is too dark or too bright for your taste.

4. **Press Set.**

   Your changes are applied.

Auto brightness relies on a sensor in the back of the camera to the lower left of the Quick Control dial that monitors the ambient brightness. If you cover this sensor with your finger, the camera adjusts the monitor brightness to compensate for what is perceived as a dark ambient lighting, and the end result probably isn't desirable.

You can also manually change the brightness of your monitor. When you choose the Manual option, the camera doesn't automatically increase or decrease monitor brightness to compensate for ambient lighting.

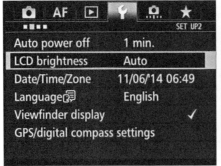
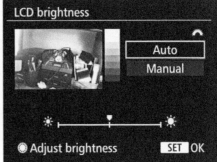

Figure 4-9: LCD brightness options.

To manually change the brightness of your LCD monitor:

1. **Press the Menu button, use the Quick Control button to navigate to the Set Up tab, and then use the multi-controller button to navigate to the Set Up2 menu.**

2. **Rotate the Quick Control dial to highlight LCD Brightness and then press the Set button.**

   The LCD Brightness menu displays (see the left image in Figure 4-10).

3. **Rotate the Main dial to highlight Manual and then press Set.**

   The options for manually increasing or decreasing monitor brightness display (see the right image in Figure 4-10). You can choose from seven brightness levels.

4. **Rotate the Quick Control dial to select the brightness level.**

   As you rotate the dial, the thumbnail image gets brighter or darker. As you look at the back of the camera, rotate the dial to the right to make the image brighter, or left to make it darker.

5. **When the thumbnail is easy to see in the current lighting conditions, press Set.**

   Your changes are applied. You may have to manually adjust the monitor again if you take pictures in a brighter or darker environment than what you manually adjusted brightness in.

Making the monitor brighter does sap more juice from your battery, so unless you have a spare battery, increase monitor brightness at your discretion.

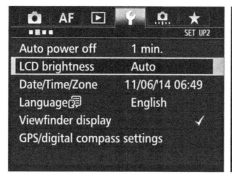
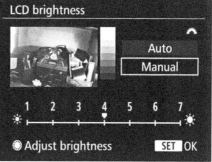

Figure 4-10: Manually setting the LCD brightness.

Deleting Images

When you review an image, you decide whether it's a keeper. If while reviewing an image, you don't like the image for any reason, you can delete it.

However, deleting images needs to be done with extreme caution because the task can't be undone. After you delete an image from your card, it's gone forever.

To delete a single image:

1. **Press the Playback button to display the last viewed image, or last photo taken, and then use the Quick Control dial to navigate to the image you want to delete.**

   Each time you rotate the dial, you display a different image. Sometimes you'll just know that an image is a clunker as soon as it appears on the LCD monitor, which is usually what happens to me. Unless I'm really pressed for time, I examine each image immediately after I shoot it.

   You can also review the images as thumbnails and delete an image. If you decide this is faster, I recommend you press the Set button to fill the monitor with the image before you delete it.

2. **Press the Erase button.**

   The Erase menu appears at the bottom of your monitor (see Figure 4-11). At the risk of being redundant, deleting an image can't be undone. At this stage, you still have the chance to stop this action by highlighting Cancel and then pressing Set.

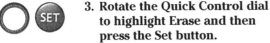

3. **Rotate the Quick Control dial to highlight Erase and then press the Set button.**

   The image is deleted.

Figure 4-11: Delete images with extreme caution.

You can also mark multiple images for deletion. This is similar to deleting a bunch of images in an image-editing program. My opinion: Images should be reviewed on a computer in which you have a bigger screen and it's easier to examine images in detail. Deleting in the camera should be used only for obvious clunkers, such as out-of-focus images, or when you photographed a moving target like a bird in flight and cut off half his body. But some may find deleting multiple images useful, and you can do so with your EOS 7D Mark II. To delete multiple images:

1. **Press the Menu button.**

   The last used camera menu displays on the camera LCD monitor.

2. **Press the Quick Control button to navigate to the Play tab and then use the multi-controller button to highlight the Play1 menu (see the left image in Figure 4-12).**

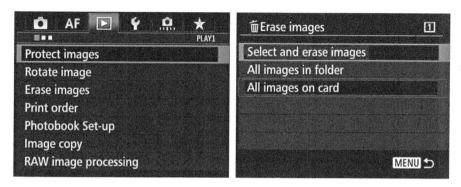

Figure 4-12: Erasing images.

3. **Rotate the Quick Control dial to highlight Erase Images and then press the Set button.**

   The options for erasing images display on the camera LCD monitor.

4. **Rotate the Quick Control dial to highlight Select and Erase Images (see the right image in Figure 4-12).**

5. **Press Set.**

   A single image displays (see the left image in Figure 4-13) on the camera LCD monitor unless you're viewing multiple thumbnails while reviewing. If you are reviewing single images and prefer to view thumbnails while marking images for deletion, press the Index/Reduce/Magnify button to view three images as thumbnails.

Figure 4-13: Marking images for deletion.

6. **Press Set to mark an image for deletion.**

   After you mark an image for deletion, a check mark appears (see the right image in Figure 4-13).

   If you're viewing multiple images as thumbnails, rotate the Quick Control dial to highlight an image and then press Set to mark it for deletion. After you mark a thumbnail for deletion, a check mark appears above it. I prefer to view one image at a time. The thumbnails are too small to give you enough information to determine whether an image needs to be deleted.

   If you accidentally select an image for deletion that you don't want to delete, press Set to deselect the image.

   If you're viewing thumbnails and want to see the bigger picture before you mark an image for deletion, press the Index/Reduce/Magnify button to display a single image on the monitor. Press the button again to zoom in, and then use the multi-controller button to pan to different parts of the image.

7. **Review other images and mark the duds for deletion.**

   A check mark appears on the display when you mark an image for deletion. The total number of images you've marked for deletion appears to the right of the word *Set* in the LCD monitor.

8. **Press the Erase button to delete the images.**

   The Erase Images menu displays (see Figure 4-14). At this stage, you still have the chance to back out if you navigate to the Cancel button and press Set.

9. **Rotate the Quick Control dial to highlight OK and then press Set.**

   Faster than a bullet from a gun, the images are toast.

Figure 4-14: Deleting selected images.

Your camera also has menu options to erase all images in a folder or on the card. This type of heavy lifting needs to be done with your computer and not in the camera because erasing images uses battery power. I always review my images after I download them to my computer and do wholesale deletion there. My computer has a bigger monitor in better light and most important, I'm seated in a comfortable chair. After all the heavy work is done on the computer, format the camera card and then you're ready to shoot up a storm.

If you do a lot of work away from your main computer and need to download cards after a day of shooting, consider investing in one of the small netbook computers, or travel with a laptop if you own one. You can install your image-editing software on the netbook, download images from a card, and then do some preliminary winnowing and editing. As of this writing, you can purchase a fairly potent netbook for less than $300.

Rotating Images

Many photographers — me included — rotate the camera 90 degrees when taking a picture of an object that's taller than it is wide. When these images are displayed on the camera LCD monitor, you must rotate the camera 90 degrees to view them in the correct orientation. If you don't like doing this, a menu command will rotate the images for you. After you invoke this command, images display on your monitor in the proper orientation. You can also use a camera menu command to rotate the images when they are down-loaded to your computer. To have the camera rotate images automatically:

1. **Press the Menu button.**

   The last used camera menu displays on the camera LCD monitor.

2. **Press the Quick Control button to navigate to the Set Up tab and then use the multi-controller button to navigate to the Set Up1 menu.**

3. **Rotate the Quick Control dial to highlight Auto Rotate (see the left image in Figure 4-15) and then press the Set button.**

   The Auto Rotate options display (see the right image in Figure 4-15).

4. **Rotate the Quick Control dial to highlight one of the following options:**

   • **Monitor and computer:** Rotates the image automatically on the camera monitor and when downloaded to the computer.

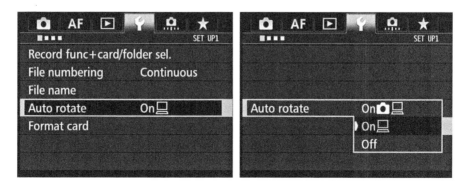

Figure 4-15: Auto-rotating images.

- **Computer only:** Rotates the image automatically on the computer monitor, but not on the camera.

- **Off:** Images are not rotated.

5. **Press Set.**

   All images taken from this point forward are rotated. Vertical images photographed before invoking this command are not rotated. If you choose to rotate the image when downloaded to your computer and it doesn't rotate, your software can't automatically rotate images from this command. If the camera is pointed up or down, an image photographed with the camera rotated 90 degrees may not rotate automatically.

Protecting Images

When you photograph a person, place, or thing, you're freezing a moment in time, a moment that may never happen again. Therefore, you need to be very careful when you delete images from a card because when deleted, an image is lost forever. That's why I recommend doing the majority of your *winnowing* (photographer-speak for separating the duds from the keepers) in an image-editing program. However, if you decide to delete lots of your images with camera erase options, you can protect any image to prevent accidental deletion. (*Note:* This also protects the image in Canon's image-editing software. This option, however, doesn't protect the image when you reformat the card.) To protect an image:

1. **Press the Menu button.**

   The last used camera menu displays on the camera LCD monitor.

2. **Press the Quick Control button to navigate to the Play tab and then use the multi-controller button to highlight the Play1 menu.**

   Protect Images is the first menu option (see the left image in Figure 4-16).

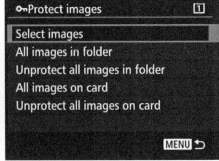

Figure 4-16: Protecting an image from accidental deletion.

3. **Press the Set button.**

The Protect Images menu displays (see the right image in Figure 4-16). You can protect images that you select, a folder of images, or all images on the card. The following steps will show you how to protect selected images.

4. **Rotate the Quick Control dial to highlight Select Images and then press Set.**

The last viewed image displays on the LCD monitor, with the last display view you selected. Remember, you can view images as thumbnails by pressing the Index/Reduce/Magnify button and then rotating the Main dial counterclockwise.

5. **Rotate the Quick Control dial to navigate to an image you want to protect and then press Set.**

The image is protected and can't be deleted. A lock icon appears on the screen when an image is protected (see Figure 4-17). Press Set again to unprotect a protected image.

You can also protect images while viewing them as thumbnails. Press the Index/Reduce/Magnify button and then rotate the Main dial counterclockwise once to view four thumbnail images or twice to view nine thumbnail images. Rotate the Quick Control dial to navigate to

Figure 4-17: Protecting an image.

the next set of thumbnails, and then use the multi-controller button to navigate to an individual thumbnail. Press Set to protect the highlighted image.

6. **Repeat Step 5 to protect additional images.**

7. **Press the Menu button to return to the main menu.**

The images you've marked enter into the Pixel Protection Program.

Third-party software is available that can rescue images that were deleted accidentally or when a card becomes corrupt. In fact, SanDisk includes rescue software with some of its cards. If you do accidentally delete a keeper, you have to use the software immediately.

Using the Quick Control Screen

A good idea is to know what all the dials and buttons on your camera do. However, at times in the heat of battle you need to make one or more changes quickly, such as when you want to change image size, enable the

10-second self-timer when shooting in Full Auto mode, or change multiple options quickly when shooting with one of the creative shooting modes. So if you're in a New York state of mind and want to change camera settings in a New York minute, follow these steps:

1. **Press the Quick Control button.**

   The Quick Control menu appears on your LCD monitor. The display varies depending on which mode you've selected from the Mode dial. Figure 4-18 shows the Quick Control screen when taking pictures in Aperture Priority mode.

2. **Press the multi-controller button right or left to navigate between shooting options and then rotate the Quick Control dial to change the setting.**

   As you rotate the dial, the setting changes. Alternatively, you can press the Set button after you select an option to display a screen showing all options. Figure 4-19 shows the screen that appears for changing ISO speed with the Quick Control screen. I discuss in detail the settings you can change with the Quick Control screen in Chapters 6 and 7.

3. **Repeat Step 2 for any other setting you want to modify.**

4. **Press the shutter button halfway to exit the Quick Control menu and begin taking pictures with the new settings.**

   Now that was quick and easy, wasn't it?

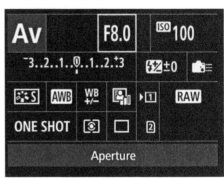

Figure 4-18: Changing shooting options with the Quick Control screen.

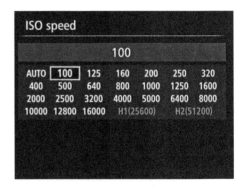

Figure 4-19: Accessing an option for a setting from the Quick Control screen.

Viewing Images as a Slide Show

If you're the type of photographer who likes to razzle and dazzle yourself and your friends by viewing images you've just shot on the camera LCD monitor — also known as *chimping* because of the noises photographers sometimes make when they see a cool image — you'll love viewing images on the camera LCD monitor as a slide show. To view images as a slide show:

1. **Press the Menu button.**

2. **Press the Quick Control button to navigate to the Play tab and then use the multi-controller button to select the Play2 menu.**

3. **Rotate the Quick Control dial to highlight Slide Show (see the left image in Figure 4-20) and then press the Set button.**

   The Slide Show menu appears (see the right image in Figure 4-20). The Set Up option is selected by default. If you decide you want to choose different images, go to Step 4. If you want to create a slide show with all images on the card, go to Step 7.

4. **To select a different viewing option, rotate the Quick Control dial to highlight All Images and then press Set.**

   Two arrows appear indicating that you have options.

5. **Rotate the Quick Control dial to scroll through the options.**

   The options vary depending on what you've captured on the card and whether you've put images into different folders. If you have multiple folders, they appear on this menu. Rotate the Quick Control dial to select the desired photos. If you have movies on the card, you can view movies on the camera monitor. You can also view stills in the slide show only.

6. **After choosing an option, press Set.**

   The images or movies you select display as a slide show after you set up the slide show.

7. **Rotate the Quick Control dial to highlight the Set Up tab.**

Figure 4-20: Slide show settings — popcorn optional.

8. **Press Set.**

   The default slide show options displays all images with a 1-second delay, and the show loops until you exit the slide show (see the left image in Figure 4-21). To accept the default slide show options, fast-forward to Step 12.

9. **Highlight Display Time and press Set.**

   The menu changes to show the options for the duration of each slide (see the right image in Figure 4-21).

10. **Rotate the Quick Control dial to select a Display Time option and then press the Menu button.**

    The previous slide show menu displays.

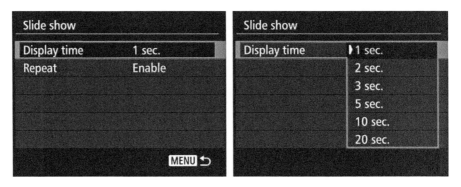

Figure 4-21: Setting playback options for the slide show.

11. **Rotate the Quick Control dial to Repeat and press Set.**

    The Repeat options display (see Figure 4-22). The default Enable option repeats the slide show until you press the shutter button halfway or press the Menu button. The Disable option plays the slide show once.

12. **After choosing the Display Time and Repeat options, press Menu.**

    The previous screen displays.

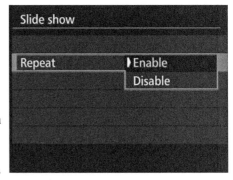

Figure 4-22: Finalizing slide show options.

13. **Rotate the Quick Control dial to highlight Start and press Set.**

    The slide show begins.

14. Press Set to pause the slide show.

Use this option to examine a single image. You can't magnify an image while in slide show mode. When the slide show is paused, you can rotate the Main dial or Quick Control dial to view a different image. You can press the Info button to show a different display with the image. Pressing Set also pauses a movie that's part of the slide show.

15. Press Set to continue the slide show.

When you're tired of watching the slide show or your battery starts running low (auto power-off is disabled when you view a slide show), press the shutter button halfway to return to picture-taking mode. Alternatively, you can press the Menu button to specify different slide show options or to view images in a different folder.

Viewing Images on a TV Set

You have a digital camera capable of capturing colorful images with an impressive resolution of 20.2 megapixels. Your television set is a grand medium on which to display your images. You can display still images or a slide show on your TV screen and knock your socks off — and for that matter, the socks of your friends and anybody else within viewing distance — by viewing your precious images onscreen. Video also looks awesome on a television set.

To view your images on an HDMI TV set:

1. Open the HDMI slot on the side of your camera.

Refer back to Figure 1-10 in Chapter 1 if you've forgotten which is the HDMI slot.

2. Insert an HDMI cable into the HDMI terminal.

The camera HDMI port accepts a male mini HDMI plug, and your TV set accepts a male HDMI plug. Canon sells an accessory cable (HTC-100), which is quite expensive, but you can purchase a video-quality cable from your favorite store that sells video equipment.

3. Connect the other end of the HDMI cable to your TV set.

Refer to your television manual to choose video as the input source.

4. Press the Playback button.

An image displays on your television set.

5. Rotate the Quick Control dial to view the next image.

You can also set up a slide show, which I outline in "Viewing Images as a Slide Show" earlier in this chapter, and view it on your TV using the preceding steps.

Shooting Pictures and Movies with Live View

In This Chapter

Exploring Live View menu options and photography

Shooting and focusing in Live View mode

Using the Quick Control menu to shoot pictures in Live View mode

Recording and previewing movies

Taking pictures while recording a movie

*P*hotographers who own point-and-shoot and mirrorless cameras use the LCD monitor to compose their pictures, which has some definite advantages. For instance, you can place the camera close to the ground and compose an image through the monitor, or hold the camera over your head to do the same. Digital SLR (single-lens reflex) owners didn't have this option until a few years ago when the Live View mode feature began popping up on digital SLR cameras. And fortunately for you, your EOS 7D Mark II has this option. Live View mode adds lots of benefits to shooting, including what-you-see-is-what-you-get. However, Live View mode has a few disadvantages as well. To use Live View mode, you hold the camera in front of you at arm's length, which, unless you work out at the gym five days a week, can be a bit tiring. Thus, many people use tripods when shooting images and movies using Live View mode.

In addition to taking great pictures in Live View mode, you can also capture high-definition (HD) movies. You can specify the size of the movie and the frame rate. So if you're ready to go live, read on. Live View shooting is enabled by default with this camera, so there's no need to invoke any menu command. In this chapter, I show you how to take pictures, capture movies, and more using the Live View mode feature.

Taking Pictures with Live View

Live View is the bee's knees when it comes to picture taking. You have a much larger view of your subject and you can compose pictures holding the camera low to the ground — which beats crawling on your belly — or over your head. To take pictures in Live View mode:

1. **Press the Start/Stop button.**

   What's in the lens's field of view appears on the camera monitor.

2. **Press the shutter button halfway to focus the scene (see Figure 5-1).**

   The autofocus square turns green when focus is achieved. You have three different autofocus modes from which to choose. FlexiZone-SingleAF was used to focus the image shown in Figure 5-1. You can also specify the type of focusing Live View uses. (See "Focusing with Live View" later in this chapter.)

   To display the electronic level while shooting pictures in Live View mode, press the Info button to cycle through the information displays until you see the level.

   Figure 5-1: Focusing in Live View mode.

   Press the depth-of-field preview button to see the depth of field while shooting in Live View mode using one of the following shooting modes: Programmed (P), Aperture Priority (Av), Shutter Priority (Tv), Manual (M), or Bulb (M).

3. **Press the shutter button fully to take the picture.**

   The LCD monitor displays the image almost immediately. After the designated image-review time, the monitor returns to Live View mode.

4. **Press the Start/Stop button to exit Live View mode.**

   If you forget to press the Start/Stop button after shooting in Live View, the camera automatically exits Live View mode after the time designated by auto power-off (see Chapter 1).

When you shoot in Live View mode, you hold the camera in front of you. Therefore, you can't hold the camera as steadily as you could when shooting through the viewfinder. Using a lens with image stabilization helps, but if you don't have one, shoot at a higher shutter speed than you normally would. For example, if you're taking pictures in Live View mode with a lens that's the

35mm equivalent of 85mm, use a shutter speed of 1/125 of a second or faster. Otherwise, mount the camera on a tripod.

Shooting images in Live View mode takes a toll on battery life. You'll get anywhere from 240 to 270 images on a fully charged battery depending upon the ambient temperature and the amount of images taken with flash.

When you shoot in Live View mode in hot conditions or in direct sunlight, the internal temperature of the camera increases. A warning icon appears when the internal temperature of the camera is at the danger point. Press the Start/Stop button to stop Live View as soon as you see this warning. After exiting Live View mode, turn the camera off for a few minutes to let it cool down.

When shooting in Live View mode, don't point the camera directly at the sun. Because the mirror is locked during Live View, exposure to the sun can damage internal components of the camera.

Displaying shooting information

Shooting information is important to many photographers. When you compose a picture in standard shooting mode, you have a lot of information at your disposal in the viewfinder and on the LCD panel. You can also display information when shooting in Live View mode by pressing the Info button. Each time you press the button, the screen changes. The default screen shows the autofocus (AF) points without minimal shooting information. Press the Info button once to display the screen, as shown in Figure 5-2.

Figure 5-2: Displaying exposure information while shooting in Live View mode.

To view additional information, press the Info button again. The second level of information (see Figure 5-3) displays all the information from the preceding screen with these additions: the Live View AF mode, the image format, exposure simulation, Auto Lighting Optimizer mode, picture style, and white balance. You see additional information if you've enabled features, such as flash exposure bracketing, automatic exposure

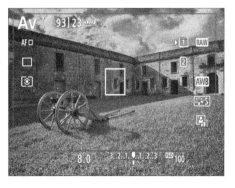
Figure 5-3: Displaying more shooting information.

bracketing, and so on. The flash icon appears if the built-in flash has popped up.

If you accept the default option of Exposure Simulation, press the button again and a histogram appears (see Figure 5-4). You can use this information to increase or decrease the exposure with exposure compensation.

Figure 5-4: Displaying the histogram.

Focusing with Live View

When you shoot in Live View mode, you have three focusing options. Two options are used for taking photographs of landscapes and objects, and the other focusing mode is used to detect faces. To specify the autofocus (AF) mode:

1. **Press the Menu button.**

2. **Use the Quick Control button to navigate to the Shoot tab and then use the multi-controller button to navigate to the Shoot5 menu.**

3. **Rotate the Quick Control dial to highlight AF Method (see the left image in Figure 5-5) and then press the Set button.**

   The Live View AF mode options display on the camera LCD monitor (see the right image in Figure 5-5).

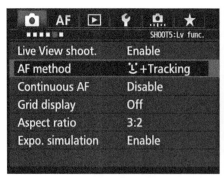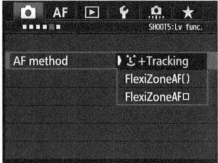

Figure 5-5: Choosing a Live View AF mode.

4. **Use the Quick Control dial to highlight one of the following options:**

   • **Face Plus Tracking:** Use this mode when photographing people. When a face is detected, the autofocus frame appears over the face. If the subject moves, the autofocus frame moves with her. If the camera detects multiple faces, you can use the multi-controller button to move the autofocus over the face you want the camera to focus on.

- **FlexiZoneAF-Multi:** This option is designated by the brackets next to its title on the camera menu. The camera uses 31 autofocus points to achieve focus. The autofocus points are divided into nine zones. The camera will automatically achieve focus, but you can press Set to toggle between automatic selection and zone selection. If you switch to zone selection, use the multi-controller button to select the zone you want to use to achieve focus.

- **FlexiZoneAF-Single:** This option is designated by the square next to its title on the camera menu, which signifies the camera uses a single autofocus point is used to achieve focus. The camera will automatically place the autofocus point over the subject with the most contrast. You can use the multi-controller button to move the autofocus point over a different part of the scene that you want to be in sharp focus, in other words, the center of attention in the photograph you are creating.

5. **Press Set.**

   The selected focusing mode is used whenever you shoot images with Live View.

After working with the camera, I find that FlexiZoneAF-Single does the best job of focusing for the type of photographs I create when shooting Live View. If you find the camera has a difficult time focusing, switch to a different autofocus mode or focus manually.

To focus the camera with Face Plus Tracking focusing:

1. **Press the Start/Stop button to enable Live View shooting.**

   An AF point appears in the center of the image.

2. **Press the shutter button halfway.**

   The camera sensor detects faces in front of the lens by placing a rect-angular AF frame over it. When the camera achieves focus, the frame turns green and the camera beeps. If the camera detects multiple faces, an AF frame with a right- and left-pointing arrow appears. Use the multi-controller button to drag the AF frame over the person who's the center of interest and should be in focus.

3. **Press the shutter button fully.**

   The camera takes the picture.

To focus the camera while using FlexiZoneAF-Single focusing:

1. **Press the Start/Stop button to enable Live View shooting.**

   An AF point appears in the center of the image.

2. **(Optional) Use the multi-controller button to move the AF point.**

   Move the AF point over the part of the image that you want the camera to focus.

3. **Press the shutter button halfway.**

   When the camera achieves focus, the AF point turns green and the camera beeps.

4. **Press the shutter button fully.**

   The camera takes the picture.

To focus with FlexiZoneAF-Multi focusing:

1. **Press the Start/Stop button to enable Live View shooting.**

   An autofocus frame point appears in the center of the image.

2. **Press the shutter button halfway.**

   The AF points for the FlexiZoneAF-Multi autofocus point mode appear on the camera LCD monitor. A white frame appears over the AF points. The point used to achieve focus turns green. If you're happy with the area the camera used to achieve focus, take the picture, if not go to Step 3.

3. **Press Set to switch to zone focusing, and then use the multi-controller button to select the desired autofocus zone.**

   This is the area of the scene that you decide must be in sharp focus.

4. **Press the shutter button fully.**

   The camera takes the picture.

Using the Quick Control menu in Live View mode

When you shoot in Live View mode, you can quickly change the Auto Lighting Optimizer, the image quality, and several more shooting options by using the Quick Control menu. If you're using the FlexZoneAF-Single autofocus (AF) mode, you can move the AF point as well. To change Live View shooting options with the Quick Control menu:

1. **Press the Start/Stop button to enable Live View shooting and then press the Quick Control button.**

   The Quick Control menu appears on the LCD monitor (see Figure 5-6).

2. **Use the multi-controller button to navigate to and highlight an option.**

   The option icon becomes orange. In Figure 5-6, the AF Method icon is highlighted. The current option is Face Plus Tracking, as noted by the highlighted icon at the bottom of the screen.

3. **Press Set to highlight the current option, and then use the multi-controller button to change the option setting.**

Figure 5-6: Using the Live View picture-taking Quick Control menu.

   As you move the multi-controller button over an option, it becomes highlighted. With the exception of the AF points at the bottom of the screen, you see text that describes what the icon represents. For example, if you're changing image quality, you see the format and size displayed.

4. **Press Set.**

   The new option is in effect.

5. **Select other options, and use the multi-controller button to change other settings as needed and then press the shutter button halfway.**

   You're ready to start shooting with your new settings.

Displaying a grid in Live View mode

When shooting in Live View mode, you can display a grid on the LCD monitor. This grid is useful when aligning objects that are supposed to be horizontal or vertical. You can also use the grid when composing your images (see Chapter 7). You have two grids from which to choose: one with 9 squares and another with 24 squares. To display a grid on the camera LCD monitor when shooting in Live View mode:

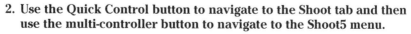

1. **Press the Menu button.**

2. **Use the Quick Control button to navigate to the Shoot tab and then use the multi-controller button to navigate to the Shoot5 menu.**

3. **Rotate the Quick Control dial to highlight Grid Display (see the left image in Figure 5-7) and then press the Set button.**

   The Grid Display options display (see the right image in Figure 5-7).

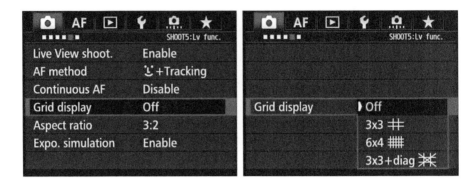

Figure 5-7: Enabling the Live View grid.

4. Rotate the Quick Control dial to highlight the desired grid.

In my opinion, the first grid display, the 3 x 3 option with nine squares, is the most useful. This is identical to the Rule of Thirds (see Chapter 8) photographers use when composing images.

5. Press Set.

The selected grid displays in the monitor when you shoot in Live View mode.

Exploring Other Useful Live View Options

In the previous sections of this chapter, I discuss menu commands that enable Live View shooting, choosing a Live View autofocus mode, and displaying a grid over the LCD monitor while shooting in Live View mode. You may find other Live View menu options and one custom function (that displays a cropping grid) useful. To take a look at the other options, follow these steps:

1. Press the Menu button.

2. Use the Quick Control button to navigate to the Shoot tab and then use the multi-controller button to navigate to the Shoot5 menu.

The Shoot5 menu displays (see the left image in Figure 5-8).

3. Rotate the Quick Control dial to review these commands:

- **Aspect Ratio:** This gives you the option to choose an aspect ratio other than the standard 3:2 aspect ratio. When you choose 4:3, 16:9, or 1:1, a black frame appears around the Live View image, which indicates what the image looks like at that aspect ratio. If you shoot using the JPEG format, the images are cropped to that aspect ratio before they are saved to the card. If you shoot using the RAW format, the images will not be cropped, but the frame is a useful visual reference if you're creating images that will be printed to an aspect ratio from this menu other than 3:2.

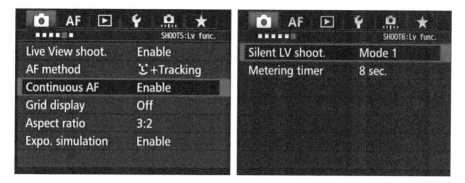

Figure 5-8: Other useful Live View menu options.

- **Expo. Simulation:** This option is selected by default and displays a histogram with one of the shooting information displays. When this command is enabled, Exposure Simulation appears on the LCD monitor when you enable Live View. Press the Info button until you see the histogram. Use the histogram to make sure the image is exposed properly.

4. **Use the Quick Control button to navigate to the Shoot6 menu (see the right image in Figure 5-8) where can choose one of these options:**

    - **Silent LV Shoot:** You have three options from which to choose. Mode 1 is considerably quieter than normal Live View shooting. When you choose this option, you can shoot continuously. If you choose high speed continuous shooting, you can capture images at 7 fps (frames per second). Mode 2 takes one shot when you press the shutter. Camera operation is suspended as long as the shutter button is pressed. When you release the shutter button, camera operation resumes. This mode is quieter than Mode 1. Your third option is to disable silent shooting.

    - **Metering Timer:** This menu command gives you the option of changing how long the exposure setting is displayed on the LCD monitor (AE Lock Time).

If you shoot with an aspect ratio other than those available with the Aspect Ratio command, you can enable a custom function that displays vertical lines that correspond to cropping size on the a LCD monitor. You can choose a specific aspect ratio that matches the paper upon which you print your images. For example, if you're shooting an image that'll be printed on 8-x-10 photographic paper, you'd use the 4:5 aspect ratio. To display a cropping grid on the camera LCD monitor:

1. **Press the Menu button.**

2. **Use the Quick Control button to navigate to the C.Fn tab and then use the multi-controller button to navigate to the C.Fn4 menu.**

3. **Rotate the Quick Control dial to highlight Add Cropping Information (see the left image in Figure 5-9) and then press the Set button.**

   The Add Cropping Information menu displays (see the right image in Figure 5-9).

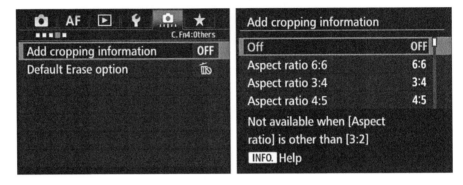

Figure 5-9: Displaying a cropping grid in Live View mode.

4. **Rotate the Quick Control dial to select the desired aspect ratio.**

   Use the Quick Control dial to scroll down if you don't see the aspect ratio that matches your paper size. The selected option is highlighted in blue.

5. **Press Set.**

   The highlighted option is put into effect.

6. **Press the shutter button halfway.**

   You exit the menu and return to shooting mode. The next time you enable Live View shooting, blue lines designate the aspect ratio. As long as you keep the important information between the lines, it appears in the final image after you crop it in your image-editing application.

Making Movies with Your Camera

With your EOS 7D Mark II you can create high-definition (HD) video. Your camera records video in Apple's QuickTime MOV format, or the .mp4 format. You can specify the dimensions of the movies you capture and the frame rate. In the following sections I show you how to capture video and perform other movie-shooting tasks with your camera.

Recording movies

Recording movies on your EOS 7D Mark II is easy. Flip a switch and push a button and you're recording. And you see the whole movie unfold on the camera LCD monitor. When you've recorded your fill, push the button again to stop recording. You can preview the movie on the camera LCD monitor to decide whether you want to keep it. When recording movies in Full Auto (A+) mode, the camera automatically determines the aperture, shutter speed, and ISO speed based on the current ambient lighting conditions. Monaural sound is recorded with your movie unless you disable sound or insert a stereo microphone into the microphone in-port on the side of the camera. To record a movie:

1. **Press the Mode Lock button and then rotate the Mode Dial to A+.**

   When you shoot in this mode, the camera makes all the decisions for you regarding aperture, shutter speed, and ISO setting.

   You can also shoot movies in Shutter Priority (Tv) mode, where you set the shutter speed and ISO and the camera provides the aperture; or Aperture Priority (Av) mode, where you provide the aperture and ISO and the camera automatically sets the shutter speed. You can also shoot in Manual mode (M) where you set the ISO, shutter speed, and aperture. This is similar to shooting still pictures with these modes as discussed the section on creating images with creative modes in Chapter 6. To start your career as a moviemaker, I suggest you let the camera make the decisions and branch out when you've achieved some success using the steps in this section.

2. **Flip the Live View/Movie Shooting switch to the left.**

   The Live/View Movie shooting switch is the circular switch that surrounds the Start/Stop button. The switch stops at the red icon that looks like a movie camera. The scene in front of your lens displays on the LCD monitor. With all the shooting information displayed, the remaining recording time displays next to the video size and frame rate information.

3. **Press the shutter button halfway to achieve focus.**

   When you record movies, you use one of the Live View autofocus modes that I discuss in "Focusing with Live View" earlier in this chapter. If the camera can't achieve focus, switch the lens to manual focus and twist the focusing ring until your subject snaps into focus.

   You can also achieve focus with the AF-On button.

   You can lock exposure to a specific part of the scene you're recording by moving the center autofocus point over the spot that you want to lock focus and then pressing the AF-On button.

4. Press the Start/Stop button.

A red dot appears in the upper-right corner of the LCD monitor when you're recording (see Figure 5-10), and the elapsed time appears above and to the left of the focusing frame. A semi-transparent frame appears around the edge of the Live View image. The area inside the frame is what the camera records. Total recording time with a fully charged battery is approximately 1 hour and 40 minutes at 73 degrees Fahrenheit. Recording time decreases when shooting in colder temperatures.

Figure 5-10: Quiet, numbskulls. You're making a movie here.

To display the electronic level while shooting video in Live View mode, press the Info button to cycle through the information displays until you see the level.

5. Press the Start/Stop button.

Recording stops and the red dot disappears.

Displaying video shooting information

When recording video, you can display a lot of shooting information, a little information, or no information. You can display the aperture and shutter speed, battery information, exposure compensation scale, autofocus mode, and much more, depending on which information screen you display. To display information when recording movies:

1. Flip the Live View/Movie Shooting switch to the left.

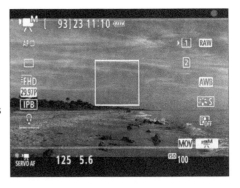

Live View movie recording is enabled.

2. Press the Info button.

A shooting information screen is displayed.

3. Press the Info button repeatedly to display different shooting information.

Figure 5-11 shows almost all of the shooting information you can

Figure 5-11: You choose how much shooting information to display.

display. You can also display a histogram. The amount of information displayed is purely subjective. I prefer a minimum amount of information so I can see what's going on and focus on the movie I'm creating.

Changing video dimensions and frame rate

Your camera can capture high-definition video with dimensions of up to 1920 x 1080 pixels and a frame rate up to 60 fps. You can modify the video dimensions and frame rate to suit your intended destination. To change video dimensions and frame rate:

1. **Flip the Live View/Movie Shooting switch to the left.**

   When you enable movie shooting, the Shoot4 and Shoot5 menus change.

2. **Press the Menu button.**

   The last used menu displays.

3. **Use the Quick Control button to navigate to the Shoot tab and then use the multi-controller button to navigate to the Shoot4 menu.**

   Your Live View video recording options display (see Figure 5-12).

4. **Rotate the Quick Control dial to highlight Movie Rec. Quality (see the left image in Figure 5-13) and then press the Set button.**

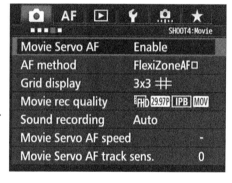

Figure 5-12: Movie Shooting Menu.

   The video dimension and frame rate options display (see the right image in Figure 5-13). The MOV/MP4 option is highlighted.

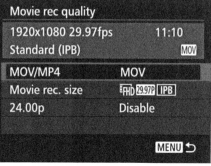

Figure 5-13: Changing video format, dimensions, and frame rate.

5. Press Set.

The MOV/MP4 options display (see the left image in Figure 5-14). MOV is the movie format for Apple QuickTime. MP4 is compatible with more playback devices.

6. Choose an option and press Set.

You're returned to the menu shown in the right image in Figure 5-13.

7. Rotate the Quick Control dial to highlight Movie Rec. Size and press Set.

The available video sizes are displayed (see the right image in Figure 5-14). As you can see, there are multiple options. The following list will make sense of the options:

- **FHD:** This stands for Full HD with a video dimension of 1920 x 1080 pixels. When you record Full HD, you can enable the 24P option shown in the right image in Figure 5-13. 24P stands for 24 fps (frames per second), which is the frame rate used in the old days when they used film to record video. 24P will give you a look that comes close to old-time video.

- **HD:** This stands for high-definition with a video dimension of 1280 x 720 pixels.

- **VGA:** This stands for Video Graphics Array with a video dimension of 640 x 480 pixels.

- **59.94P:** This is a frame rate of 59.94 (60) frames per second.

- **29.97P:** This is a frame rate of 29.97 (30) frames per second.

- **ALL-1:** This compression method compresses one frame at a time while recording. This results in the largest file size, but is most suitable for editing in an application like iMovie or Premiere Pro.

- **IPB:** Compresses multiple frames while recording. This results in a smaller file size, which means you can record more video on a card. However, the fact that the video is compressed means it's not suitable for further editing.

- **IPB Light:** Compresses multiple frames while recording, and is only available when recording in the MP4 format. This format enables you to record more on a card than any other compression format, but is not suitable for further editing.

8. Choose the desired option and press Set.

You're returned to the menu shown in the right image in Figure 5-13.

9. Press the shutter button halfway.

You're ready to record video with the specified dimension and frame rate.

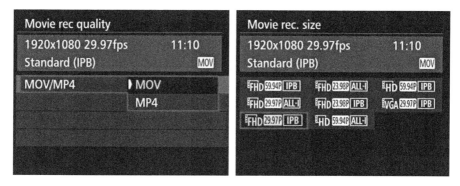

Figure 5-14: Choosing a file format, video dimensions, and compression method.

Unfortunately, providing details about shooting video is beyond the scope of this book. For more information, check out *Digital SLR Video and Filmmaking For Dummies* by John Carucci.

Taking a still picture while recording a movie

You can take a picture while recording a movie. This option is handy when you're making a recording and something interesting happens that you want to save as a still picture. The still image uses the exposure settings displayed in the Live View shooting information. The image is the format and quality you specify with the camera menu. To take a still picture while recording a video:

1. **Begin recording a movie.**

2. **Press the shutter button when you see something you want to record as a still image.**

   The Live View turns black while the camera takes the picture. You may notice a glitch at that point in the video unless you're using a fast UDMA (Ultra Direct Memory Access) CF card.

Using the Quick Control menu while shooting movies

You can make a few changes in video settings with the Quick Control menu. The options are limited but useful when you need to change one of the available Quick Control menu options on the fly. To use the Quick Control menu while shooting video:

1. **Flip the Live View/Movie Shooting switch to the left.**

   You're ready to shoot some video, Mr. Spielberg.

2. Press the Quick Control button.

The Quick Control menu options display on the camera LCD monitor (see Figure 5-15). You can change the following with the Quick Control menu: **AF Method, video dimensions, Drive Mode**, Recording Level (set manually only), **Volume** (with headphones attached), **Recording/Playback card, image quality** (still photos), White Balance, Picture style, and Auto Lighting Optimizer. When shooting in Full Auto (A+) mode, only the boldfaced options can be set.

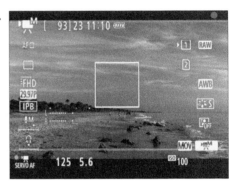

Figure 5-15: Using the Quick Control menu for movies.

3. Use the multi-controller button to highlight an option.

The highlighted item setting is displayed on the screen.

4. Rotate the Quick Control dial or use the multi-controller button to change the setting, then press the shutter button halfway.

You're ready to record video with the new settings.

Changing audio recording options

When you record video with your EOS 7D Mark II, you record audio as well. You can change the record level, disable audio, and enable a wind filter and a sound attenuator. And you thought those little holes in the front of the camera were just a dinky microphone. To beef up the audio in your movies:

1. Flip the Live View/Movie Shooting switch to the left.

You can change video menu options only when video recording is enabled.

2. Press the Menu button.

The last used menu appears.

3. Use the Quick Control button to navigate to the Shoot tab and then use the multi-controller button to navigate to the Shoot4 menu.

4. Use the Quick Control dial to navigate to Sound Recording (see the left image in Figure 5-16) and then press Set.

The Sound Recording options appear (see the right image in Figure 5-16).

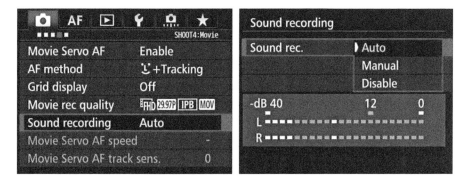

Figure 5-16: Changing the sound recording option.

5. **Use the multi-controller button or Quick Control dial to highlight Manual and then press Set.**

   The Manual recording menu appears. This menu gives you a right and left meter, which you use to accurately set the recording level. The meters record the highest decibel rating and hold it for three seconds.

6. **While looking at the peak-level meter, rotate the Main dial until the loudest sound recorded is −12 on the scale.**

   If the sound exceeds 0, the sound will be clipped (distorted).

7. **Press Menu to apply the changes.**

   The recording level is optimum for the scene you are recording. You'll have to reset the levels when you record a scene in a louder or quieter environment.

You can also enable a wind filter, which will eliminate some wind noise when you're recording video in windy conditions, and a sound attenuator, which is useful for suppressing loud sounds when recording.

Previewing Movies on the Camera LCD Monitor

You can preview movies in all their glory on the camera's LCD monitor. When you preview a movie, buttons appear that let you play the movie at full speed or in slow motion, pause the movie, preview it frame by frame, and navigate to the first or last frame. You can also edit movies in the camera, which I show you how to do in Chapter 9. To preview a movie on the camera LCD monitor:

1. **Press the Playback button to navigate to the desired movie.**

   You can preview images and movies as single images or thumbnails. A movie is designated by an old-fashioned movie camera icon when you view single images or with a filmstrip border when you view them as thumbnails.

2. Press the Set button.

Buttons appear beneath the movie.

3. Rotate the Quick Control dial to select one of the following options:

- **Exit:** Exits movie playing mode.
- **Play:** Plays the movie at full speed.
- **Slow Motion:** Plays the movie in slow motion.
- **First Frame:** Rewinds the movie to the first frame.
- **Previous Frame:** Rewinds the movie to the previous frame.
- **Next Frame:** Fast-forwards to the next frame.
- **Last Frame:** Fast-forwards to the last frame.
- **Edit:** Edits the movie.

4. Press Set.

After you finish viewing the movie, press the Menu button to return to single image display.

About the Handy Pad

For serious videographers, Canon added an option known as the Handy Pad to the EOS 7D Mark II. The Handy Pad, shown in Figure 1-2 in Chapter 1, is operational when you enable Silent Control from the Shoot5 menu when shooting movies in any mode except A+ (Full Auto), in which case you find the command on the Shoot3 menu. After you enable Silent Control, you display the Quick Control menu on the LCD monitor. With the Quick Control menu displayed, touch the top, bottom, left, or right side of the Handy Pad to silently change the following: shutter speed (when recording movies in Shutter Priority or Manual modes), aperture (when recording movies in Aperture Priority or Manual modes), ISO speed (when recording in Manual mode), exposure compensation (when shooting in any mode except Full Auto), recording audio level (when shooting in any mode except Full Auto), and headphone volume (when shooting in any mode). Your camera should be mounted on a sturdy tripod when using the Handy Pad and Silent Control.

Tips for Movie Shooting

Your camera captures awesome video. I've used my EOS 7D Mark II to capture some beautiful video from the nearby beaches. In January I'll send a copy of the video to my relatives who live north of the Mason-Dixon Line to show them how the other half lives. I've also seen some awesome videos on the web that were shot with this camera. Here are a few movie-shooting tips:

- For the best results, consider purchasing a high speed UDMA card that writes data at a speed of 8MB per second.

- Don't point the camera directly at the sun when shooting video, which can damage the camera sensor.

- Mount the camera on a tripod; it's hard to hold a camera steady for a long time while recording video. If your tripod has a pan head, you're in business.

- Pan slowly. If you pan too fast, your video looks very amateurish.

- If you plan on doing a lot of video recording with your camera, consider purchasing a device that steadies the camera (such as SteadiCam) while you move. You can find these at your favorite camera retailer that also sells video equipment.

- Remember to push the Start/Stop button when you're finished recording. Otherwise, you get several minutes of very choppy video as you move to the next scene. Worst-case scenario, you capture video of your feet shuffling on the sidewalk.

Part II
Going Beyond Point-and-Shoot Photography

In this part . . .

- Find out how to use some of the very cool features of your Canon EOS 7D Mark II. Gain the ability to shoot photographs outside of Full Auto mode and take full advantage of the high-powered technology that Canon is very proud of.

- Learn all about the advanced features your camera has to offer, including changing the autofocus system, changing the way the camera meters the scene, and more.

- Explore how to use the creative shooting modes to photograph action, wildlife, people, pets, places, and things.

- Check out the articles "Creating a Mood with Your Images" and "The Genius of Digital Photography" online at www.dummies.com/extras/canoneos7dmark2.

6

Getting the Most from Your Camera

In This Chapter

Using two memory cards

Clarifying metering

Using the creative shooting modes

Using exposure compensation

Locking your focus

Choosing a Drive mode

Working with and clearing custom functions

*Y*our camera has a plethora of features that are designed to enable you to capture stunning images. You can shoot images continuously, which is great for action photography. In fact, the camera has two speeds for continuous shooting: low and high. The Hi Speed Continuous mode lets you capture images at up to 10 frames per second (fps), which means you can capture a bunch of images really fast. In addition, your camera has two drive modes that significantly reduce camera noise, which is great if you photograph weddings or meetings, or any other event where silence is indeed golden. Your camera also has modes that take you way beyond point-and-shoot photography. When you take photographs with either Aperture Priority (Av) mode or Shutter Priority (Tv) mode, you supply one part of the exposure equation and your EOS 7D Mark II supplies the other part. Plus, you can do all sorts of things to hedge your bet and make sure you get stellar photos from your camera. You can use exposure compensation when you need to tweak the exposure the camera meters. You can also bracket exposure and tweak the white balance.

If you're a geek photographer like me who likes complete control over every aspect of your photography, you'll love the features I show you in this chapter.

Shooting with Two Cards

The fact that your camera has two memory card slots gives you a tremendous amount of flexibility. You can use the second card as overflow when you fill up the first card with images, or you can store different image formats on each card. The latter is a wonderful option for professional and semi-professional photographers. For example, if you're shooting a sporting event where you want to post images online immediately, you can store images in the JPEG format on one card and in the RAW format on the other card. When someone orders an image from your online gallery, you can edit the RAW image to pixel perfection in your favorite image-editing application. To specify how your camera writes images to two cards, follow these steps:

1. **Insert two cards in the camera.**

   For more information on inserting cards into the camera, see Chapter 1.

2. **Press the Menu button.**

   The previously used menu displays.

3. **Use the Quick Control button to navigate to the Set Up tab and then use the multi-controller button to navigate to the Set Up1 menu.**

4. **Rotate the Quick Control dial to highlight Record Func+Card/Folder Sel (see the left image in Figure 6-1) and then press Set.**

   The Record Func+Card/Folder Sel menu displays (see the right image in Figure 6-1).

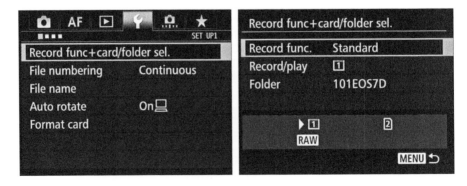

Figure 6-1: Specifying options when shooting with two cards.

5. Press Set again and choose one of the following options (see Figure 6-2):

- **Standard:** Images will be recorded to the card you specify with the Record/Play menu command, which I show you in the next set of steps. Images will only be recorded to the card you specify. When the card becomes full, you must invoke the Record/Play menu command again to select the other card for recording images and playing them back.

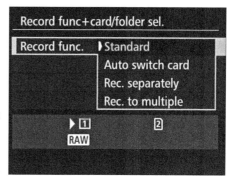

Figure 6-2: Who's on Card 1 and what's on Card 2?

- **Auto switch card:** Similar to the Standard method, but the camera automatically switches to the other card when the card you specify for recording and playback with the Record/Play command becomes full.

- **Rec. separately:** When you choose this option, you can specify the image format that is recorded to each card (see Chapter 1). For example, you can record images in the RAW format to one card for editing and record images in one of the JPEG formats for displaying on the web. When you specify this option the number of images you can record (burst) when choosing the Low Speed Continuous or High Speed Continuous drive option decreases.

- **Rec. to multiple:** When you choose this option, each image is recorded simultaneously to the CF and SD cards at the same size and format. You can specify JPEG and RAW. This option is handy when you're shooting lots of images that will be used by two parties, or will be edited by two parties. When the cards are full, simply hand the duplicate card to the other party that will be using or editing the images.

When you shoot with cards of different capacities, the number of shoots remaining, which is displayed on the LCD panel, will be for the smaller capacity card. When you fill the smaller card, it will not be possible to record additional images. Therefore, it makes sense to use cards with the same capacity.

6. Press Set.

You're ready to shoot up a storm with two cards.

When you record with multiple cards, you need to specify which card records and plays back images first. To specify which card records and plays back, follow these steps:

1. **Specify the method by which the camera writes images to two cards.**

   If you're flummoxed, read the previous set of steps.

2. **Press the Menu button.**

   The previously used menu displays.

3. **Use the Quick Control button to navigate to the Set Up tab and then use the multi-controller button to navigate to the Set Up1 menu.**

4. **Rotate the Quick Control dial to highlight Record Func+Card/Folder Sel (see the left image in Figure 6-3).**

5. **Press Set.**

   The Record Func+Card/Folder Sel menu displays.

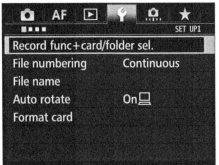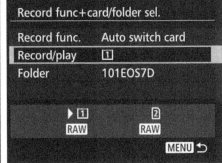

Figure 6-3: Specifying which card is selected for recording or playback.

6. **Rotate the Quick Control dial to highlight Record/Play (see the right image in Figure 6-3).**

7. **Press Set and choose the desired card (see Figure 6-4).**

   • If you choose the Standard or Auto Switch option for writing images to the CF and SD cards, select the card that will record and play back images.

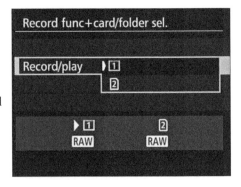

Figure 6-4: To SD or CF? That is the question.

• If you choose Rec. separately or Rec. multiple, select the card that will play back the images.

8. Press Set.

You're ready to start creating beautiful images.

Understanding Metering

Your camera's metering device examines the scene and determines which shutter speed and f-stop combination will yield a properly exposed image. The camera can choose a fast shutter speed and large aperture, or a slow shutter speed and small aperture.

When you take pictures in Full Auto mode, the camera makes both decisions for you. But you're much smarter than the processor inside your camera. If you take control of the reins and supply one piece of the puzzle, the camera will supply the rest. When you're taking certain types of pictures, it makes sense to determine which f-stop will be best for what you're photographing. In other scenarios, it makes more sense to choose the shutter speed and let the camera determine the f-stop. In the upcoming sections, I show you how to use the creative shooting modes your camera has to offer. In Chapter 8, I show you how to use these modes for specific picture-taking situations.

Taking Pictures with Creative Modes

You bought an EOS 7D Mark II because you're a creative photographer. The Full Auto shooting mode is useful when you're getting used to the camera. But after you know where the controls are, branch out and use shooting modes in which you control the manner in which your images are exposed. In the upcoming sections, I show you how to expose images with the creative shooting modes: P (Programmed Auto Exposure), Av (Aperture Priority), Tv (Shutter Priority), M (Manual), and B (Bulb).

The following list describes each mode in detail:

- **Programmed Auto Exposure mode (P):** This mode is like stepping out of the kid's pool into the shallow end of the deep pool. The camera still determines what shutter speed and aperture will yield a perfectly exposed image, but you can change the values to suit the type of scene you're photographing.

- **Aperture Priority mode (Av):** When you switch to this mode, you supply the f-stop value (aperture), and the camera determines what shutter speed will result in a perfectly exposed image.

✔ **Shutter Priority mode (Tv):** In this mode, you determine the shutter speed, and the camera does the math to determine what f-stop value (aperture) is needed to create a pixel-perfect image.

✔ **Manual mode (M):** When you decide to shoot in this mode, you supply the shutter speed and f-stop, but the camera does give you some help in determining whether the combination you provide will yield a perfectly exposed image.

✔ **Bulb mode (B):** If you've been a photographer for any length of time, you know that the Bulb mode enables you to shoot *time exposures,* which means the shutter can stay open longer than the slowest shutter speed provided by the camera, which is 30 seconds, or longer if you use the Bulb Timer menu command (see Chapter 10).

Before you can determine which mode is best for you, you need to understand how exposure works, which is the topic of the next section.

Understanding how exposure works in the camera

Your EOS 7D Mark II exposes images the same way film cameras did. Light enters the camera through the lens and is recorded on the sensor. The amount of time the shutter is open and the amount of light entering the camera determines whether the resulting image is too dark, too bright, or properly exposed.

The duration of the exposure is the *shutter speed.* Your camera has a shutter speed range from as long as 30 seconds in duration to as fast as 1/8000 of a second. A fast shutter speed stops action, and a slow shutter speed leaves the shutter open for a long time to record images in low-light situations.

The *aperture* is the opening in the lens that lets light into the camera when the shutter opens. You can change the aperture diameter to let a lot, or a small amount, of light into the camera. The *f-stop value* determines the size of the aperture. A low f-stop value (large aperture) lets a lot of light into the camera, and a high f-stop value (small aperture) lets a small amount of light into the camera. Depending on the lens you're using, the f-stop range can be from f/1.8, which sends huge gobs of light into the camera, to f/32, which lets in a miniscule splash of light into the camera. The f-stop also determines the depth of field, a concept I explain in "Controlling depth of field" later in this chapter.

The duration of the exposure (shutter speed) and aperture (f-stop value) combination determines the exposure. For each lighting scenario you encounter, several different combinations render a perfectly exposed photograph. Use different combinations for different types of photography. The camera's metering device examines the scene and determines which shutter speed and f-stop combination will yield a properly exposed image. The camera can choose a fast shutter speed and large aperture, or a slow shutter speed and small aperture.

Using Programmed Auto Exposure mode

When you take pictures with the Programmed Auto Exposure mode, the camera determines the shutter speed and aperture (f-stop value) that yields a properly exposed image for the lighting conditions. Even though this sounds identical to Full Auto mode, with this mode you can change the AF (autofocus) mode, Drive mode, ISO speed, picture style, and more. You can also change the shutter speed and aperture to suit the scene you're photographing. You cannot shift programmed exposure when using flash. To take pictures in Programmed Auto Exposure mode:

1. **Press the Mode Lock button and then rotate the Mode dial to P (see Figure 6-5).**

2. **Press the Flash Compensation/ISO button and then rotate the Main dial to change the ISO speed to the desired setting.**

   Higher ISO speeds make the camera sensor more sensitive to light, which is ideal when you're photographing in dim light or at night. For more information on changing ISO speed, see Chapter 7.

Figure 6-5: Rotating the Mode dial to P.

3. **Press the shutter button halfway to achieve focus.**

   The green dot on the right side of the viewfinder appears when the camera achieves focus. If the dot is flashing, the camera can't achieve focus and you must manually focus the camera.

4. **Check the shutter speed and aperture.**

   You can use the viewfinder or LCD panel (see Figure 6-6) to check the shutter speed and aperture. If you notice a shutter speed of 8000 and the minimum aperture for the lens blinking, the image will be overexposed. If you notice a shutter speed of 30 seconds and the maximum aperture for the lens blinking, the image will be underexposed.

Figure 6-6: Check the shutter speed and aperture.

5. Press the shutter button fully to take the picture.

The image displays almost immediately on your LCD monitor.

You can shift the exposure and choose a different shutter speed and aperture combination. Use this option when you want to shoot with a faster shutter speed to freeze action or a different aperture to control depth of field. To shift the Programmed Auto Exposure:

1. Follow Steps 1–3 of the preceding instructions and then press the shutter button halfway.

The camera achieves focus.

 2. With the shutter button depressed halfway, rotate the Main dial.

This can be a bit of a juggling act, but is manageable if you use your middle finger to press the shutter button and your forefinger to rotate the Main dial. As you rotate the dial, you see different shutter speed and aperture combinations in the viewfinder and LCD panel (see Figure 6-7). If you notice that the shutter speed is too slow for a blur-free picture, you have to put the camera on a tripod or increase the ISO speed setting.

3. When you see the desired combination of shutter speed and aperture, press the shutter button fully to take the picture.

The image appears almost immediately on your LCD monitor.

Figure 6-7: You can shift programmed exposure.

Using Aperture Priority mode

If you like to photograph landscapes, Aperture Priority mode is right up your alley. When you take pictures with Aperture Priority mode, you choose the desired f-stop and the camera supplies the proper shutter speed to achieve a properly exposed image. A large aperture (small f-stop value) lets a lot of light into the camera, and a small aperture (large f-stop value) lets a small amount of light into the camera. The benefit of shooting in Aperture Priority mode is that you have complete control over the depth of field (see "Controlling depth of field" later in this chapter). You also have access to all the other options, such as setting the ISO speed, choosing a picture style,

working in an AF mode or a Drive mode, and so on. To take pictures with
Aperture Priority mode:

1. **Press the Mode Lock button and then
   rotate the Mode dial to Av (see Figure 6-8).**

2. **Press the Flash Compensation/ISO button
   and then rotate the Main dial to change the
   ISO speed to the desired setting.**

   When choosing an ISO speed, choose the
   slowest speed for the available lighting conditions. For more information on changing
   ISO speed, see Chapter 7.

3. **Rotate the Main dial to select the desired
   f-stop.**

   As you change the aperture, the
   camera calculates the proper
   shutter speed to achieve a properly exposed image. The change
   appears in the LCD panel and the
   viewfinder. As you rotate the dial,
   monitor the shutter speed in the
   viewfinder (see Figure 6-9). If you
   notice that the shutter speed is
   too slow for a blur-free picture,
   you have to put the camera on a
   tripod or increase the ISO speed
   setting. If you see the minimum
   shutter speed (30 seconds) blinking, the image will be underexposed with the selected f-stop.
   If you see the maximum shutter
   speed (1/8000 second) blinking,
   the image will be overexposed
   with the selected f-stop.

Figure 6-8: Rotating the Mode
dial to Av.

Figure 6-9: Make sure the shutter speed is fast
enough for a blur-free picture.

4. **Press the shutter button halfway to achieve focus.**

   A green dot appears in the viewfinder when the camera achieves focus.

5. **Press the shutter button fully to take the picture.**

   The image appears on your LCD monitor almost immediately.

Controlling depth of field

Depth of field determines how much of your image looks sharp and is in apparent focus in front of and behind your subject. When you're taking pictures of
landscapes on a bright sunny day, you want a depth of field that produces
an image in which you can see the details for miles and miles and miles . . .

Other times, you want to have a very shallow depth of field in which your subject is in sharp focus but the foreground and background are a pleasant out-of-focus blur. A shallow depth of field is ideal when you're shooting a portrait, for example.

You control the depth of field in an image by selecting the f-stop in Aperture Priority mode and letting the camera do the math to determine what shutter speed will yield a properly exposed image. You get a limited depth of field when using a small f-stop value (large aperture), which lets a lot of light into the camera. A fast lens:

✔ Has an f-stop value of 2.8 or smaller

✔ Gives you the capability to shoot in low-light conditions

✔ Gives you a wonderfully shallow depth of field

When shooting at a lens's smallest f-stop value, you're letting the most amount of light into the camera, which is known as shooting *wide open*. The lens you use also determines how large the depth of field will be for a given f-stop. At the same f-stop, a wide-angle lens has a greater depth of field than a telephoto lens. When you're photographing a landscape, the ideal recipe is a wide-angle lens and a small aperture (large f-stop value). When you're shooting a portrait of someone, you want a shallow depth of field. Therefore, a telephoto lens with a focal length that is the 35mm equivalent of 85mm with a large aperture (small f-stop value) is the ideal solution.

Figure 6-10 shows two pictures of the same subject. The first image was shot with an exposure of 1/640 second at f/1.8, and the second image was shot with an exposure of 1/80 second at f/10. In both cases, I focused on the subject. Notice how much more of the image shot at f/10 is in focus. The detail of the flowers in the second shot distracts the viewer's attention from the subject. The first image has a shallow depth of field that draws the viewer's attention to the subject.

Using depth-of-field preview

When you compose a scene through your viewfinder, the camera aperture is wide open, which means you have no idea how much depth of field you'll have in the resulting image. You can preview the depth of field for a selected f-stop by pressing a button on your camera, which closes the aperture to the f-stop you use to take the picture. To preview depth of field:

1. **Compose the picture and choose the desired f-stop in Aperture Priority mode.**

   See "Using Aperture Priority mode" earlier in this chapter if you need help.

Figure 6-10: The f-stop you choose determines the depth of field.

2. **Press the shutter button halfway to achieve focus.**

   A green dot shines solid on the right side of the viewfinder when the camera focuses on your subject.

3. **Press the Depth-of-Field Preview button (see Figure 6-11).**

   The button is conveniently located on the front right side of the camera when your camera is pointed toward your subject. You can easily locate the button by feel. When you press the button, the image in the viewfinder may become dim, especially when you're using a small aperture (large f-stop number) that doesn't let a lot of light into the camera. Don't worry, the camera chooses the proper shutter speed to compensate for the f-stop you select.

Depth of Field Preview button

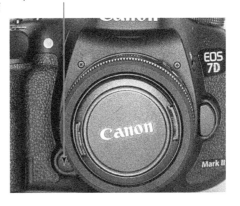

Figure 6-11: The Depth-of-Field Preview button.

When you use depth-of-field preview, pay attention to how much of the image is in apparent focus in front of and behind your subject. To see what the depth of field looks like with different f-stops, select what you think is the optimal f-stop for the scene you're photographing. Then, press the shutter button halfway to achieve focus, as I outline earlier, and then rotate the Main dial to choose different f-stop values.

As long as you hold down the Depth-of-Field Preview button while you're choosing different f-stops, you can see the effect each f-stop has on the depth of field.

Using Shutter Priority mode

When your goal is to accentuate an object's motion, choose Shutter Priority mode. When you take pictures in Shutter Priority mode, you choose the shutter speed and the camera supplies the proper f-stop value to properly expose the scene. Your camera has a shutter speed range from 30 seconds to 1/8000 of a second. When you choose a slow shutter speed, the shutter is open for a long time. When you choose a fast shutter speed, the shutter is open for a short duration and you can freeze action. To take pictures in Shutter Priority mode:

1. **Rotate the Mode dial to Tv (see Figure 6-12).**

2. **Rotate the Main dial to choose the desired shutter speed.**

   As you change the shutter speed, the camera determines the proper f-stop to achieve a properly exposed image. If you notice that the shutter speed is too slow for a blur-free picture, you have to put the camera on a tripod or increase the ISO speed setting. If you see the minimum aperture (largest f-stop value) for the lens blinking, the image will be underexposed with the selected shutter speed. If you see the maximum aperture (smallest f-stop number) blinking, the image will be overexposed with the selected shutter speed. If you choose a shutter speed that's too slow for a blur-free picture, mount the camera on a tripod or choose a higher ISO speed setting.

   Figure 6-12: Rotating the Mode dial to Tv.

3. **Press the Flash Compensation/ISO button and then rotate the Main dial to change the ISO speed to the desired setting.**

   Choose an ISO setting that enables you to achieve the desired shutter speed. For more information on changing ISO speed, see Chapter 7.

4. Rotate the Main dial to choose the desired shutter speed.

As you rotate the dial, the shutter speed value changes on the LCD panel and in the viewfinder. I rarely look at the LCD panel when changing shutter speed or aperture. I like to see my subject while I make the changes.

5. Press the shutter button halfway to achieve focus.

A green dot appears in the right side of the viewfinder. If the dot is flashing, the camera can't achieve focus. If this occurs, switch the lens to manual focus and twist the focusing barrel until your subject snaps into focus. Figure 6-13 shows the viewfinder when working in Shutter Priority mode.

6. Press the shutter button fully to take the picture.

Figure 6-13: Adjusting the shutter speed.

Shutter Priority mode is the way to go whenever you need to stop action or show the grace of an athlete in motion. You'd use Shutter Priority mode in lots of scenarios. Figure 6-14 shows the effects you can achieve with different shutter speeds. The image on the left was photographed with a slow shutter speed, and the image on the right was photographed with a fast shutter speed to freeze the action. For more information on using Shutter Priority mode when photographing action, check out Chapter 8.

Figure 6-14: A tale of two shutter speeds.

Using Manual mode

You can also manually expose your images. When you choose Manual mode, you supply the f-stop value and the shutter speed. You can choose from several combinations to properly expose the image for the lighting conditions. Your camera meter gives you some assistance to select the right f-stop and shutter speed combination to properly expose the image. (If you fast-forwarded to this section and don't understand how your camera determines shutter speed and exposure, check out "Understanding how exposure works in the camera" earlier in this chapter.) To manually expose your images:

1. **Rotate the Mode dial to M (see Figure 6-15) and then rotate the Main dial to set the shutter speed.**

   The shutter speed determines how long the shutter stays open. A slow shutter speed is perfect for a scene with low light. A fast shutter speed freezes action. As you change the shutter speed, review the exposure indicator in the LCD panel, or if you have the shutter button pressed halfway, in the viewfinder.

Figure 6-15: Manually exposing the image.

   When the exposure is correct for the lighting conditions, the exposure level mark aligns with the center of the scale (see Figure 6-16). If the exposure level mark is to the right of center, the image will be overexposed. If to the left of center, the image will be underexposed. In the viewfinder, you use the exposure indicator on the right side of the viewfinder. If the indicator is in the center, the image is properly exposed, below the center, the image will be underexposed, or on top of the center, the image will be overexposed. Of course, you're in control. You may want to intentionally

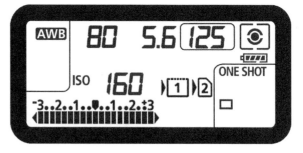

Figure 6-16: Monitor the exposure in the LCD panel.

   overexpose or underexpose for special effects. For example, if you slightly underexpose the image, the colors will be more saturated. You can also monitor exposure in the viewfinder using the scale on the right side of the viewfinder.

2. **Rotate the Quick Control dial to set the f-stop value.**

   The f-stop value determines how much light enters the camera. A small f-stop value, such as f/2.8, lets a lot of light into the camera and also gives you a shallow depth of field. A large f-stop value lets a small amount of light into the camera and gives you a large depth of field. As you change the f-stop value, review the exposure indicator in the LCD panel, or if you have the shutter button pressed halfway, in the viewfinder. When the exposure is correct for the lighting conditions, the exposure level mark aligns with the center of the scale. If the exposure level mark is to the right of the center, or above center when viewing the exposure scale in the viewfinder, the image will be overexposed. If to the left of center, or below center when viewing the exposure scale in the viewfinder, the image will be underexposed.

3. **Press the shutter button halfway to achieve focus.**

   A green dot appears in the viewfinder when the camera has achieved focus. If the dot is flashing, the camera can't achieve focus and you must focus manually.

4. **Press the shutter button fully to take the picture.**

Shooting time exposures with Bulb mode

When you switch to Bulb mode, the shutter stays open as long as you press the shutter button. If you've ever seen night pictures in which you can actually see trails from stars that follow the curvature of the earth, you've seen a photograph that was taken with the Bulb mode. The photographer left the shutter open for a long period of time, and the earth rotated while the photograph was taken. These types of images are known as *time exposures* because the image was exposed over a long period of time. To shoot time exposures:

1. **Mount the camera on a tripod.**

   The lens will be open for a long time. The slightest movement will show up as a blur in the final image. Unless you want the image blurred for a creative effect, you need to stabilize the camera on a tripod.

2. **Rotate the Mode dial to B (see Figure 6-17).**

   B means Bulb mode. Back in the old days of film cameras, photographers would open the shutter with a pneumatic device that looked like a bulb. The shutter opened

Figure 6-17: Rotate the Mode dial to B to select Bulb mode.

when the photographer squeezed the device and remained open until the photographer released his grip.

3. **Rotate the Quick Control dial or the Main dial to set the f-stop value.**

   A small f-stop value such as f/2.8 (large aperture) lets a lot of light into the camera and gives a shallow depth of field. A large f-stop value (small aperture), such as f/16, lets a small amount of light into the camera and gives a large depth of field. You also need to leave the shutter open longer when using a large f-stop value, which in most instances is desirable. However, a longer exposure can add digital noise to the image. When you have an exposure that leaves the shutter open for several seconds, or perhaps minutes, use an ISO speed setting of 100 to minimize digital noise.

4. **Connect a remote switch to the camera.**

   If you hold the shutter button open with your finger, you'll transmit vibrations to the camera, which yields a blurry image. A remote switch, such as the Canon RS-80N3, or a remote timer and switch, such as the Canon TC-80N3, triggers the shutter remotely and no vibration is transmitted to the camera. Both plug into a port on the side of your camera. (For the location of this port, refer back to Figure 1-10 in Chapter 1.)

5. **Press the button on the remote switch to open the shutter.**

   The shutter remains open as long as you hold the button. The time is noted in the LCD panel.

6. **Release the button on the remote switch to close the shutter.**

7. **Review the image on your LCD monitor.**

   I find it useful to take one picture, note the time the lens remained open, and examine the image carefully on the LCD monitor. If I'm not pleased, I take another shot, leaving the lens open longer if the test image is underexposed or for a shorter duration if the test image is overexposed.

Time exposures can be a lot of fun. You can use them to record artistic depictions of headlight patterns on a curved stretch of road (see Figure 6-18) or capture the motion of the ocean at night. The possibilities are limited only by your imagination. You can also manually set the number of seconds for which the shutter is open using the bulb timer, a task I show you how to do in Chapter 10.

Figure 6-18: A time exposure that records headlight trails at night.

Modifying Camera Exposure

Your camera has a built-in metering device that automatically determines the proper shutter speed and aperture to create a perfectly exposed image for most lighting scenarios. However, at times, you need to modify the exposure to suit the current lighting conditions. Modify camera exposure for individual shots, or hedge your bets and create several exposures of each shot. You can also lock focus and exposure to a specific location in the scene you're photographing. I show you how to achieve these tasks in the upcoming sections.

Using exposure compensation

When your camera gets the exposure right, it's a wonderful thing. At times, however, the camera doesn't get it right. When you review an image on the camera LCD monitor and it's not exposed to suit your taste, you can compensate manually by increasing or decreasing exposure. To manually compensate camera exposure:

1. **Choose P, Av, or Tv from the Mode dial (see Figure 6-19).**

   Exposure compensation is available only when you take pictures with Programmed Auto Exposure, Aperture Priority, or Shutter Priority modes.

2. **Press the Shutter button halfway.**

   The camera meters the scene.

3. **Rotate the Quick Control dial while looking in the viewfinder or at the LCD panel.**

   Rotate the dial counterclockwise to decrease exposure or clockwise to increase exposure. As you rotate the dial, you see the exposure indicator in the viewfinder and LCD panel move, which shows you the amount of exposure compensation you're applying (see Figure 6-20).

4. **Press the shutter button fully to take the picture.**

5. **To cancel exposure compensation, rotate the Quick Control dial until the exposure indicator is in the center of the exposure compensation scale.**

   You see the exposure compensation scale in the viewfinder and on the LCD panel.

Figure 6-19: Use exposure compensation with these shooting modes.

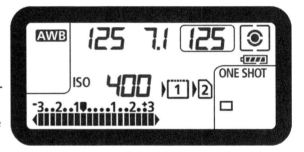

Figure 6-20: Using exposure compensation.

TIP

Exposure compensation stays in effect even after you power off the camera. You can inadvertently add exposure compensation by accidentally rotating the Quick Control dial when you have the shutter button pressed halfway. You can safeguard against this by keeping the Quick Control switch (below the Quick Control dial) in the locked position when you don't need to use the Quick Control dial.

Bracketing exposure

When you're photographing an important event, properly exposed images are a must. Many photographers get lazy and don't feel they need to get it right in the camera when they have programs like Adobe Photoshop or Adobe Photoshop Lightroom. However, you get much better results when you process an image that's been exposed correctly. Professional photographers bracket their exposures when they photograph important events or places they may never visit again. When you bracket an exposure, you take three pictures: one with the exposure as metered by the camera, one with exposure that's been decreased, and one with exposure that's been increased. You can bracket up to plus or minus 3 EV (exposure value) in ⅓ EV increments. To bracket your exposures:

1. **Press the Menu button.**

   The previously used menu displays.

2. **Use the Quick Control button to navigate to the Shoot tab and then use the multi-controller button to navigate to the Shoot2 menu.**

   Expo Comp/AEB (automatic exposure bracketing) is the first command (see the left image in Figure 6-21).

3. **Press the Set button.**

   The Expo Comp/AEB setting menu appears.

4. **Rotate the Main dial to set the amount of bracketing.**

   When you rotate the dial, a new mark appears on each side of the center of the exposure indicator scale (see the right image in Figure 6-21). Each mark indicates 1/3 f-stop correction.

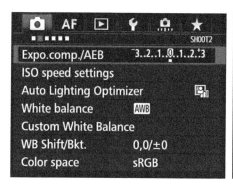 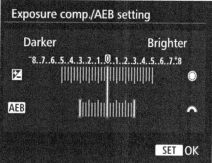

Figure 6-21: Setting automatic exposure bracketing.

5. **(Optional) Rotate the Quick Control dial to apply exposure compensation to the settings determined by the camera meter.**

   This step is not necessary if you're comfortable with the way the camera has been setting exposure. If you are not happy with the way the camera has been calculating exposure settings for the lighting conditions, you can use exposure compensation to increase or decrease the exposure metered by the camera. When you add exposure compensation to the mix, the automatic exposure bracketing (AEB) marks move as well. In other words, the exposure will be increased and decreased relative to the compensated exposure.

6. **Press Set.**

The settings are applied. The Expo Comp/AEB menu option shows the amount of bracketing and exposure compensation you've applied. The AEB icon appears in the viewfinder and LCD panel (see Figure 6-22).

AEB icon

Figure 6-22: These icons appear after you set AEB.

7. **Press the Drive-AF button and rotate the Quick Control dial to choose one of the Continuous Drive modes.**

When I use AEB, I generally use the low speed Continuous mode.

8. **Press the shutter button halfway to achieve focus and then press the shutter button fully.**

When you press the shutter button, the camera creates three images: one with standard exposure, one with decreased exposure, and one with increased exposure. To cancel AEB, turn off the camera.

Locking exposure

You can also lock exposure on a specific part of the frame, which is handy when you want a specific part of the frame exposed correctly. For example, recently I was photographing a beautiful sunset. The camera meter averaged the exposure for the scene, and the image ended up with blown-out highlights around the sun and clouds that weren't as dark and colorful as I saw them. To compensate for this, I locked exposure on the blue sky, and the picture turned out perfect. To lock exposure:

1. **Look through the viewfinder and move the camera until the center of the viewfinder is over the area to which you want to lock exposure.**

2. **Press the AE Lock button.**

 The auto-exposure lock icon appears in the viewfinder (see Figure 6-23).

3. **Press the shutter button half-way to achieve focus.**

 A green dot in the viewfinder tells you that the camera has achieved focus. You also see black rectangles that designate the areas on which the camera has focused.

4. **Press the shutter button fully to take the picture.**

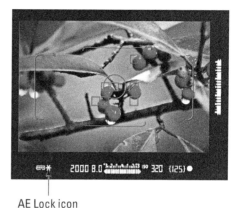

AE Lock icon

Figure 6-23: This icon notifies that exposure lock is enabled.

Locking Focus

You can choose from two ways to lock focus on an object that isn't in the center of the frame: the shutter button or the AF-On button. This option comes in handy when your center of interest isn't in the center of the frame.

To lock focus with the shutter button:

1. **While looking through the viewfinder, move your camera until the center of the viewfinder is over the subject that you want the camera to lock focus on.**

2. **Press the shutter button halfway.**

 Make sure that a black autofocus square appears over your subject. When I'm photographing people who aren't in the center of the frame, I switch to a single autofocus point that's in the center of the frame, and then lock focus on the subject's eye that is closest to the camera. When the camera achieves focus, a green dot appears in the viewfinder. (For more information on selecting and modifying autofocus points, see Chapter 7.)

3. **While holding the shutter button halfway, recompose your picture.**

4. **Press the shutter button fully to take the picture.**

You can also lock focus with the AF-On button on the top of your camera. This is a little easier because you don't have to hold the shutter button halfway while composing your picture. To lock focus with the AF-On button:

1. **Look through the viewfinder and move the camera until the center of the viewfinder is over the subject that you want the camera to lock focus on.**

2. **Press the AF-On button.**

Red autofocus squares appear momentarily in the viewfinder over the objects that the camera will lock focus on. The squares turn black after the camera achieves focus. Make sure the autofocus points that display are over the object that you want the camera to lock focus on. I find it useful to switch to a single autofocus point in the center of the frame when I'm photographing a person or subject that isn't in the center.

3. **Move the camera to recompose the picture and then press the shutter button fully.**

An image appears almost instantaneously on the camera LCD monitor. Review the image to make sure the camera locked focus on the desired object.

Choosing a Drive Mode

Your camera can capture multiple images when you press the shutter button in the P (Programmed Auto Exposure), Av (Aperture Priority), Tv (Shutter Priority), or M (Manual) shooting modes. Your camera also has a Hi Speed Continuous mode that captures images at the blindingly fast rate of 10 fps, which is ideal for any situation that requires you to capture a bunch of images in a short period of time. To specify the Drive mode, follow these steps:

1. **Choose one of the following shooting modes from the Mode dial: P (Programmed Auto Exposure), Av (Aperture Priority), Tv (Shutter Priority), or M (Manual).**

When you shoot in Full Auto mode, you can capture only a single shot each time you press the shutter button. You can capture images at up to 10 fps when shooting in one of the other aforementioned shooting modes.

2. **Press the Drive-AF button.**

3. **Rotate the Quick Control dial while looking at the LCD panel and then choose one of the following:**

- **Single Shot:** You capture one picture each time you press the shutter button. (See the left image in Figure 6-24.)

- **Low Speed Continuous Shooting:** You can capture up to 3 fps when you press and hold the shutter button. (See the right image in Figure 6-24.)

- **Hi Speed Continuous Shooting:** You can capture up to 10 fps when you press and hold the shutter button. (See the left image in Figure 6-25.)

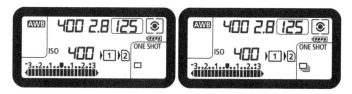

Figure 6-24: Single Shot and Hi Speed Continuous Drive modes.

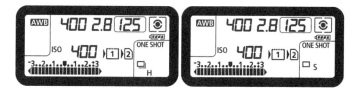

Figure 6-25: Low Speed Continuous and Silent Single Shooting.

- **Silent Single Shooting:** You can capture one picture when you press the shutter button and the camera will make less noise than when shooting in Single Shot mode. (See the right image in Figure 6-25.) When shooting movies, or shooting in Live View mode, shooting will not be silent even if this option is selected.

- **Silent Continuous Shooting:** You can capture up to 4 frames and the camera will make less noise than when shooting in than when shooting in Low Speed Continuous mode. (See Figure 6-26.)

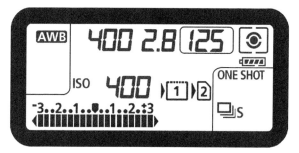

Figure 6-26: Silent Continuous Shooting.

4. **Take some pictures.**

   The Drive mode you select stays in effect until you change it. If you power off the camera, the Drive mode still stays in effect. Switch back to Single Shot mode when you no longer need to capture images continuously.

Using Custom Functions

Your camera has almost as many custom functions as there are Smiths in the New York City phone book. Well, almost. At any rate, I find some custom functions extremely useful. In fact, I've already covered a couple of custom functions in earlier chapters. Unfortunately, I'd have to buy my editor a year's supply of her favorite hair-coloring product if I covered every custom function. In the upcoming sections, I show you how to access and use a custom function. I leave it to you, dear reader, to explore the other custom functions when the weather's not conducive to photography. But then again, when the weather's bad, you may prefer to try some still-life photography on common household items instead of exploring custom functions.

Custom functions enable you to modify the camera to suit your shooting style and the subjects you photograph. If this is your first Canon digital SLR, or you've never explored customs functions, consider this your baptism by fire. One useful custom function is *Safety Shift*. When you shoot in Aperture Priority or Shutter Priority mode, this function shifts the exposure instantly if the lighting changes dramatically and the subject gets considerably brighter or darker. This custom function also shifts ISO if a proper exposure cannot be obtained with the currently selected ISO. Here's how to enable it:

1. **Press the Menu button.**

    The previously used menu displays on the camera LCD monitor.

2. **Use the Quick Control button to navigate to the C.Fn tab and then use the multi-controller button to navigate to C.Fn1 menu.**

3. **Rotate the Quick Control dial to highlight Safety Shift (see the left image in Figure 6-27) and then press Set.**

    The default Safety Shift option displays (see the right image in Figure 6-27).

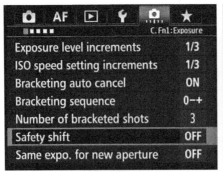
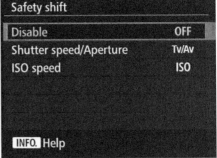

Figure 6-27: The Safety Shift options.

4. **Rotate the Quick Control dial to highlight the one of the following options.**

   • **Disable:** The default option disables safety shift.

   • **Shutter speed/Aperture:** If the correct exposure cannot be obtained, the camera will shift the shutter speed if you're shooting in Shutter Priority mode, or the aperture if you're shooting in Aperture priority mode to obtain a correctly exposed image.

   • **ISO speed:** If the correct exposure cannot be obtained using the ISO setting you choose, the camera will automatically shift the ISO to obtain a correctly exposed image.

5. **Press Set.**

   The custom function is highlighted in blue and remains in effect until you disable it.

Clearing Custom Functions

Enabling custom functions and customizing your camera can be quite useful. However, sometimes you get carried away and go over the top. Other times you've experimented with a bunch of custom functions and decide they no longer suit your style of photography. You can wipe out all the custom functions and any changes you've applied to camera buttons by doing the following:

1. **Press the Menu button.**

   The previously used menu displays.

2. **Use the Quick Control button to navigate to the C.Fn tab and then use the multi-controller button to navigate to the C.Fn5 menu.**

3. **Rotate the Quick Control dial to highlight Clear All Custom Func (C.Fn) (see the left image in Figure 6-28).**

4. **Press the Set button.**

   A dialog box appears asking you to confirm clearing all custom functions (see the right image in Figure 6-28).

5. **Rotate the Quick Control dial to highlight OK and press Set.**

   Any custom function you've enabled has been cleared.

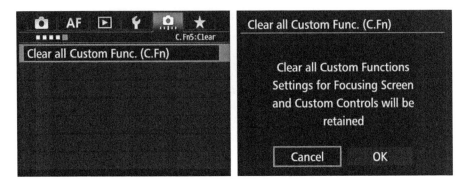

Figure 6-28: Clearing all custom functions.

Useful Menu Commands for Images

The new Canon EOS 7D Mark II has a plethora of custom functions. If you're a veteran user of the camera's predecessor, you may have scoured the custom functions looking for Long Exposure Noise Reduction, High ISO Noise Speed Reduction, and Image Highlight Tone Priority. Not to worry. They've just found a different home in the EOS 7D Mark II. In the upcoming sections, I show you where they are now and how to use them.

Enabling Long Exposure Noise Reduction

If you take pictures using the B (Bulb) mode, the lens is open for a long time, which causes noise — the scourge of digital photography — to raise its ugly head. When you enable Long Exposure Noise Reduction, the camera greatly reduces the amount of noise in the resulting image. To apply noise reduction to images with an exposure duration of 1 second or longer:

1. **Press the Menu button.**

   The previously used menu displays.

2. **Use the Quick Control button to navigate to the Shoot tab, use the multi-controller button to navigate to the Shoot3 menu, and then use the Quick Control dial to highlight Long Exp Noise Reduction (see the left image in Figure 6-29).**

3. **Press Set.**

   The Long Exp Noise Reduction menu appears (see the right image in Figure 6-29).

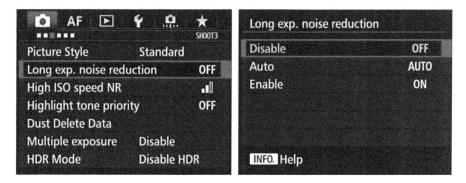

Figure 6-29: Enabling Long Exposure Noise Reduction.

4. Choose one of the following options:

- **Disable:** Does not apply noise reduction regardless of the exposure duration.

- **Auto:** Applies noise reduction to images with an exposure duration of 1 second or longer when noise typical of long exposures is detected.

- **Enable:** Applies noise reduction to all images with an exposure duration of 1 second or longer. This option may do a better job of cleaning up long exposure noise than the Auto option.

5. Press Set.

The Long Exposure Noise Reduction option of your choice is now in effect.

When you enable Long Exposure Noise Reduction, the camera takes longer to save the image to the memory card because the noise reduction is applied before the image is saved.

Enabling High ISO Speed Reduction

If you shoot in dim lighting conditions — some wedding photographers shoot in rooms just slightly brighter than caves — you need to bump the ISO to achieve a shutter speed capable of freezing motion. Even though you're able to capture the image, you'll find noise in the darker areas of the image. Enabling High ISO Speed Reduction helps get rid of the nasty noise, resulting in an almost squeaky-clean image. To enable high speed noise reduction:

1. Press the Menu button.

The previously used menu displays.

2. **Use the Quick Control button to navigate to the Shoot tab, use the multi-controller button to navigate to the Shoot3 menu, and then use the Quick Control dial to highlight High ISO Speed NR (see the left image in Figure 6-30).**

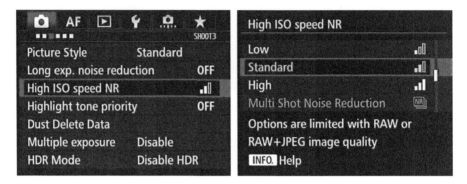

Figure 6-30: Enabling High ISO Speed Noise Reduction.

3. **Press Set.**

   The High ISO Speed NR menu displays (see the right image in Figure 6-30).

4. **Choose one of the following options:**

   • **Low:** Applies minimal noise reduction to images photographed with a high ISO speed.

   • **Standard:** The default option applies noise reduction to all images.

   • **High:** Applies the maximum amount of noise reduction to images photographed with high ISO speed. This option may be ideal if you shoot lots of images with a high ISO speed.

   • **Multi Shot Noise Reduction:** This option is available when you use the camera's multi-shot option(see Chapter 10). It applies more noise reduction than the High option.

5. **Press Set.**

   Your favorite flavor of high ISO speed noise reduction is applied to every image you shoot until you reset the camera to its default settings or choose a different high ISO speed noise reduction option.

I haven't performed extensive tests on these options. Change these custom functions at your discretion and with however many grains of salt you choose.

Enabling Highlight Tone Priority

Another custom function that's found a new home is Highlight Tone Priority. This option is very useful if you do a lot of photography in bright conditions. In essence, the camera gives priority to the bright parts of your scene or subject you are photographing, which prevents them from being overexposed. If you do wedding photography, this feature enables you to capture images with subtle details such as the bride's veil. It also extends the dynamic range. To enable Image Highlight Tone Priority:

1. **Press the Menu button.**

   The previously used menu displays.

2. **Use the Quick Control button to navigate to the Shoot tab, use the multi-controller button to navigate to the Shoot3 menu, and then use the Quick Control dial to select Highlight Tone Priority (see the left image in Figure 6-31).**

3. **Press Set.**

   Choose one of the following options (see the right image in Figure 6-31):

   - **Disable:** The default option disables Highlight Tone Priority.

   - **Enable:** Enables Highlight Tone Priority, which boost the dynamic range of the image by approximately 18 percent, the increase noticeable in the bright tones of the image.

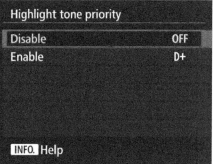

Figure 6-31: Enabling the Highlight Tone Priority custom function.

4. **Rotate the Quick Control dial to highlight Enable and press Set.**

   The option is displayed in blue. Highlight Tone Priority is in effect until you disable the option or reset all custom functions.

You can't use ISO expansion when Highlight Tone Priority is enabled. With this option, you're limited to an ISO range from 200 to 6400.

7

Using Advanced Camera Features

In This Chapter

Keeping tabs on your battery

Optimizing lighting automatically

Choosing a metering mode

Using the grid and level

Modifying autofocusing and metering

Selecting a picture style

Specifying the color space

Setting white balance and ISO speed

Exploring flash photography

Using eternal Speedlites

Your camera has lots of features that enable you to take great pictures. When you shoot in one of the creative modes, you can modify lots of things. If the light is a bit dim and you don't feel like flashing your subject, you can increase the ISO speed setting. You can also change the autofocus system to suit your taste and the type of photography you do. You can also change the way the camera meters the scene before you. In short, the sky's the limit when you employ the advanced features of your camera.

To bring you up to speed on all the advanced features you can use, read the sections in this chapter in which I show you how to harness all the cool features.

Viewing Battery Information

Your camera provides gobs of useful information about pictures and camera settings. You also have a *smart battery* powering your EOS 7D Mark II. For instance, you can access information about how much charge is left in your battery, how many shutter actuations have occurred since you inserted it, and the battery's condition. View the battery information on your LCD monitor. To check your battery's condition:

1. **Press the Menu button.**

   The last used menu displays.

2. **Use the Quick Control button to navigate to the Set Up tab and then use the multi-controller button to navigate to the Set Up3 menu (see the left image in Figure 7-1).**

3. **Rotate the Quick Control dial to highlight Battery Info and then press the Set button.**

   The following battery information displays (see the right image in Figure 7-1):

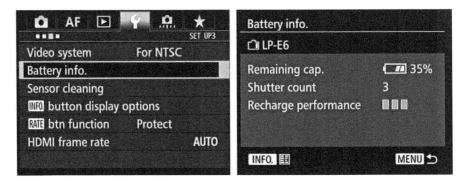

Figure 7-1: Displaying battery information.

- **Model:** Displays the battery model or household power source being used to power the camera.

- **Remaining cap:** Displays the remaining power capacity in 1 percent increments.

- **Shutter count:** Displays the number of shutter actuations for the current battery. When a recharged battery is inserted, the count resets to zero.

- **Recharge performance:** Displays the recharge performance. Three green bars indicate excellent recharging performance, two green bars indicate the recharging performance is slightly degraded, and one red bar indicates poor performance. When you see one red bar, think about replacing the battery.

4. **Press the shutter button halfway.**

   You're ready to take pictures.

Using the Auto Lighting Optimizer

If you capture images in JPEG mode, you can invoke a menu command that gives you better-looking images when you're shooting in dark conditions. Instead of getting a shot with too much contrast, you end up with a brighter shot. This option may add *digital noise* to the image. Digital noise comes in two flavors:

- **Color:** Shows up as specks of color.
- **Luminance:** Shows up as random gray clumps.

Digital noise is most prevalent in areas of solid color, such as the dark shadow areas in your image. If you shoot images in the RAW format, you can adjust image brightness with Canon's Digital Photo Professional or with Adobe Photoshop Lightroom, which I introduce you to in Chapter 10. To enable the Auto Lighting Optimizer:

1. **Press the Menu button.**

   The last used menu displays.

2. **Use the Quick Control button to navigate to the Shoot tab and then use the multi-controller button to navigate to the Shoot2 menu.**

3. **Rotate the Quick Control dial to highlight Auto Lighting Optimizer (see the left image in Figure 7-2) and then press Set.**

   The Auto Lighting Optimizer menu displays (see the right image in Figure 7-2).

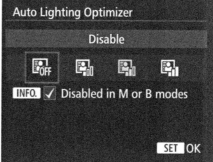

Figure 7-2: Selecting the Auto Lighting Optimizer.

4. **Rotate the Quick Control dial to highlight one of the following options:**

   • **Disable:** Brightness and contrast isn't corrected when photographing backlit subjects.

   • **Standard:** The default option adjusts the lighting to create a picture that brightens backlit subjects.

   • **Low:** This option adds a minimal amount of brightness to a backlit subject.

   • **Strong:** This option adds a considerable amount of brightness to a backlit subject.

5. **Press Set.**

   The change is applied, and you return to the Shoot2 menu.

6. **Press the shutter button halfway to return to take pictures.**

   The Auto Lighting Optimizer setting you choose remains in effect until you select a different option. In some cases, digital noise may be apparent when the Auto Lighting Optimizer is used.

Reducing Lens Flicker

When you use a high shutter speed to take a picture of a scene illuminated by one or more fluorescent lights, the blinking of the light source may cause uneven exposure vertically. Fortunately, there is a menu command that when invoked senses the rate of flicker from the light source and adjusts the exposure so that it is even. Here's how to reduce lens flicker:

1. **Press the Menu button.**

   The last used menu displays.

2. **Use the Quick Control button to navigate to the Shoot tab and then use the multi-controller button to navigate to the Shoot4 menu.**

3. **Rotate the Quick Control dial to highlight Anti-Flicker Shoot (see the left image in Figure 7-3) and press Set.**

   The Anti-Flicker Shoot menu displays(see the right image in Figure 7-3).

4. **Rotate the Quick Control dial to highlight Enable and then press Set.**

   You are now ready to take pictures illuminated by fluorescent light. Just remember to disable the option when you start taking pictures illuminated by a different light source.

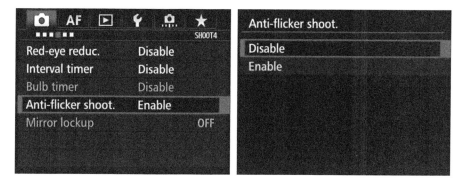

Figure 7-3: Just flicker. I dare you!

Choosing a Metering Mode

When you press the shutter button halfway, your camera meters the scene you photograph to determine the optimal exposure settings. The default metering mode (Evaluative) works well for most lighting conditions. When you shoot in Full Auto mode, the Evaluative metering mode is used, however, when you shoot in one of the creative modes, you can change the metering to suit the lighting and situation. To change the metering mode:

1. **Press the White Balance/Metering button on the top of your camera.**

   This button is in front of the LCD panel and to the left when you point the camera toward your subject.

2. **Rotate the Main dial to choose one of the following metering options:**

   - **Evaluative:** This is the default mode for your camera. You can use this mode for most of your work, including backlit scenes. The camera divides the scene into several zones and evaluates the brightness of the scene, direct light, and backlighting, factoring these variables to create the correct exposure for your subject.

   - **Partial:** This mode meters a small area in the center of the scene. This option is useful when the background is much brighter than your subject. A perfect example of this is a beach scene at sunset when you're pointing the camera toward the sun and your subject is in front of you.

   - **Center-Weighted Average:** This metering mode meters the entire scene, but gives more importance to the subject in the center. Use this mode when one part of your scene is significantly brighter than the rest; for example, when the sun is in the picture. If your bright light source is near the center of the scene, this mode prevents it from being overexposed.

- **Spot:** This mode meters a small area in the center of the scene. Use this mode when your subject is in the center and is significantly brighter than the rest of your scene. You camera may have the option to spot-meter where the autofocus frame is. If your camera can move the autofocus frame to your subject, you can accurately spot-meter a subject that isn't in the center of the frame.

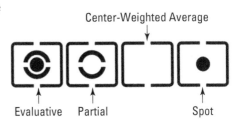

Figure 7-4 shows the icons you see in the LCD panel for each metering mode.

Figure 7-4: You can change the metering mode to suit different picture-taking scenarios.

Displaying the Grid

The *grid* is a visual reference that appears in your camera LCD monitor. Use the vertical and horizontal lines on the grid to ensure you're holding the camera straight. When the gridlines are aligned with lines in the scene that you know should be vertical or horizontal, the resulting image looks correct. To display the grid:

1. **Press the Menu button.**

   The last used menu displays.

2. **Use the Quick Control button to navigate to the Set Up tab and then use the multi-controller button to navigate to the Set Up2 menu.**

3. **Rotate the Quick Control dial to highlight Viewfinder Display (see the left image in Figure 7-5) and press Set.**

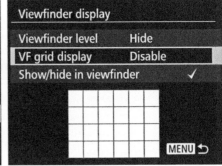

Figure 7-5: Viewfinder display options.

The Viewfinder Display options display in the camera LCD monitor (see the right image in Figure 7-5).

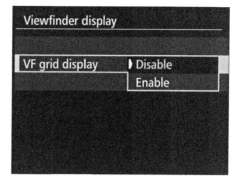

4. **Rotate the Quick Control dial to highlight VF Grid and press Set.**

   The default option, Disable, is selected (see Figure 7-6).

5. **Rotate the Quick Control dial to highlight Enable and then press Set.**

Figure 7-6: Enabling the viewfinder grid.

6. **Press the shutter button halfway.**

You're ready to take pictures with the grid displayed in your viewfinder.

Using the Electronic Level

The electronic level enables you to take pictures with your camera level and plumb. This ensures that the camera isn't tilted right or left, or up or down. The end result is you get images that look correct and not like they were photographed by a drunken sailor. When you're not shooting in Live View mode, the electronic level is most useful when you have the camera mounted on a tripod. To display the electronic level on your LCD monitor:

1. **Mount your camera on a tripod.**

   You can also use the electronic level when handholding the camera. However, it's more difficult to get accurate results, and you can't hold the camera as steady because it's away from your body.

2. **Press the Info button twice.**

   The electronic level displays on your LCD monitor. The left image shown in Figure 7-7 illustrates what the level looks like when the camera isn't level horizontally and not plumb.

3. **Adjust the legs of your tripod until a solid green line appears in the center of the level.**

   This tells you the camera is level and plumb (see the right image shown in Figure 7-7).

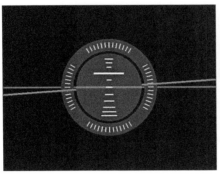
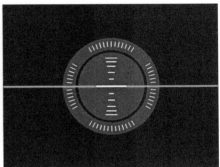

Figure 7-7: A level camera is a wonderful thing.

Tailoring Autofocus to Your Shooting Style

Your camera has a truly advanced autofocus system that is highly customizable. You can choose the autofocus mode, choose how autofocus points are displayed in the viewfinder, choose the type of autofocus, and much more. In the following sections I show you how to tailor the camera autofocus to shoot the types of subjects you photograph and your shooting style.

Choosing the autofocus mode

Your camera focuses automatically on objects that intersect autofocus points. You have three autofocus modes on your camera. One is ideally suited for still objects and another is ideally suited for objects that are moving. You have yet a third autofocus mode, which is a chameleon: you use it for still objects that may move. To choose an autofocus mode:

1. **Press the Drive-AF button (it is located on top of your camera and directly in front of the LCD panel).**

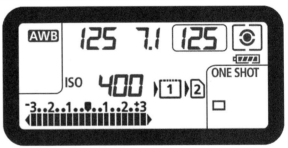

   Figure 7-8 shows the LCD panel as it appears when you're using One Shot mode.

Figure 7-8: Photographing in One Shot AF mode.

2. **Rotate the Main dial while viewing the LCD panel to select one of the following autofocus modes:**

   • **One Shot:** Use this autofocus mode for objects that don't move. It's ideally suited for shooting portraits and landscapes.

- **AI Focus:** Use this chameleon autofocus mode for objects that are stationary but may begin to move. The camera locks focus using One Shot but switches to AI Servo if the subject starts moving. This option is ide- ally suited for macro photog- raphy of objects like flowers on a windy day. Figure 7-9 shows the LCD panel when you're shoot- ing in AI Focus mode.

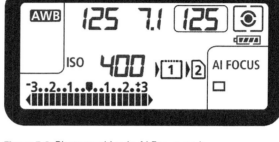

Figure 7-9: Photographing in AI Focus mode.

- **AI Servo:** Use this autofo- cus mode for objects in motion. After the camera locks focus on the object, the camera updates the focus as the subject moves. This mode is ideally suited for objects that are moving toward or away from you. Figure 7-10 shows the LCD panel when you're shooting in AI Servo mode.

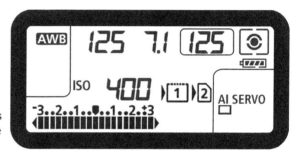

Figure 7-10: Photographing in AI Servo mode.

You may find that none of the autofocus modes are effective on fast-moving objects, such as racecars or airplanes. To capture blur-free shots of objects like these that move toward or away from you, switch the lens to manual focus and then focus on a spot your subject will cross. Press the shutter button shortly before your subject reaches the point on which you have focused. The amount of time varies depending on how fast your subject is moving.

Choosing the autofocus point mode

The M-Fn button makes it possible to switch between autofocus point modes. The default autofocus mode uses 65 points to achieve autofocus. You can switch to a single autofocus point when you need the camera to focus on a specific point in the frame. You can also switch to an autofocus zone that uses several autofocus points within a zone. I cover the single-point autofocus and zone autofocus in upcoming sections. However, I familiarize you with the M-Fn button and the AF Point Selection lever here so you can switch between the default autofocus mode to zone or single autofocus zones at Will — whoever he was. To switch between autofocus point selection modes:

1. **Press the AF Point Selection button.**

2. **While looking in the viewfinder, press the M-Fn button or tilt the AF Point Selection lever.**

   The default autofocus mode with the autofocus frame displays in your viewfinder (see Figure 7-11). In this mode, the camera can use any combination of the 65 autofocus points to achieve focus. The mode is used automatically when you shoot in Full Auto (A+) mode.

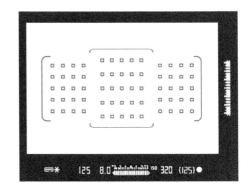

Figure 7-11: The default autofocus frame.

3. **Press the M-Fn button or tilt the AF Point Selection Lever again.**

   The autofocus mode that enables you to select a single autofocus point displays in your viewfinder (see Figure 7-12). I show you how to select a specific autofocus point in the next section.

4. **Press the M-Fn button again or tilt the AF Point Selection Lever.**

   The display changes to reflect zone autofocus points (see Figure 7-13). This figure shows the center autofocus zone.

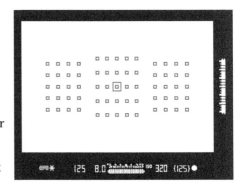

Figure 7-12: Selecting a single autofocus point.

Switching to a single autofocus point

By default, your camera displays 65 autofocus points. The camera focuses on well-defined edges that

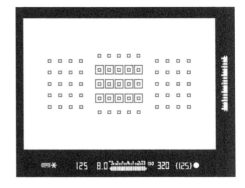

Figure 7-13: Selecting zone autofocus.

intersect these grid points. The default number of autofocus points works fine for most picture-taking situations. However, at times, it makes sense to switch to a single autofocus point that you align with a single object. This option is useful when you want to focus selectively on a single subject in a scene that has other objects that the camera may lock focus on. Your camera also has the option to switch to an autofocus group. To change the autofocus point:

1. Press the AF Point Selection button.

2. While looking at the view-finder, press the M-Fn button until you see a single autofocus point in the center.

3. Press the multi-controller button to navigate to the desired autofocus point.

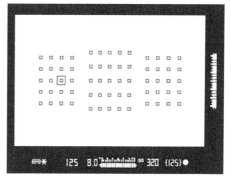

Figure 7-14: Choosing an autofocus point.

You can navigate to any of the autofocus targets (the small red squares) to designate the point from which the camera will focus. Figure 7-14 shows one of the side autofocus points selected. The camera focuses on an object under that autofocus point.

4. Press the shutter button halfway.

You're ready to take pictures with a single autofocus point. The autofocus point is the default autofocus point until you use the AF Point Selection button to designate another autofocus point, or you use the AF Point Selection button in conjunction with the M-Fn button to select the default autofocus or zone autofocus option.

After selecting a single autofocus point that is not in the center of the frame, press the multi-controller button down to select the center autofocus point.

Using zone autofocus

Zone autofocus lets you use several autofocus points that are in a zone. The camera focuses on any object that's directly beneath an autofocus point in the zone you specify. The camera has nine autofocus zones, three on the left side, three in the middle, and three on the right. Each autofocus zone is comprised of 15 autofocus points. I find the middle zone in the middle is great for many picture-taking tasks, including portrait photography. To choose an autofocus zone:

1. **Press the AF Point Selection button.**

2. **While looking at the viewfinder, press the M-Fn button or tilt the AF Zone Selection lever until you see 15 autofocus points in the center.**

   This is the middle autofocus zone.

3. **Press the multi-controller button to the left, right, up, or down to select the desired autofocus zone.**

   Figure 7-15 shows the top center autofocus zone selected. The zone you select remains in effect until you change it or switch to the default display.

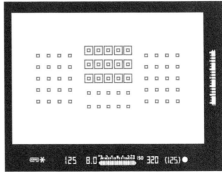

Figure 7-15: Choosing an autofocus zone.

Modifying autofocus to suit shooting style

No two photographers are alike. We shoot different subject matter and we have different interests and goals. Your EOS 7D Mark II makes it possible for you to apply a great deal of customization to the autofocus. There are lots of different autofocus characteristics you can modify. In fact there's an AF tab with five menu lists. If the standard autofocus doesn't suit your fancy, try experimenting with some of the settings in the following AF menus:

✔ **AF-1:** Lets you fine tune the autofocus for AI Servo mode, which is used when you want the camera to track a moving object and update focus as the object moves. There are six different cases to suit different photography scenarios. With each case you can fine-tune tracking sensitivity, acceleration and deceleration tracking, and how the autofocus points are switched when the camera tracks the subject. Each case is highly specialized. Fortunately, you can press the Info button to get help. The six cases are:

   • **Case 1:** The settings you change suit any moving object.

   • **Case 2:** The settings you change are applicable when photographing tennis players, swimmers, skiers, and so on.

   • **Case 3:** The settings you change are applicable when photographing bicycle racers, downhill skiers, and so on.

- **Case 4:** The settings you change are applicable when photographing a soccer game, motor sports, and so on. However, even when you tweak the settings in this case, you'll have a hard time freezing the action of a racecar heading toward you. I show you how to effectively photograph racecars in Chapter 8.

   - **Case 5:** The settings you change are applicable when photographing figure skaters and similar subjects.

   - **Case 6:** The settings you change are applicable when photographing gymnasts and similar subjects.

✓ **AF-2:** This menu lets you further fine tune AI Servo characteristics. This menu lets you decide the priority between shutter release and achieving focus. Press the Info button to get help with these choices as well.

✓ **AF-3:** This menu applies to specific Canon lenses. You can decide whether you can fine-tune the focus manually after pressing the shutter button halfway or not. If you choose to fine-tune the focus, you do so by turning the focusing ring on the lens while looking through the viewfinder at the most important part of the scene. You can also enable or disable the AF assist beam when shooting with flash. Another menu choice lets you determine whether the shutter will release only when focus is achieve, or release immediately when you press the shutter button. The latter enables you to take pictures quickly, but you may end up with some out-of-focus images.

✓ **AF-4:** This menu further fine-tunes autofocus by letting you decide whether the lens autofocus motor will continue trying to achieve focus in difficult conditions, or whether it will stop searching to prevent a horribly out-of-focus picture. There are also menu commands to let you determine the number of selectable autofocus points, determine the autofocus zones you can select, the manner in which you select an autofocus area, and so on.

✓ **AF-5:** The final AF menu lets you determine how autofocus points are displayed in the viewfinder, how focus status is displayed in the viewfinder, and lets you micro-adjust the influence of each autofocus point.

The autofocus menu is extremely specialized, and not for the feint of heart. I'd love to get down to the nitty-gritty on each command on the AF menus, but many readers will not have use for these specialized options. The previous list is your introduction, and my way of saving a tree or six in a rain forest. If you decide you absolutely have to tinker with the autofocus system on your camera, most of the menu commands offer assistance that can be accessed by pressing the Info button. And if you should happen to tweak the autofocus and it doesn't suit your needs, you can restore the camera to its default settings (see Chapter 9).

Choosing a Picture Style

When you photograph a scene or image, your camera sensor captures the colors and subtle nuances of shadow and light to create a faithful rendition of the scene. At times, however, you want a different type of picture. For example, when you're photographing a landscape, you want vivid blues and greens in the image. You can choose from a variety of picture styles and create up to three custom picture styles. When you take pictures in Full Auto mode, this option isn't available. To choose a picture style:

1. **Press the Creative Photo/Comparative Display button.**

   The Creative Photo options display and the Picture Style option is selected by default (see the left image in Figure 7-16). Note that you can also access this option by choosing Picture Style from the Shoot3 menu.

2. **Press Set.**

   The Picture Style menu displays on your LCD monitor (see the right image in Figure 7-16).

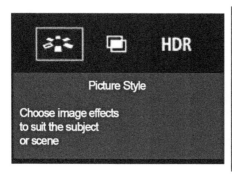
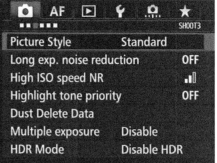

Figure 7-16: Choosing a Picture Style option.

3. **Press Set again and then rotate the Quick Control dial to choose one of the following styles (see Figure 7-17):**

   • **Auto:** The color tone will be adjusted automatically to suit the scene or subject matter you are photographing. Images photographed with this style will have vivid colors. This is a great mode for landscape photography to ensure vivid blue skies and crisp bright greens.

   • **Standard:** The default style captures crisp, sharp images and is suitable for most photography situations.

- **Portrait:** This style renders a soft image with flattering skin tones. This style is ideally suited for portraits of women and children.

- **Landscape:** This style renders an image with vivid blues and greens. Landscape is ideally suited for — you guessed it — landscapes. I love truth in advertising.

- **Neutral:** This style renders an image with no in-camera enhancement and is ideally suited for photographers who will be editing and enhancing their images with a computer image-editing application, such as Adobe Photoshop or Photoshop Lightroom. The resulting image has natural colors.

- **Faithful:** This is another style ideally suited for photographers who like to edit their images with a computer image-editing application. When you photograph a subject in daylight with a color temperature of 5200K, the camera automatically adjusts the image color to match the color of your subject.

- **Monochrome:** This style creates a black and white image. If you use this style and choose JPEG as the file format, you can't convert the image to color with your computer. If you use this style when using the JPEG format, make sure you switch back to one of the other picture styles when you want to capture images with color again.

Picture Style	$\mathbb{O}, \mathbb{O}, \&, \mathbb{O}$
🅰 Auto	3 , 0 , 0 , 0
🆂 Standard	3 , 0 , 0 , 0
🅿 Portrait	2 , 0 , 0 , 0
🅛 Landscape	4 , 0 , 0 , 0
🅝 Neutral	0 , 0 , 0 , 0
🅕 Faithful	0 , 0 , 0 , 0
INFO. Detail set.	SET OK

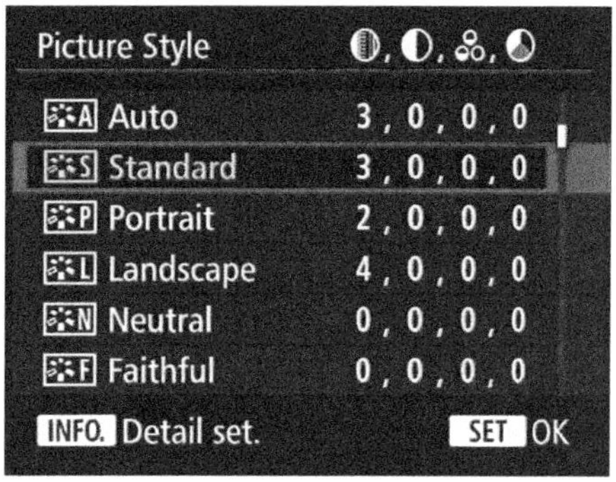

Figure 7-17: Decisions, decisions!

- **User-Created Styles:** These slots are for styles you've created. I show you how to create custom picture styles in Chapter 9.

4. **After choosing the desired option, press Set.**

All JPEG images will have the style applied to them until you change the style or restore camera settings to their defaults.

Figure 7-18 shows a comparison of the different picture styles.

If you use the JPEG mode, the picture style will be applied to the saved image. However if you use the RAW picture style, the picture style will show up in the preview on your LCD monitor, but will not be applied to the image when it is saved to your card. In other words, what you see on the monitor is not what you'll get when you shoot RAW. If you shoot RAW, I suggest you use the Faithful style.

Figure 7-18: A comparison of the picture styles.

Specifying the Color Space

Several color spaces are used in photography and image-editing applications. The *color space* determines the range of colors you have to work with. The default color space (sRGB) in your camera is ideal if you're not editing your images in an application like Photoshop or Photoshop Lightroom. However, if you do edit your images in an image-editing application and want the widest range of colors (also known as *gamut*) with which to work, you can specify Adobe RGB. To specify the color space that your camera records images with, follow these steps:

1. **Press the Menu button.**

   The last used menu displays.

2. **Use the Quick Control button to navigate to the Shoot tab and then use the multi-controller button to navigate to the Shoot2 menu.**

3. **Rotate the Quick Control dial to highlight Color Space (see the left image in Figure 7-19) and then press Set.**

   The Color Space menu displays (see the right image in Figure 7-19).

4. **Rotate the Quick Control dial to highlight one of the following:**

   - **sRGB:** The default color space is ideal if you don't edit your images or do minimal editing.

   - **Adobe RGB:** Use this color space if you're editing your images in an application, such as Photoshop or Photoshop Lightroom.

Figure 7-19: Choosing a color space.

5. **Press the shutter button halfway.**

   You exit the menu and are ready to shoot pictures with your desired color space.

After you edit images that were created with the Adobe RGB color space, you must convert them to sRGB in your image-editing application before printing them or displaying them on the web. For more information, see a *For Dummies* book about the software application you're using to edit your work.

Setting White Balance

The human eye can see the color white without a colorcast no matter what type of light the white object is illuminated with. Your digital camera has to balance the lighting in order for white to appear as white in the captured image. Without white balance, images photographed with fluorescent light have a green colorcast and images photographed with tungsten light sources have a yellow/orange colorcast. Yup, your subject would be "green around the gills," or have some other ghastly colorcast, depending on the light sources used to illuminate the scene.

Your camera automatically sets the white balance, or you can choose a white balance setting to suit the scene you're photographing. You can also change white balance when you want to create an image with some special effects. If you shoot images with the RAW format and inadvertently choose the wrong white balance setting or your camera doesn't get it right, you can change the white balance setting in an application like Photoshop or Canon's Digital Photo Professional or Photoshop Lightroom. To set white balance:

1. **Press the White Balance/Metering Mode button.**

2. **Rotate the Quick Control dial while looking at the left side of your LCD panel (see Figure 7-20) and choose one of the following white balance options:**

   - **Auto White Balance:** The camera automatically sets the white balance based on the lighting conditions.

   - **Daylight:** Use this option when photographing subjects on a bright, sunny day.

   - **Shade:** Use this option when photographing subjects in shaded conditions.

   - **Cloudy:** Use this option when photographing subjects on a cloudy day.

   - **Tungsten:** Use this option when photographing subjects illuminated by tungsten light.

Figure 7-20: Choosing a white balance option.

- **White Fluorescent:** Use this option when photographing subjects illuminated by fluorescent lights.

- **Flash:** Use this option when photographing subjects with the on-camera flash or an auxiliary flash unit.

- **Custom:** Use when creating a custom white balance. See "Creating a Custom White Balance" later in this chapter.

- **K:** Use when using a color temperature specified with a menu command. See the next section, "Specifying Color Temperature."

Specifying Color Temperature

If you use studio lighting, you can set the color temperature to the same temperature as the light emitted from your strobes. Color temperature is measured on the Kelvin scale. For example, most studio strobes have a color temperature of 5200 K. You can easily set the color temperature for the camera white balance to match the color temperature of your studio lights with a menu command. To specify a color temperature:

1. **Press the Menu button.**

   The last used menu displays.

2. **Use the Quick Control button to navigate to the Shoot tab and then use the multi-controller button to navigate to the Shoot2 menu.**

3. **Rotate the Quick Control dial to highlight White Balance (see the left image in Figure 7-21) and then press the Set button.**

   The White Balance menu appears on the LCD monitor (see the right image in Figure 7-21).

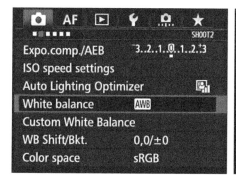
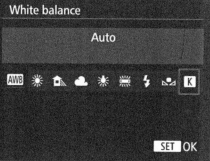

Figure 7-21: Specifying the color temperature.

4. Rotate the Quick Control dial to highlight K and then rotate the Main dial to specify the color temperature.

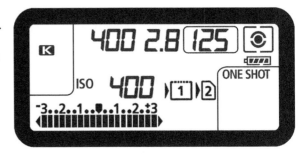

Figure 7-22: Using the K white balance mode.

The K white balance icon appears on the LCD panel (see Figure 7-22), and the specified color temperature is used whenever you choose the K option for white balance.

Creating a Custom White Balance

When you photograph a scene that's illuminated with several different light sources, your camera may have a hard time figuring out how to set the white balance. And if the camera has a hard time, chances are you can't use one of the presets to accurately set the white balance. You can, however, set a custom white balance by following these steps:

1. Photograph a white object and then press the Menu button.

Photograph the object under the light source that will be used to illuminate your scene. Photograph something that's pure white, such as a sheet of paper without lines. You won't get accurate results if you photograph something that's off-white. You'll also get better results if you use the Neutral picture style. If you use the Monochrome picture style, you can't obtain a white balance reading.

Note: Some papers contain optical brighteners. If you use one of those to set your white balance, your images may be a little warmer (more reddish-orange in color) than normal.

You can purchase an 18-percent gray card from your favorite camera retailer and use this in place of a white object in Step 1. The 18-percent gray card gives you extremely accurate results.

2. Use the Quick Control button to navigate to the Shoot tab, use the multi-controller button to navigate to the Shoot2 menu, and then rotate the Quick Control dial to highlight Custom White Balance (see the left image in Figure 7-23).

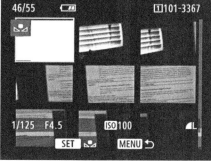

Figure 7-23: Setting a custom white balance.

3. **Press the Set button.**

   The image you just photographed displays onscreen (see the right image in Figure 7-23).

4. **Press Set.**

   A dialog box appears asking you to confirm that you want to use the image to set the white balance (see the left image in Figure 7-24).

5. **Rotate the Quick Control dial to highlight OK and press Set.**

   The camera calculates the color temperature for the light source. After the camera completes the calculation, a dialog box appears asking you whether you want to assign the color temperature derived from the calculation to the custom white balance setting (see the right image in Figure 7-24).

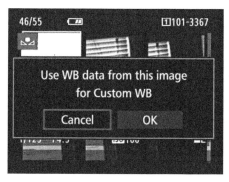

Figure 7-24: Finalizing the custom white balance.

6. Rotate the Quick Control dial to select OK and then press Set.

7. When the menu reappears, press the Menu button to exit the Custom White Balance menu and then press the White Balance/Metering button.

8. While viewing the LCD panel, rotate the Quick Control dial to select Custom White Balance, which appears in a rounded rectangle on the left side of Figure 7-25.

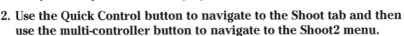

Figure 7-25: Creating a custom white balance.

Your custom white balance is used to determine white balance until you select a different white balance option.

The custom white balance remains in effect and is used whenever you select the Custom White Balance option. You can register only one custom white balance. When you encounter a different lighting scenario that requires a custom white balance, repeat these steps.

Using white balance compensation

If you find that images photographed with a custom white balance have a colorcast, you can apply compensation to remove that colorcast. This is pretty advanced stuff, so unless you know a lot about color correction, color temperatures, and so on, stick to AWB (auto white balance) and do any necessary color correction in your favorite image-editing application. But if you're dying to know what it's all about, follow these steps:

1. Press the Menu button.

   The previously used menu displays on the camera LCD monitor.

2. Use the Quick Control button to navigate to the Shoot tab and then use the multi-controller button to navigate to the Shoot2 menu.

3. Rotate the Quick Control dial to highlight WB Shift/Bkt (see the left image in Figure 7-26) and then press the Set button.

   The White Balance Correction dialog box appears (see the right image in Figure 7-26). Notice there are four letters: one at the center top (*G* for green), one at the center bottom (*M* for magenta), one at the left center

 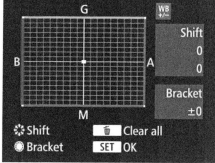

Figure 7-26: Correcting a custom white balance.

(*B* for blue), and one at the right center (*A* for amber).

4. **Use the multi-controller button to move the dot.**

   You can move the dot toward one color and then move it up or down to shift the white balance toward a combination of amber and green. When you move the dot, the color shift is designated in the dialog box (see Figure 7-27). In this case, the white balance has been shifted two levels toward green.

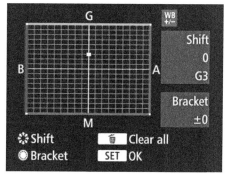

Figure 7-27: Applying a color shift to a custom white balance.

5. **Press Set.**

   Your changes are applied.

 6. **Press the White Balance/Metering Mode button and then rotate the Quick Control dial to select Custom White Balance.**

   The custom white balance icon displays on the LCD panel (see Figure 7-28).

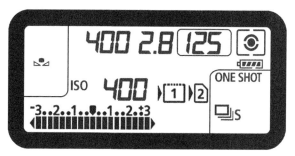

Figure 7-28: White balance compensation in action.

7. Press the shutter button fully to take a picture.

The color shift is applied to your custom white balance. The colorcast is no more, quoth the raven.

To remove white balance compensation, repeat the preceding Steps 1–3 and then press the Info button.

Bracketing white balance

If you're the type of photographer who likes to hedge her bets, you may consider using white balance bracketing. When bracketing white balance, you end up with three images: one with your custom white balance setting, and two that have color shifts applied to them. You can also apply a white balance correction to your custom white balance, which will be the new custom white balance. To bracket a custom white balance:

1. Press the Menu button.

The previously used menu displays on the camera LCD monitor.

2. Use the Quick Control button to navigate to the Shoot tab and then use the multi-controller button to navigate to the Shoot2 menu.

3. Rotate the Quick Control dial to highlight WB Shift/Bkt. (see the left image in Figure 7-29) and then press the Set button.

The White Balance Correction/Bracketing dialog box appears (see the right image in Figure 7-29).

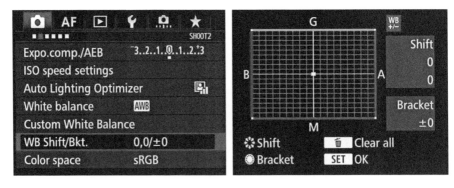

Figure 7-29: Setting up white balance bracketing.

4. (Optional) Apply white balance compensation to your custom white balance, as I outline in the preceding section.

The corrected white balance is the starting point for bracketing.

5. Rotate the Quick Control dial to set bracketing.

When you move the dial, two dots appear. Each click of the dial adds another level of bracketing (see Figure 7-30). Rotating the dial clockwise moves the bracketing further from center along the B/A scale, while rotating the dial counterclockwise moves the bracketing further from center along the M/G scale. The bracketing in Figure 7-30 produces one image with a color shift of −2 BA, and one image with a color shift of +2BA.

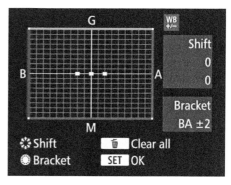

Figure 7-30: Setting the amount of bracketing.

6. Press Set.

Your changes are applied.

7. Press the shutter button halfway to return to shooting mode.

8. Press the White Balance/Metering Mode button and then rotate the Quick Control dial to select the Custom White Balance option.

The custom white balance icon is flashing, which indicates that white balance will be bracketed.

9. Press the Drive-AF button and then rotate the Quick Control dial to select Low Speed Continuous.

10. Press the shutter button halfway to achieve focus and then press the shutter button fully.

The camera takes three pictures with the white bracketing you specify.

Setting the ISO Speed

The ISO speed determines how sensitive your camera sensor is to light. When you specify a high ISO speed, you can capture images when in dark conditions and extend the range of the camera flash. However, when you specify a high ISO speed, you also run the risk of adding digital noise to your images. To change the ISO speed:

1. Press the Flash Compensation/ISO button.

The button is convex with a little dimple inside so you can find it by feel.

2. Rotate the Main dial to specify the ISO setting while viewing the LCD panel to see the settings as you rotate the dial.

The default ISO for the camera is A (Automatic). You can choose an ISO setting from 100 to 6400 or use the extended ISO range (see the following section, "Extending the ISO Range," for more details). Figure 7-31 shows the LCD panel after setting the ISO to 640.

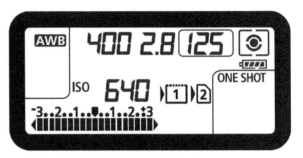

Figure 7-31: Choosing the ISO setting.

Extending the ISO Range

Your camera has an ISO range from 100 to 16000. However, if you take pictures in very dark places and don't want to use flash, you can extend the ISO range to 512000. This setting creates digital noise in shadow areas. Before deciding whether the extended ISO range is useful for your photography, I suggest taking some test shots with this setting at night in an area that has lights and areas of complete shadow. Examine the images on your computer and zoom to 100-percent magnification. Pan to areas with lots of shadow and look for evidence of digital noise, which will show up as clumps of gray (*luminance* noise) or random areas of colored specks (*color* noise). To extend the ISO range:

1. **Press the Menu button.**

   The last used menu displays.

2. **Use the Quick Control button to navigate to the Shoot tab and then use the multi-controller button to navigate to the Shoot2 menu.**

3. **Rotate the Quick Control dial to highlight ISO Speed Settings and press the Set button.**

   The ISO Speed Settings menu displays.

4. **Rotate the Quick Control dial to highlight ISO Speed Range (see the left image in Figure 7-32) and then press Set.**

   The ISO Speed Range menu displays.

5. **Rotate the multi-controller button to highlight the default maximum ISO setting (1600) and then press Set.**

   An arrow appears above and below the maximum ISO setting (see the right image in Figure 7-32).

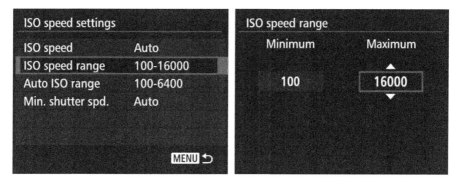

Figure 7-32: Increasing the maximum ISO speed.

6. **Rotate the Quick Control dial to highlight H1 (ISO 25600) or H2 (ISO 51200) and then press Set.**

   The maximum ISO setting you select can now be enabled when using the Flash Compensation/ISO button.

7. **Press the shutter button halfway.**

   You're ready to shoot with a higher maximum ISO speed.

Flash Photography and Your EOS 7D Mark II

Your camera is equipped with a popup flash — a very intelligent popup flash. When you take pictures in Full Auto mode, the flash pops up when the camera determines that not enough light is available to properly expose the scene. When you take pictures using the creative modes I discuss in Chapter 6, you have full control over how the flash is used. In the upcoming sections, I show you how to use the flash unit that's built into your camera, how to use auxiliary flash units, and how to modify the amount of light your flash unit delivers.

Using the built-in flash

When you shoot in Full Auto mode, pop goes the flash unit when the camera decides extra light is needed to properly expose the scene. You also have a handy little button on the side of the camera with an icon that looks like a lightning bolt; this is how you make the flash pop up when you decide it's needed. To use your flash in Full Auto (A+) mode, you don't have to do anything because the flash is fully automatic. The popup flash can be used to illuminate a scene or fill in the shadows. Popup flash also comes in handy when you want to warm up an image. The flowers in the top image of Figure 7-33 were taken with the ambient light. The flowers on the bottom of Figure 7-33 were illuminated with ambient light and then filled from the popup flash. I also used exposure compensation on the bottom image to decrease the brightness of the background and saturate the image.

Figure 7-33: Spritzing flowers with fill flash.

To use your popup flash:

 1. Press the Flash button.

The flash unit pops up (see Figure 7-34).

2. Compose the scene in your viewfinder and then press the shutter button halfway.

The camera achieves focus and fires a pre-flash to determine how much illumination is needed to properly expose the scene.

3. Take the picture.

The flash fires. The flash unit remains in the locked and loaded position until you close it.

Figure 7-34: Pop goes the flash unit.

4. Gently press your fingers on the top of the flash unit to close it.

The effective range of the built-in flash varies depending on the ISO speed setting you use and the f-stop. Choosing a higher ISO speed setting and large aperture (small f-stop value) extends the range of the built-in flash. For example, using the flash with a 3.5 f-stop value and a 100 ISO setting yields a range of approximately 12 feet. If you use the same f-stop with an ISO setting of 6400, the range increases to approximately 85 feet.

Changing the flash-sync speed in Av mode

When you're shooting in Aperture Priority (Av) mode, by default the camera shutter speed is set between 30 seconds and 1/250 of a second when the flash is enabled. The flash duration is very short and fires when the shutter opens, which gives you a sharp image of your subject. However, if the shutter speed is slow, you see motion trails if your subject moves during the long exposure. This can be very artistic. However, if you want to eliminate the possibility of motion trails, you can use a custom function to change the shutter speed used when a flash unit fires. Choosing one of the options that uses a higher shutter speed prevents motion trails, but the background will be dark. To change the flash-sync speed when shooting in Av mode:

1. Press the Menu button.

The last used menu displays.

2. Use the Quick Control button to navigate to the Shoot tab and then use the multi-controller button to navigate to the Shoot1 menu.

3. Rotate the Quick Control dial to highlight Flash Control (see the left image in Figure 7-35) and then press the Set button.

The Flash Control displays.

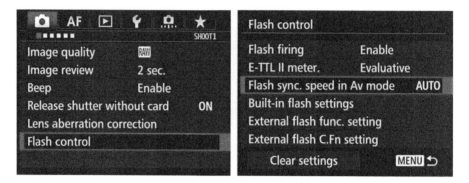

Figure 7-35: Controlling camera flash.

4. **Rotate the Quick Control button to highlight Flash Sync Speed in Av Mode (see the right image in Figure 7-35) and then press the Set button.**

   The Flash Sync Speed in Av Mode options display (see Figure 7-36).

5. **Rotate the Quick Control dial to highlight one of the following:**

   • **Auto:** The camera chooses a shutter speed between 30 seconds and 1/250 of a second when a flash unit is used in Av mode.

   • **1/250–1/60Sec. Auto:** The camera automatically chooses a shutter speed between 1/60 of a second and 1/250 of a second when a flash unit is used in Av mode.

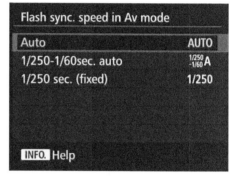

Figure 7-36: Choosing a flash-sync speed.

   • **1/250Sec. (Fixed):** The camera sets the shutter speed to 1/250 of a second when a flash is used in Av mode.

6. **After choosing an option, press Set.**

   The text for the selected option is blue.

Choosing second-curtain sync

The built-in flash for your camera fires when the shutter opens. This is all well and good when you're photographing people or objects that are standing still. However, when you use flash to photograph a moving object, the duration of the flash is much shorter than the shutter speed of the camera, especially when you're photographing in dim conditions or at night. The movement of the object after the flash fires shows up as a blur of motion, but the blur is going away from the object. When you enable second-curtain sync, the flash fires just before the shutter closes, creating a natural-looking motion trail that goes to the object instead of away from it. To enable second-curtain sync:

1. **Press the Menu button.**

   The last used menu displays.

2. **Use the Quick Control button to navigate to the Shoot tab and then use the multi-controller button to navigate to the Shoot1 menu.**

3. **Rotate the Quick Control dial to highlight Flash Control (see the left image in Figure 7-37) and then press the Set button.**

   The Flash Control menu displays.

4. **Rotate the Quick Control dial to highlight Built-In Flash Settings (see the right image in Figure 7-37) and then press Set.**

   The Built-In Flash Settings menu displays.

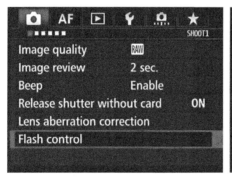
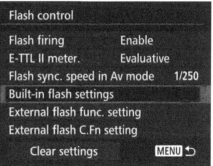

Figure 7-37: Changing built-in flash settings.

5. **Rotate the Quick Control dial to highlight Shutter Sync (see the left image in Figure 7-38) and then press Set.**

   The Shutter Sync options display (see the right image in Figure 7-38).

6. **Rotate the Quick Control dial to highlight 2nd Curtain and then press Set.**

   Your camera flash fires just before the shutter closes.

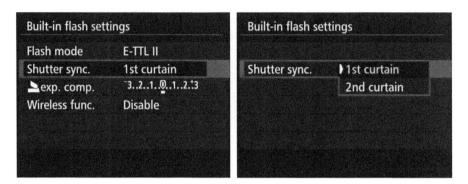

Figure 7-38: Enabling second-curtain shutter sync.

7. Press the shutter button halfway.

You're now ready to photograph with second-curtain sync.

Using auxiliary flash

Canon manufactures several flash units that are compatible with your EOS 7D Mark II. Some third-party units may also fit in your camera hot shoe. However, the camera can have an intelligent conversation with the auxiliary flash units that are dedicated to your beloved EOS 7D Mark II. You can control the amount of illumination emitted from dedicated flash units with flash compensation (see the upcoming section, "Using flash compensation"). The following Canon Speedlites work hand in hand with your EOS 7D Mark II: 90EX, 270 EXII, 320 EX, 430EX II, and 600EX-RT. To attach an auxiliary flash unit to your camera, slide it in the hot shoe. Most Canon flash units have a thumbwheel that you use to firmly lock the flash unit in the hot shoe (see Figure 7-39).

Figure 7-39: Attaching an auxiliary flash to your camera.

Using flash compensation

You can increase or decrease the amount of illumination coming from the popup flash or a dedicated EOS flash inserted in the camera hot shoe. You can increase or decrease flash illumination by up to three stops in 1/3 stop increments. To use flash compensation:

1. **Press the Flash Compensation/ISO button.**

2. **Rotate the Quick Control dial while looking at the LCD panel.**

   As you move the dial, the exposure level mark moves along the exposure indicator (see Figure 7-40). Rotate the dial clockwise to increase flash exposure and counterclockwise to decrease flash exposure.

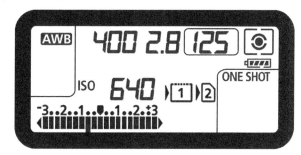

Figure 7-40: Specifying the amount of flash compensation.

3. **Press the shutter button halfway to achieve focus.**

   When flash compensation is enabled, you see the flash compensation icon in the LCD panel (see Figure 7-41).

Figure 7-41: Enabling flash compensation.

4. **Press the Flash button.**

   The built-in flash makes a cameo appearance.

5. **Press the shutter button fully to take the picture.**

   The flash fires with the amount of compensation you added or subtracted.

   Note: Flash compensation stays in effect even when you power off the camera. Remember to disable flash compensation when it's no longer needed.

Locking the flash exposure

Another handy lighting option at your disposal is locking the flash exposure to a certain part of the frame. This option is handy when your main subject isn't in the center of the frame or you want to throw some extra light on a specific part of the scene you're photographing. Locking flash exposure also works when you have a Canon Speedlite in the hot shoe. To lock flash exposure:

1. **Press the Flash button.**

   The built-in flash unit pops up.

2. **Move your camera until the center autofocus point is centered over the part of the scene that you want to lock flash exposure.**

3. **Press the M-Fn button.**

   The camera fires a preflash to calculate exposure for the area over which you pointed the autofocus point. The flash icon in the viewfinder flashes on and off, and the FE lock icon appears (see Figure 7-42).

Figure 7-42: Locking flash exposure.

4. **Recompose the scene through the viewfinder and then press the shutter button halfway to achieve focus.**

   A green dot appears in the right side of the viewfinder when the camera achieves focus.

5. **Press the shutter button fully to take the picture.**

   The flash unit fires, properly exposing the area over which you locked flash exposure.

Controlling External Speedlites from the Camera

The following Canon flash units can be controlled with camera menu settings: 420EX, 430EX, 430EX II, 550EX, 580EX, 580EX II, and 600EX-RT. You have more control with the EX II units and the 600EX that have new bells and whistles engineered for newer cameras. And yes, your camera is a newer model. But even if you own one of the older EX Speedlites, you can still do some cool stuff from the camera menu after you attach the unit to your camera hot shoe. You can also control all the aforementioned Speedlites wirelessly. That's right, you can do sophisticated stuff, such as bouncing light into shadows, bouncing the light off walls, and more.

In the upcoming sections, I show you how to control a Speedlite mounted in the hot shoe and use the built-in flash as a master to control Speedlites wirelessly. Hmmm . . . Maybe I should've called this section, "Flashing for Fun and Profit." At any rate, a whole lot of flashing is going on in the upcoming sections.

Controlling a flash in the hot shoe

When you mount a Canon EX Speedlite in the camera hot shoe, you can control the output with the camera menu and much more. If you have an EX II Speedlite, you have gobs of control. The following steps show the options you have available with an EX II Speedlite. The options may be different for your Canon Speedlite. Refer to your Speedlite manual for additional instructions. To control flash with camera menu commands:

1. **Insert a Canon EX or EX II Speedlite in your camera's hot shoe.**

2. **Press the Menu button.**

   The last used menu displays.

3. **Use the Quick Control button to navigate to the Shoot tab and then use the multi-controller button to navigate to the Shoot1 menu.**

4. **Rotate the Quick Control dial to highlight Flash Control (see the left image in Figure 7-43) and then press the Set button.**

   The Flash Control options display.

5. **Rotate the Quick Control dial to highlight External Flash Func Setting (see the right image in Figure 7-43) and then press Set.**

   The options you can use to control your Speedlite display (see Figure 7-44).

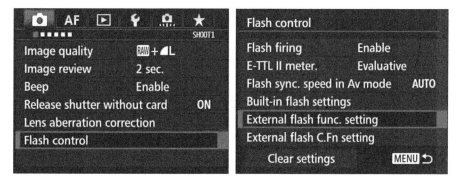

Figure 7-43: Controlling your external Speedlite with menu commands.

6. **Rotate the Quick Control dial to highlight a command and then press Set to set to see the options.**

   The following is a brief rundown of each option:

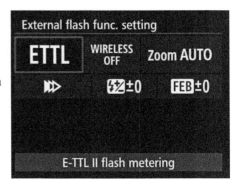

Figure 7-44: Controlling your Speedlite with camera menu commands.

   - **E-TTL II:** This option determines how the camera meters the scene, which determines the amount of illumination the flash uses to properly expose the picture. Your options are Evaluative or Average. These options are identical to the metering options that I discuss in "Choosing a Metering Mode" earlier in this chapter The default option is E-TTL II on most Speedlites. The other options vary depending on the flash unit attached to the hot shoe.

   - **Wireless:** This option determines whether the flash can be controlled wirelessly or optically by the light from another flash unit. This option varies depending on the Speedlite you use. For more information, refer to your Canon Speedlite manual.

   - **Zoom:** Enables you to specify the flash zoom of supported EX II Speedlites from the menu. By default (the Auto option), the flash unit inherits the level of zoom from the camera lens. Press Set and rotate the Quick Control dial to choose an option supported by your Speedlite. This option comes in handy when you want to add a splash of light to a specific part of the scene. For example, if you're photographing someone with a lens that is the 35mm equivalent of 85mm, change the zoom setting of the flash to 105mm and you send a splash of light to a focused point in the center of the image.

   - **Shutter Sync:** Choose from 1st Curtain (the default) or 2nd Curtain shutter sync. The second-curtain sync option may not be available for your Speedlite. For more information on second-curtain sync, see "Choosing second-curtain sync" earlier in this chapter.

   - **Flash Exposure Compensation:** This option gives you the capability to increase or decrease the amount of light emitted from the flash unit. Press Set to enable the exposure compensation scale and then rotate the Quick Control dial to increase or decrease the amount of illumination from the flash unit. Each mark represents 1/3 stop.

- **Flash Exposure Bracketing:** This option is available only with certain Speedlites: It isn't supported on EX units or the 430EX II. If this option is available for your Speedlite, you can take three pictures with different amounts of illumination. This is similar to automatic exposure bracketing.

7. Press the shutter button halfway.

You're back in shooting mode and ready to put your new flash settings to work.

If you're really into controlling your Canon Speedlite through the camera, check out the External Flash C.Fn Setting menu. This menu has options for custom functions that you can use to gain further control over your Speedlite. The available functions vary depending on the Speedlite you own. Refer to your Speedlite manual for more information.

Going wireless

The EOS 7D Mark II built-in flash can turn you into a real control freak. As I mention previously, you can control the output of the flash. With a few menu commands, you can turn the built-in flash into a control freak. The built-in flash acts as the master, and any Canon EX Speedlite capable of functioning as a slave can be fired in conjunction with it. Just think of the possibilities with multiple flash units illuminating a scene.

The possibilities are limited only by your imagination. You can even set up a portable studio with a couple Canon Speedlites and your EOS 7D Mark II. Unfortunately a detailed discussion showing you how to use Canon Speedlites as slave units is beyond the scope of this book. If you have one or more Canon Speedlites or you want to know more about flash photography with Canon Speedlites, pick up a copy of *Canon Speedlite System Digital Field Guide* by Michael Corsentino. If you purchase that book, you can disregard the ST-E2 wireless transmitter because with a few menu commands, you can get your EOS 7D MARK II's built-in flash to act as a wireless transmitter.

The first type of wireless shooting enables you to fire one or more external Speedlites that are controlled by the built-in flash unit. The built-in flash unit fires a beam to trigger the external flash unit and also adds illumination to the exposure. With this option, you can control the ratio of the built-in flash to the off-camera flash units. In other words, you determine whether the on-camera flash fires at full power and the off-camera flash fires at half power, and so on. You can also make the off-camera flash units more powerful than the built-in flash unit. To control one or more external Speedlites with the built-in flash:

1. Position one or more Canon Speedlites that can operate as a slave unit.

Canon Speedlites come with a small stand that can be screwed into a light stand. The positioning depends on where you want to add light to a scene. Some standard lighting patterns are used by portrait and fashion photographers. Unfortunately, coverage of these patterns is beyond the scope of this book.

2. **Switch the external Speedlite(s) to slave mode and then set the channel that the slave will receive instructions from the camera's built-in flash.**

   On many Canon Speedlites, you use a switch to have the unit operate as a slave. Refer to your Speedlite manual for more instructions. Make sure the external flash unit(s) sensor (the red plastic rectangle on the front of the unit) faces the camera. You can swivel the Speedlite head so that the flash is aimed at your subject and the sensor faces the camera.

3. **Press the Flash button.**

   The built-in flash pops up, and you're now ready to take a picture illuminated by one external Speedlite that's controlled by the camera's built-in flash.

4. **Press the Menu button.**

   The last used menu displays.

5. **Use the Quick Control button to navigate to the Shoot tab and then use the multi-controller button to navigate to the Shoot1 menu.**

6. **Rotate the Quick Control dial to highlight Flash Control (see the left image in Figure 7-45) and then press the Set button.**

   The flash options display on your LCD monitor.

7. **Rotate the Quick Control dial to highlight Built-In Flash Settings (see the right image in Figure 7-45) and then press Set.**

   The settings for the built-in flash display.

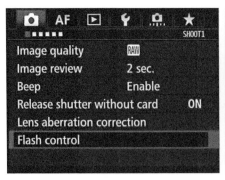
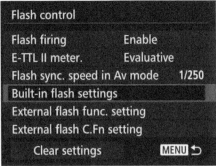

Figure 7-45: Getting control of your built-in flash unit.

8. **Accept the default Flash mode option of ETTL-II, rotate the Quick Control dial to highlight Wireless Func (see the left image in Figure 7-46), and then press Set.**

   The Wireless Func. options for your built-in flash display.

9. **Rotate the Quick Control dial to select the third option (see the right image in Figure 7-46) and press Set.**

   The third option is when you use multiple external Speedlites. If you're only using a single external Speedlite, choose the first option after Disable. You can also control one or more external Speedlites without the onboard flash firing if you choose the second option after Disable. After choosing an option Channel options become available.

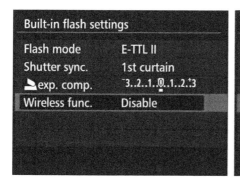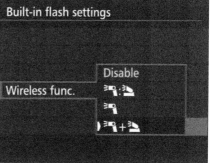

Figure 7-46: Choosing a wireless option.

10. **Rotate the Quick Control dial to highlight Channel and then press Set.**

    The Channel options display.

11. **Rotate the Quick Control dial to select the desired channel (1-4) and then press Set (see the left image in Figure 7-47).**

    I know this is a no-brainer, but make sure you select the same channel as that to which you set your external Speedlite. After you press Set, the camera is set to communicate with an external Speedlite on the same channel.

12. **Rotate the Quick Control dial to highlight the Firing Group option (see the right image in Figure 7-47) and then press Set.**

    The Firing Group options display on the camera LCD monitor.

Built-in flash settings		Built-in flash settings	
Flash mode	E-TTL II	Shutter sync.	1st curtain
Shutter sync.	1st curtain	Wireless func.	⁼◪+◪
Wireless func.	⁼◪+◪	Channel	1
Channel	1	◪exp. comp.	⁻3..2..1..0..1..2.:3
◪exp. comp.	⁻3..2..1..0..1..2.:3	Firing group	◪All and ◪
		◪exp. comp.	⁻3..2..1..0..1..2.:3
		INFO. Test flash firing	

Figure 7-47: Choosing the Channel and Firing Group.

13. Rotate the Quick Control dial to highlight All and the built-in flash, and then press Set.

The LCD monitor displays the selected options (see Figure 7-48). Note that you can also dial in exposure compensation for the built-in flash and the external Speedlites.

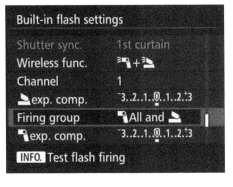

Built-in flash settings	
Shutter sync.	1st curtain
Wireless func.	⁼◪+◪
Channel	1
◪exp. comp.	⁻3..2..1..0..1..2.:3
Firing group	◪All and ◪
◪exp. comp.	⁻3..2..1..0..1..2.:3
INFO. Test flash firing	

14. Press the Info button to fire a test flash.

If you've set up everything cor- Figure 7-48: All fired up and ready to flash.
rectly, the built-in flash and your
external Speedlites fires.

If the external flash doesn't fire, make sure the sensor (the red dome on the front of the flash) can see the signal from the camera flash. If not, swivel the flash head so that it's pointing toward your subject, and the red dome is facing the camera.

15. Take the picture.

When you press the shutter button, the built-in flash and the external Speedlite(s) fires.

The previous set of steps fire all flash units at once at the same power. The flash strength is automatically set to ensure a properly exposed image.

To clear all wireless flash settings, return to the Flash Control menu, high-light Built-in Flash Func. Settings, and then press the Menu button.

8

Mastering Your EOS 7D Mark II

In This Chapter

- Choosing the right settings
- Photographing moving objects
- Taking photos of landscapes and sunsets
- Shooting portraits and wildlife
- Enhancing your creativity
- Composing and visualizing images

*I*n earlier chapters, I show you all the bells and whistles on your camera that you can use in your photography. Bells and whistles are cool, but if you don't know when to ring or blow them, they don't do you much good. In this chapter, I cut to the chase and show you how to use these features for specific types of photography.

Of course, you may not be interested in all the types of photography I discuss in this chapter, but I like to practice several different photography disciplines. I find that different disciplines keep me on my toes and keep my work fresh. Not to mention that they help me get to know my camera better. Try diversifying and shooting different subjects — you might like it. In this chapter, I show you what settings to use for specific types of photography. I also sprinkle in some tips that will take your photography to the next level.

Choosing the Optimal Settings for Specific Situations

Your camera has settings for every conceivable type of photography. You have the option of letting the camera take the reins and shoot in Full Auto mode (the A+ dial on the camera, also known as Scene Intelligent). But when shooting fully automatic, the camera doesn't really know if you're photographing a pet rock or the Grand Canyon. When you take off the training wheels and start using the really cool settings your camera has, you're in control, and with practice (plus the sage advice of your friendly author), you'll create some great images. All you need to do is attach the right lens to the camera and you're ready for action. You can take pictures of just about any object, from a small insect to a racing car traveling at a high rate of fuel consumption. But the trick is knowing what settings to use for a specific picture-taking situation. For example, say you're photographing your significant other and want her to be the center of attention with a soft blurry background. That's easy to achieve with the right camera setting and the right lens.

In addition to the right settings, you have to be creative so your photograph of a known person, place, or thing doesn't look like someone else's photograph of the same person, place, or thing. To take great pictures, you have to examine everything in the viewfinder and determine whether it's something you should include in the photograph. With a bit of thought and keen observation, you'll notice that light pole sticking out of your significant other's head and ask her to move to a different position, or you'll move to a different position.

Photographing Action

Your camera is well-equipped to photograph action, whether your subject is a flock of flying birds or the Blue Angels in formation. When you photograph an object in motion, your goal is to portray motion artistically. The camera settings and lens you use depend on the type of subject you're photographing. If you're photographing a marathon runner, you want to depict the beauty and grace of his fluid stride and athletic body. If you're photographing a racecar, your goal is the same, you want to depict the beauty of a beautifully sculpted racecar at speed. So the type of settings you use depends on whether your subject is moving toward you or parallel to you, and whether your subject is moving very fast or very slowly.

Photographing fast-moving subjects

When people see my photographs of racecars, they always assume I'm using a fast shutter speed because the car looks so clear and they can see every detail, including the driver's name on the side of the car. But I do just the opposite. I shoot with a relatively slow shutter speed when the car is traveling parallel to me. To photograph a fast-moving subject:

1. **Attach a telephoto lens to your camera.**

   The focal length of the lens depends on how far away your subject is. When I photograph racecars, I use a Canon 70–200 mm f/4 lens. If the cars are relatively close to me, I can zoom out and still get the whole car. If they're far away, I zoom to 200mm, which brings the action to me.

2. Point the camera where your subject will be when you take the picture and then zoom in.

If you're photographing an automobile race, you can compose your picture a lap before you take it. I generally zoom to almost fill the frame with the car and then zoom out a little, leaving a little distance in front of the car to give the impression that the car is going somewhere.

3. Press the Drive-AF button and then rotate the Main dial to switch to AI Servo autofocus mode so that your camera focuses continually on your subject as it moves toward or away from you.

If your camera has a hard time keeping fast-moving subjects in focus, you can focus manually on the spot where the object will be when you take the picture.

4. Switch to a single autofocus point in the center of the frame.

When you use multiple autofocus points, the camera may focus on an object other than the one you want to photograph. For more information on choosing an autofocus point, see Chapter 7.

5. Press the Mode Lock button and then rotate the camera shooting Mode dial to Tv (Shutter Priority mode).

6. Press the shutter button halfway and then rotate the Main dial to select a shutter speed of 1/160 second.

You may have to use a slightly higher shutter speed if you're using a lens with a focal length of 200mm or longer. The aperture really doesn't matter with this technique. The background is stationary, but the car and camera are moving at the same relative speed. Therefore, the background will be a blur caused by the motion of the camera relative to the background. However, if you are photographing a race on an overcast day, and the f-stop value selected by the camera is lower than f/6.3, increase the ISO setting until you have an f-stop value of f/6.3 or higher. If you shoot with too large an aperture, the side of the car will be in focus, but the driver's helmet will be out of focus.

7. Spread your legs slightly and move your elbows to the side of your body. Cradle the barrel of the lens with your left hand and position your right forefinger over the shutter button. Look through the viewfinder and point the camera toward the area where your subject will first appear.

This helps stabilize the camera as you pan with your subject. In this position, you're the human equivalent of a tripod.

8. Pivot from your waist toward the direction from which your subject will be coming.

9. When your subject comes into view, press the shutter button halfway to achieve focus.

Sometimes the camera has a hard time focusing on a fast-moving object, such as a fighter jet traveling at several hundred miles per hour. If this is the case, switch to One Shot AF mode, switch your lens to manual focus, and focus on the place where your subject will be when you press the shutter button. Press the shutter button just before your subject reaches the spot on which you've focused.

10. **Pan the camera with your subject to keep it in frame.**

    When you're photographing an object in motion, a good idea is to keep more space in front of the object than behind it. This shows your viewer the direction in which your subject is traveling.

11. **Press the shutter button when your subject is in the desired position and follow through.**

    If you stop panning when you press the shutter button, your subject won't be sharp. Figure 8-1 is a photograph of a racecar speeding through a corner. I used the panning technique to catch the essence of speed. At this point, the car was traveling well over 100 mph.

Freezing action

When your subject is rapidly traveling toward or away from you, your goal is to freeze the action. Another time you want to freeze action is when you want the photo to depict the beauty and grace of your subject. An example of this

Figure 8-1: Depicting the beauty of speed.

is a close-up of a tennis player with the ball just leaving her racket or a water skier slicing through the water. To freeze action:

1. **Attach a telephoto lens to your camera.**

   The focal length of the lens depends on how far away your subject is. I generally use a focal length that is 300mm or longer when photographing racecars coming toward me. This puts some distance between me and the subject. A telephoto lens also does a great job of compressing the background. For example, if you're photographing a gaggle of racecars, a long focal length makes them look like they're closer to each other than they actually are.

2. **Point the camera where your subject will be when you take the picture, bring the viewfinder to your eye and then zoom in.**

   When you compose the picture, leave some room in front of your subject to give the appearance that it's going somewhere. I generally try to include some of the background to give viewers an idea of the locale in which the photograph was taken.

3. **Press the Drive-AF button and then rotate the Main dial to switch to AI Servo autofocus mode so that your camera focuses continually on your subject as it moves toward or away from you.**

   Your camera may have a hard time focusing on a fast-moving vehicle. I had this problem when photographing the start of an automobile race. The cars were traveling well over 100 mph at the place I wanted to photograph them, so I switched to manual focus and focused on an expansion joint. I snapped the shutter just before the car crossed the expansion joint. (For more information on switching focus modes, see Chapter 7.)

4. **Press the AF Point Selection button and then use the multi-controller button to select a single autofocus point in the center of the frame.**

   With multiple autofocus points, the camera may focus on something other than your subject. (For more information on switching to a single autofocus point, see Chapter 7.)

5. **Press the Mode Lock button, rotate the shooting Mode dial to Tv (Shutter Priority mode), press the shutter button halfway, and then rotate the Main dial to choose a shutter speed of 1/1000 of a second.**

   Choose a higher shutter speed when trying to freeze the motion of something like a pitcher throwing a fastball. When you set the shutter speed, make note of the f-stop. If you can get a 5.6 or 7.1 f-stop, the background will be recognizable but not in sharp focus. You may have to experiment with different ISO speed settings to achieve the optimal shutter speed and aperture combination. Note that if you're shooting in low ambient light, you may see the maximum aperture (smallest f/stop value) blinking in the viewfinder, which means the image will be underexposed at the current shutter speed. Either choose a slower shutter speed, or increase the ISO until the aperture stops blinking.

6. Press the Drive-AF button and then rotate the Quick Control dial to switch to Continuous shooting mode.

With this mode, you can capture a sequence of images as long as your finger is on the shutter button at up to 10 fps (frames per second). This is a great way to capture an image sequence of your dog catching a Frisbee. For more information on choosing a Drive mode, see Chapter 6.

7. Press the shutter button halfway to achieve focus.

A green dot appears on the right side of the viewfinder when you achieve focus. When shooting in AI Servo autofocus mode, the camera updates focus as your subject moves toward or away from you.

If the dot is flashing, the camera can't achieve focus. You may experience this when you try to focus on a subject that's traveling very fast. If this happens, switch to One Shot AF mode, switch the lens to manual focus and then pre-focus on the place your subject will be when you take the picture.

8. Press the shutter button fully to take the picture.

If you switched to manual focus, press the shutter button just before the subject moves to where you focused. Figure 8-2 was photographed at the start of an automobile race. In this case, I switched to manual focus and focused on an expansion strip in the race track (which began life as a WWII airport).

Figure 8-2: Freezing motion.

To get the knack of this technique, photograph one of your family members bouncing a ball, or photograph your son or daughter throwing a knuckleball at baseball practice.

Photographing slow-moving subjects

I cover freezing motion and capturing the essence of speed in previous sections in this chapter. Here I show you techniques to photograph subjects that move slower, such as horses, runners, and bicyclists. When you freeze the motion of subjects like these, the end result is kind of boring. When you photograph slow-moving subjects like runners or cyclists, you can use blur creatively to capture a compelling photograph of your subject. This technique also works great for photographing birds in flight. To photograph slow-moving objects:

1. **Attach a telephoto zoom lens to your camera.**

   You can do this technique with a lens with a shorter focal length of 50mm. However, a longer focal length compresses the background. I like to use my 70–200mm lens when photographing slow-moving subjects.

2. **Point the camera where your subject will be when you take the picture and zoom in.**

3. **Press the Drive-AF button and then rotate the Main dial to switch to AI Servo autofocus mode.**

   After the camera locks focus, your camera updates focus continually as your subject moves toward you. (For more information on switching autofocus modes, see Chapter 7.)

4. **Press the AF Point Selection button and use the multi-controller button to switch to a single autofocus point in the center of the frame.**

   When you use multiple autofocus points, the camera may inadvertently focus on an object other than the one you want to photograph. (For more information on switching to a single autofocus point, see Chapter 7.)

5. **Press the Mode Lock button, rotate the shooting Mode dial to Tv (Shutter Priority mode), press the shutter button, and then rotate the Main dial to select a shutter speed of 1/30 second or slower.**

   This shutter speed is a good starting point, but don't be afraid to choose a slower shutter speed. I often photograph runners and bicyclists at a shutter speed of 1/6 second.

6. **Spread your legs slightly and move your elbows to the side of your body.**

   This stabilizes the camera, which is important when you're shooting at a slow shutter speed.

7. **Pivot from your waist toward the area from which your subject will be coming.**

8. **When your subject comes into view, press the shutter button halfway to achieve focus.**

   A green dot appears in the right side of your viewfinder when you achieve focus. When you shoot in AI Servo autofocus mode, the camera updates focus as your subject moves.

9. **Pan the camera with your subject and then press the shutter button when your subject is at the desired spot.**

   Remember to follow through.

When you use this technique, certain parts of your subject are in relatively sharp focus, but body parts, such as a runner's arms and legs, are a blur of motion. The technique works well with many objects in motion such a horse and rider (see Figure 8-3).

Figure 8-3: Using motion blur creatively.

Photographing Landscapes

If you live in an area like mine, where you can discover lots of lovely landscapes — thank you, Joni — capturing compelling pictures of the landscape is an excellent way to use your camera. Landscape photography is a time-honored tradition. The fact that you own a camera capable of capturing images with a 20.2 megapixel resolution means that you can create some very big prints of your favorite landscapes. My home is decorated with photographs I've shot since moving to the Gulf Coast of Florida in December 2008. To photograph landscapes:

1. **Attach a wide-angle zoom lens to your camera.**

   When you're photographing landscapes, you want to capture the wide expanse. Use a lens that can zoom out to a focal length that is 28mm or less. My favorite lens for shooting landscapes has a focal length that is 24mm.

2. **Press the Mode Lock button, rotate the shooting Mode dial to Av (Aperture Priority mode), press the shutter button, and then rotate the Main dial to choose the smallest aperture (highest f-stop value) possible for the lighting conditions.**

   A small aperture gives you a large depth of field. When you're photographing something like the Grand Canyon, you want to see everything from foreground to background. When I photograph landscapes, I use an aperture of f/11.0 or smaller. Keep in mind, you may have to increase the ISO speed setting when photographing in cloudy or overcast weather. For more information on Aperture Priority mode, see Chapter 6.

3. **Press the shutter button halfway to achieve focus.**

   A green light appears in the viewfinder when the camera achieves focus. Take note of which autofocus points glow red. In spite of the large depth of field you get with a small aperture, you don't want the camera focusing on items in the foreground.

4. **Press the shutter button fully to take the picture.**

Landscape photography is rewarding. The preceding steps get you started in the right direction, but the time of day is also very important. If you think morning is for eating breakfast and the time before sunset is for eating dinner, you have it all wrong. These are the times you need to be chasing the clouds with your camera in hand. And yes, I do mean "chasing the clouds" because clouds add interest to any landscape. If you have a still body of water into which the clouds can reflect, you have an even more compelling picture. The light in the morning just after sunrise and the light just before sunset is warm, almost golden in color. That's why the hour after sunrise and the hour before sunset is called the *Golden Hour.* This is when you need to photograph your landscapes (see Figure 8-4).

Figure 8-4: Photographing landscapes in the Golden Hour.

Composition is a very important part of photography, especially when you photograph a landscape. Your goal is to draw your viewer into the image. For more information on composing your photographs, check out "Composing Your Images" later in this chapter.

Photographing the Sunset

Sunset is an awesome time of day for photographers. The sun is low on the horizon, casting warm orange light. Add clouds to the equation and you have the recipe for great sunset pictures. When you photograph a sunset, the sun is obviously a key player, but you need other ingredients, such as clouds and an interesting landscape, for a great shot. Without clouds, you have a boring picture of an orange ball sinking in a cerulean sky. You can take pictures of sunsets with the skyline of your town in silhouette. You can get an even better sunset shot when you have a body of water such as a lake, a river, or an ocean. The water will reflect the colorful clouds. If the water is still, you have a wonderful mirror reflection of the clouds and the setting sun.

You can get some great sunset pictures in the final few minutes before the sun sets. After the sun sets, many photographers pack up their gear and head home. This is a mistake. As long as the clouds don't go all the way to the horizon, the sun will reflect warm colors on the underside of the clouds for about 10 to 15 minutes after setting. If you want really great sunset pictures, wait a few minutes after the sunset and get ready to take some pictures when the clouds are bathed in giddy shades of pink, orange, and purple (see Figure 8-5).

Figure 8-5: Catching the perfect sunset.

The camera settings for a sunset are almost identical to those you use for landscapes, with the exception of lens choice. If you're going for the grand view, use a wide-angle lens with a minimum of 28mm or less, and choose the smallest possible aperture for a large depth of field. Sometimes you may need to go the other route and choose a telephoto focal length and a fairly large aperture for a limited depth of field.

Recently I photographed a sunset at a picturesque beach a few minutes from my home. I used my Canon 24–105mm F 4.0 L lens and zoomed to 105mm, with an aperture of f/7.1. I focused on some nearby sea oats. The sea oats were in silhouette and in sharp focus, the clouds were a little soft, and the sun was a soft out-of-focus orange orb, as shown in Figure 8-6. But due to the telephoto lens, the sun is relatively large in the resulting photo, which makes it clear I took the photo as the sun was setting.

When you photograph a sunset, the camera metering system may make the scene much brighter than it actually is. If you notice this when reviewing the image on the camera LCD monitor, lock exposure on the sky and then take the picture. Alternatively, you can use exposure compensation to reduce exposure by one stop or more. (For more information on exposure compensation and locking focus, see Chapter 6.)

Figure 8-6: Photographing the sun.

When you photograph the sun, don't look directly at the sun through your viewfinder or you may damage your vision. If you photograph sunsets with Live View mode or with the mirror locked, don't point the camera at the sun for a long period of time because you may damage some of the sensitive components in your camera.

Developing a style

Photographers are attracted to different subjects and do things in different ways. Casual photographers tend to produce similar images, but die-hard photographers like to do things differently. Die-hards have a different way of seeing things, and therefore, produce different-looking images, even when they photograph the same subjects. They experiment with different lenses, different vantage points, different lighting, and so on.

Each year thousands of photographs are taken of Yosemite National Park, yet most of them pale in comparison with the memorable images photographed by Ansel Adams. The key to developing your own style is to study the work of the masters. If you're a landscape photographer, check out Ansel Adams's work. If you like the gritty, down-to-earth, street-journalism style of photography, look at Henri Cartier-Bresson's work. The next step is to shoot what you love as often as you can.

Photographing People and Things

You have a great camera that can do many things. Photographing people and the world around you is another great way to use your camera. When you photograph people and things, your goal is to create a compelling photo of the object or person, a portrait if you will. In the upcoming sections, I offer some advice for photographing people and things.

Photographing people and pets

With the right lens, your camera can capture stunning photos of people or pets. You can photograph formal or candid portraits, or use Live View mode to shoot from the hip. When you photograph people and pets, here are some things to keep in mind:

Figure 8-7: Photographing your subject against a plain background.

- Use a telephoto lens with a focal length that is 85mm or longer.

- Switch to Aperture Priority (Av) mode. (For more information on Aperture Priority mode, see Chapter 6.)

- Switch to a single autofocus point or the middle autofocus zone. (For more information on modifying autofocus, see Chapter 7.)

- Choose your largest aperture (smallest f-stop value). Choosing a large aperture gives you a small depth of field. Your subject is in focus, but the background is a soft, out-of-focus blur.

- If you're taking the picture indoors, photograph your subject against a solid color wall. You can also tack a solid color bed sheet to a wall and use that as a backdrop.

- If you're photographing your subject outdoors, photograph her against a nondescript background, such as distant foliage. If you photograph your subject with a telephoto lens with a large aperture and shoot *wide open* (photographer-speak for using your largest aperture), the background will be a pleasant out-of-focus blur that won't distract your viewer's attention from your subject (see Figure 8-7).

✔ If possible, don't use a flash when photographing people because this produces a harsh light that isn't flattering for portraits. Available light from a window is your best bet if you photograph indoors, and diffuse shade is best if you photograph the portrait outdoors. Photographing portraits on a cloudy overcast day is also ideal. If you do use a flash, use it with a diffuser, which spreads the light out and makes it appear as though your subject is illuminated with a larger light source. You can find flash diffusers at your favorite camera retailer, or purchase them online. A company called LumiQuest (`www.lumiquest.com`) manufactures a line of very portable and very affordable flash diffusers.

✔ When you're shooting portraits of a friend, relative, or your pet, take lots of pictures. Your subject will give you more natural expressions as he relaxes.

✔ If you have a Canon Speedlite, mount it in the hot shoe and then bounce it off a white surface, such as a wall or the ceiling. When you bounce the flash off a large surface, you end up with a soft diffuse light similar to that of a cloudy day.

✔ When using flash to illuminate your subject, make sure she's not too close to the wall; otherwise you'll get a nasty shadow.

✔ Use Live View mode when you want candid shots of friends or your pet. After enabling Live View, place the camera on a table with the end of the lens just off the table. When you see something interesting happen, take a picture. Your friends won't be as intimidated by the camera on the table as they would if you held the camera to your face.

✔ Never photograph pets with flash. The bright light scares them, and the light reflecting from the back of their eyes makes them look like they're possessed.

✔ When you photograph a person or a pet, make sure the eyes are in focus. To do so:

1. *Switch to a single autofocus point when photographing a head-and-shoulders portrait.*

2. *In the viewfinder, align the autofocus point with the person's (or pet's) eye that is closest to the camera, and press the shutter button halfway to achieve focus.*

3. *Recompose the shot and take the picture.*

Remember that the eyes are the windows to the soul.

You need to consider lots of things when you photograph people and pets, much more than I can include in this book. If you want more information on portrait photography, check out *Digital Portrait Photography For Dummies* by yours truly.

Exploring selective focus

When you own a camera like the EOS 7D Mark II and a lens with a large aperture with an f/stop value of 2.8 or smaller, you can create some wonderfully artistic photos by using the *selective focus* technique. When you take pictures with the largest aperture on a lens with a focal length 85mm or longer, you have a wonderfully shallow depth of field. You can use this to your advantage by focusing on one spot that will be your center of interest. The rest of the image will be out of focus, and your viewer's attention will be drawn to the point in sharpest focus. To create images with this technique:

1. **Switch to a single autofocus point and Aperture Priority mode.**

   See Chapter 7 for more on autofocus points and see Chapter 6 for more on the Aperture Priority mode.

2. **Look through the viewfinder and position the autofocus point over your center of attention.**

3. **Press the shutter button halfway to achieve focus and then recompose the image.**

   I photographed Figure 8-8 with a Canon 85mm f/1.8 lens. I switched to a single autofocus point and focused on the Harley Davidson badge.

Figure 8-8: The selective focus technique with a telephoto lens and a large aperture.

Exploring macro photography

Extreme close-up photography, also known as *macro photography,* can be a tremendous source of enjoyment. With a macro lens, you can get close to small insects, flowers, and other objects that look interesting when magnified to life-size proportions. Keep the following in mind when working with macro photography:

- Canon makes a wonderful lens for macro photography — the 100mm EF f/2.8 lens — that is compatible with your EOS 7D Mark II. You can also choose from lots of third-party macro lenses available for your camera. Tamron (www.tamron-usa.com) makes a great 90mm macro lens and 180mm macro lens.

- Focus is extremely important because when you use a macro lens and get very close to your subject, you're dealing with a very limited depth of field.

- Macro photography is almost impossible to do when the weather is windy because your subject keeps moving in and out of focus. If it's not too windy, switch the autofocus mode to AI Focus. If the camera achieves focus and the item you're photographing moves, the camera switches to AI Servo and updates focus.

- When you decide to get small and go macro, shoot in Aperture Priority (Av) mode (see Chapter 6) and choose the smallest aperture possible for the lighting conditions. This gives you a slightly larger depth of field.

- A good tripod is a handy accessory when shooting macro photography because it keeps the camera steady. If you're not using a tripod, shoot at a higher shutter speed than you normally would. Keep as steady as possible, focus, and gently squeeze the shutter button when you exhale.

Photographing Wildlife

With a camera like the EOS 7D Mark II, you can capture stunning photos of wildlife, whether the animals are moving or standing still. Photographing wildlife can be challenging, but the results are extremely rewarding. When you shoot wildlife with a camera and get a great shot, the animal lives to see another day and you have a wonderful trophy to matte and frame. The following sections offer some tips for photographing wildlife in different locations.

Photographing animals at state parks

The easiest way to find spots to photograph wildlife near your home is to do an Internet search for *state park* followed by the name of the town or county in which you live. Another good source for information are the people in your local camera store or camera club. Be nosy and ask them where their favorite wildlife photography spots are. Make friends with them and ask whether you can tag along on one of their photo shoots. I live in an area that has many state parks. When I moved to my current stomping grounds I had the good fortune to find a photography buddy who has shown me many of the wonderful wildlife hot spots near my home. Here are some things I've figured out about photographing wildlife in a state park:

- **Photograph animals with a long lens.** Unless you're photographing large animals, you'll need a long lens with a focal length that is 300mm or greater. State parks are animal sanctuaries. Even though the animals are protected, they're wary of humans. A long lens may be the only way you can get close-ups of the animals.

- **Switch to Shutter Priority (Tv) mode (see Chapter 6) and choose the proper shutter speed.** When you're photographing wildlife with a long lens, camera shake due to operator movement is magnified. Choose a shutter speed that's equal to the reciprocal of focal length of the lens you're using. If you're using a lens with a focal length that is 300mm, you have to choose a shutter speed that is at least 1/300 of a second. If your lens has image stabilization, enable it when photographing wildlife. You may have to increase the ISO speed (see Chapter 7) to get the proper shutter speed, especially if you're photographing wildlife in a forest or in dense foliage. A tripod is also useful to stabilize the camera.

- **Use a large aperture (small f-stop number) when you create wild-life portraits.** The shallow depth of field you get with a large aperture ensures that your viewer's attention is drawn toward the animal, and not the background (see Figure 8-9). To get the desired f-stop when you want to use a specific shutter speed, change the ISO setting. If you photograph toothy critters like the alligator eating the fish in Figure 8-9, make sure you're in a safe position. Predators like alligators can move amazingly fast. Alligators in many state parks have lost their natural fear of humans, because people have broken the law and fed them.

- **Switch to a single autofocus point (see Chapter 7) and focus on the animal's eyes.** If the eyes aren't in focus, you've missed the shot. When you're shooting wildlife with a long lens and using a large aperture, you have a very shallow depth of field, which makes accurate focus a necessity. If the animal's eyes are in focus, your viewer assumes the entire animal is in focus.

Figure 8-9: Use a large aperture when creating wildlife portraits.

✓ **Always travel with a photo buddy.** Many of the animals in state parks are fairly benign. However, some of the inhabitants can be dangerous if you're not careful. Many state parks have bears, alligators, and other animals that can be hazardous to your health when provoked. While you're in the moment photographing a bird, your buddy can watch your back and make sure a dangerous animal like an alligator isn't sneaking up on you. An alligator can pop out of the water like a rocket.

Stabilizing the camera when using long telephoto lenses

When you photograph wildlife with a long telephoto lens, any operator movement is magnified. The simple act of pressing the shutter button, no matter how gently you do it, vibrates the camera. The vibration degrades the resulting images slightly; they don't appear to be tack-sharp. A tripod is a huge help when using a long lens, but it doesn't stop the vibration. Here are two techniques you can use to minimize the vibration transmitted after you press the shutter button.

Stabilizing the camera with the self-timer

An easy way to stop vibration from reaching the camera is to delay the shutter opening after you press the shutter button. You do this with the self-timer as follows:

1. **Press the Drive-AF button.**

2. **While looking at the LCD panel, rotate the Quick Control dial until the 2-Second Timer icon appears.**

3. **Mount the camera on a tripod.**

4. **Compose your scene and press the shutter button halfway to achieve focus.**

   When the camera focuses on your subject, a green dot appears in the viewfinder.

5. **Press the shutter button fully.**

   Press the shutter button gently, don't stab it with your finger. After you press the shutter button, the timer counts down. When you press the shutter button gently, two seconds is enough time to stabilize any vibration transmitted to the camera.

If you frequently use the tripod to steady your camera, consider investing in the Canon RS-80N3 remote switch, which plugs into the side of the camera and enables you to release the shutter without touching the camera.

Using Mirror Lockup to stabilize the camera

Your camera can also lock the mirror in the up position before the picture is taken. This helps minimize the transmission of any vibration that occurs when the mirror moves up prior to opening the shutter. This vibration can cause your image to be less than tack sharp. You can enable Mirror Lockup using a custom function as follows:

1. **Press the Menu button.**

   The previously used menu displays.

2. **Use the Quick Control button to navigate to the Shoot tab and then use the multi-controller button to navigate to the Shoot4 menu.**

3. **Use the Quick Control dial to highlight Mirror Lockup (see the left image in Figure 8-10).**

4. **Press the Set button.**

   The options for Mirror Lockup appear on your camera LCD monitor (see the right image in Figure 8-10).

5. **Use the multi-controller or Quick Control dial to highlight Enable and then press Set.**

   Mirror Lockup is enabled.

6. **Press the shutter button halfway to return to shooting mode.**

7. **Compose the scene and then press the shutter button halfway to achieve focus.**

   A green dot appears in the right side of the viewfinder.

8. **Press the shutter button fully.**

   The mirror locks up.

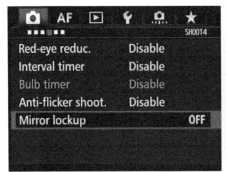
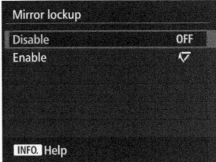

Figure 8-10: Enabling Mirror Lockup.

9. Press the shutter button again.

The picture is taken, and the mirror drops down.

When you're using Mirror Lockup in bright conditions, press the shutter button as soon as possible after the mirror locks up. Excessive exposure to bright light or the sun can damage the sensor. Make sure you disable Mirror Lockup as soon as you no longer need it.

Photographing animals at the zoo

If you live in a big city or don't have any nearby nature reserves, you can still get some great shots of wildlife at your local zoo. Visit the zoo on an off day when there will be fewer crowds to contend with and get there just before feeding time. The animals are likely to be more active prior to feeding time. When you find an animal you want to photograph, make sure no humans (or other signs that you're at a zoo) are in the frame. Switch to Aperture Priority (Av) mode (see Chapter 6) and choose your largest aperture. Move around to compose the best possible picture and then zoom in on the animal. Patiently wait until the animal does something interesting and then take the picture. Stick around for a few minutes, and the animal may do something else that's interesting or amusing. If possible, compose your image so that no telltale signs, such as fence posts or signs, give away that the image was shot at a zoo. If you're forced to take pictures with these objects, crop them out in your image-editing program.

Photographing birds

Birds run the gamut from downright ugly — the turkey vulture comes to mind — to beautiful and graceful. If you've ever witnessed a snowy egret preening, you've seen a truly elegant bird. When you photograph birds, it's almost like shooting a portrait of a person. Here are some tips for photographing birds with your EOS 7D Mark II:

- **If you're photographing flying birds, switch to the middle autofocus zone and switch to AI Servo autofocus mode (see Chapter 7).** When the camera achieves focus, it updates the focus as the bird flies.

- **If you're photographing flying birds, switch to Shutter Priority (Tv) mode (see Chapter 6), and choose a shutter speed of 1/250 of a second or faster.** This freezes the bird's motion. You can also go the other way and choose a slow shutter speed of 1/30 of a second. If you choose the slower shutter speed route, pan the camera with the bird and then the bird's wings will be blurred, giving you an artistic photograph of a bird in flight.

- **Photograph birds in the morning or late in the afternoon.** The light is warmer and more pleasing at these times of day. The harsh midday sunlight isn't a good light for any subject, even your fine feathered friends.

✔ **Use a long telephoto lens with a focal length that's the 35mm equivalent of 200mm or greater.** If the lens has a large aperture (small f-stop value), you're in business. The telephoto lens gets you close to your subject without spooking the bird. Even protected birds in a city park are unnerved by the sight of a human at close range. Shooting in Aperture Priority (Av) mode (see Chapter 6) and choosing a large aperture helps to blur the background. After all, you want photographs of birds, not the buildings in the background.

If you don't have a long telephoto lens, purchase a 2X tele-converter for your camera. This effectively doubles the focal length of any lens you attach to it. Unfortunately, it also doubles the f/stop, which lets less light into the camera. In spite of this, a good tele-converter is an excellent option, especially when you consider the price of a long telephoto lens.

✔ **Crouch down to the bird's level for a more natural-looking photograph.** This often means kneeling in wet grass. Wear a pair of old jeans when you photograph wildlife and watch where you kneel; you may kneel in a great blue heron's bathroom. The photograph of a burrowing owl (see Figure 8-11) was shot with a long telephoto lens. When you photograph birds, give them some distance and you won't spook them.

Figure 8-11: Photograph birds in their natural habitat.

- ✏ **Photograph birds on a cloudy day or a foggy morning.** You'll have beautiful diffuse light that won't cast harsh shadows. If the sky is completely overcast, you have no shadows. Photograph birds in heavy fog and you have no signs of civilization. When you photograph birds in low light, you may have to increase the ISO speed setting to get a shutter speed fast enough to take pictures while hand-holding the camera. Alternatively, you can use a tripod.

- ✏ **Take one shot and then move closer.** Get as close as you think you can without spooking the bird and then take a picture. With one picture in the bank, move closer and take another picture. If you approach the bird cautiously, you won't spook him and may end up getting an extreme close-up.

Enhancing Your Creativity

Great photographs are made by creative photographers who stretch the envelope. You can enhance your creativity by trying new things. Schedule a time each week when you experiment with new techniques or new equipment. Julia Cameron, author of *The Artist's Way,* calls this an "Artist's Date."

When I do this, I limit myself to one or two lenses and I often visit familiar territory. When you photograph a familiar place and the goal is to enhance your creativity, do things differently. Shoot from a different vantage point and use a different lens than you'd normally use for the subject.

When I was out on a recent "Artist's Date," I spotted this colorful mask while visiting the Ringling Museum. Normally I'd photograph something like this with a 50mm lens. Instead I put my Lensbaby Composer with the Double Glass optic on the camera with and composed the scene through the camera viewfinder (see Figure 8-12).

Great photos always inspire me to get out the camera and take some pictures. Great photos can also help you become more creative. When you see a really great photo, dissect the image and try to figure out what the photographer did to

Figure 8-12: Look at things in a new way to enhance creativity.

make it so compelling. Was it a camera technique, or did the photographer do some editing after the fact to make the image pop? You can find great photos on the Internet in lots of places. One of my favorite places is Photo. net (`http://photo.net`). At this website, you'll find many types of inspirational photographs from portraits to drop-dead gorgeous landscapes. You can even join Photo.net and upload your own images. Next time you need something to spark your creativity, look at some great photographs.

You can enhance your creativity while you're taking pictures. Stretching the envelope is a wonderful way to create interesting photographs. The following points can help you stretch your creativity:

- **Simplify the scene to its lowest common denominator.** A great way to do this is to use a large aperture (small f-stop value) and focus your camera on the most important part of the scene. Or you can compose your picture so the viewer's eye is drawn to a single element in the image.

- **Look for patterns.** Patterns are everywhere. For instance, migrating birds in flight create a unique pattern; scattered leaves in the gutter create interesting random patterns; and flower petals create compelling symmetrical patterns. Of course nothing says you have to compose an image symmetrically.

- **Don't fall in love with your first shot.** Before moving on, think of other ways you can capture the scene. Perhaps you can move to a different vantage point, switch lenses, or select a different aperture. Milk a scene for all it's worth and remember to look down. An interesting photograph may be beneath your feet.

- **Explore your favorite subject and create a theme of photographs.** For example, if you're a cat lover, photograph your cat and then photograph the neighborhood cats. When you photograph the same subjects or places frequently, you think of new ways to create interesting pictures. Your creative juices start flowing and before you know it, you see your favorite subject in a different way. Photographing your favorite subjects and photographing them often helps you master your camera.

My favorite subject happens to be landscapes. I live near the ocean and not very far from a picturesque river, so lately this has been my theme.

Composing Your Images

A photographer's job is to create a compelling image, an image that makes the viewer take more than a casual glance. When you compose an image properly, you draw your viewer into the image. Lots of rules exist for composing a photo. I mention many of them in this section. Your job as a photographer is to figure out which one best suits your subject. This section is designed to make you think about composition when you look through the viewfinder of your EOS 7D Mark II. You can use the camera viewfinder grid or one of the Live View grids as a visual reference. For more information on the Live View grid, see Chapter 5.

When you compose an image, look for naturally occurring curves that you can use to draw your viewer into the photograph. Curves are everywhere in nature: Birds have curved necks, and roads and paths have curves. The trunk of a tree curves to cope with Mother Nature like the trees in the tundra regions of the Rocky Mountain National Park. Look for naturally occurring curves and compose your image so that the curve draws the viewer's eye into the picture.

Many photographers take pictures in *landscape* format — the image is wider than it is tall. When you're photographing a scene like a waterfall, a person, or anything that's taller than it is wide, rotate the camera 90 degrees. This is known as *portrait* format. The photograph of a Black-Crowned Night Heron in Corkscrew Sanctuary swamp (see Figure 8-13) is an example of shooting in portrait format. A couple other compositional elements are in this picture: The curve of the bird's body draws you to the bird's eye and the branch is another entryway into the image.

Figure 8-13: Using curves as part of your composition.

Many photographers place the horizon line smack-dab in the middle of the picture. Boring! When you're photographing a landscape, take a deep breath and look at the scene. Where is the most important part of the scene? That part of the scene should occupy roughly two-thirds of the image. For example, if you're photographing a mountain, the mountain base should be in the lower third of the image. When you're photographing a sunset, place the horizon line in the lower third of the image to draw your viewer's attention to the sky. In Figure 8-14, I wanted to draw the viewer's eye to the majestic peaks from Tunnel View in Yosemite National Park, so I place the horizon line in the lower third of the image and the majestic mountains dominate the image.

Figure 8-14: Placing the horizon line.

When you're composing an image, you want to draw the viewer's eye to a center of interest in your photo. In a composition rule known as the *Rule of Thirds,* imagine your scene is divided into thirds vertically and horizontally, creating a grid, as shown in Figure 8-15. Compose your picture so a center of interest intersects two gridlines. The grid you can enable in the viewfinder doesn't quite get the job done, but it does give you a point of reference. Figure 8-15 shows a grid overlay on an image I photographed at Sanibel Island. Notice where the boy is placed in the sunset image. The middle of his body intersects two gridlines. This image, therefore, is composed according to the Rule of Thirds.

Figure 8-15: Aligning an image according to the Rule of Thirds.

Visualizing your images

Anybody can point a camera at something or somebody, press the shutter button, and create a photograph. The resulting photograph may or may not be good, but that's not really photography. True photography is studying your subject and then visualizing the resulting photograph in your mind's eye. When you visualize the photograph, you know the focal length needed to capture your vision, the camera settings to use, and the vantage point from which to shoot your image.

Seeing, Thinking, and Acting

To take a good picture, you need a great camera like the EOS 7D Mark II. But even the EOS 7D Mark II doesn't guarantee you'll get a good, or even a mediocre, picture. Getting a good picture is all about you: Your unique personality, vision, and creativity is what separates your photographs from those taken by the guy down the street who also owns an EOS 7D Mark II. Have you ever looked at two photographs of the same subject, yet they look completely different? That's where the skill and unique vision of each photographer comes into play as well as the photographer's comfort level with his equipment. Compare Ansel Adams's fine-art photographs of Yosemite to tourist snapshots from there, and you'll see what I mean.

Being in the moment

Some people think of photography as a religion. They approach their equipment and their subject with reverence, awe, and wonder. I'm sure you've seen photographs that have brought out those feelings in you. There's no reason you can't create your own jaw-dropping images. One of the best skills you can develop is being *in the moment* — experiencing the present moment and not thinking about anything else but the subject you're about to photograph. If you're distracted by things you have to do later, you can't devote your total focus to the subject you're photographing. When you aren't thinking about anything in particular but are instead observing what's around you, you notice things that'd normally pass you by. When you're in the moment, you notice small details, such as the photogenic pile of leaves in the gutter or the way the sun dapples through the leaves to create an interesting pattern on the wall. You get better pictures when you're focused on what you're doing and not fretting about what you're going to cook for dinner or wear to work the next day.

Practicing 'til your images are pixel-perfect

If you use your camera only once in a blue moon, your pictures will show it. Letting your gear gather dust in the closet won't help you become a better photographer. Instead, use your camera every chance you get. Consider joining a local camera club because networking with other photographers is a wonderful way to get new information. You may also find a mentor there. Simply strike up a friendship with an experienced photographer and tell her you want to tag along the next time she does a photo shoot.

The best way to practice photography is to take pictures of people, places, and things that interest you every chance you get. Practice your photography when you see something that inspires you, such as a compelling image in a magazine or a picture on the web. With that inspiration fresh in your mind, grab your camera and take lots of pictures of similar subjects.

I often do a photo walk-about. I grab one or two lenses, my trusty camera, and my imagination and then drive to a part of town I haven't photo-graphed. I then park the car and start exploring. This photo walkabout gives me a chance to learn how to use a new piece of gear or experi-ment with a new tech-nique, which enhances my creativity. Figure 8-16 shows an image I created with a 90mm macro lens shortly after I received it.

Figure 8-16: Practice makes perfect.

Becoming a student of photography

When you decide to seriously pursue photography, you can find a lot of resources. Great portrait photography is all around you. For instance, you'll find portraits of the rich and famous in magazines like *People* and *US Weekly,* or you can find great pictures of places in magazines like *Outdoor Photographer* or *National Geographic.* You can find great pictures of things in magazine advertisements. Your local newspapers and magazines are also great resources for great images.

When you see an interesting image in a magazine, study it carefully. Try to determine the type of lens the photographer used and then try to determine whether the photographer shot the picture in Aperture Priority or Shutter Priority mode. After you ascertain which shooting mode the photographer used:

✓ **In Shutter Priority mode,** try to determine whether the photographer used a fast or slow shutter speed.

✏ **In Aperture Priority mode,** try to determine whether the photographer
used a large or small aperture.

Also try to determine how the photographer illuminated the subject. Did he
use available light, camera flash, or fill flash. If you study great images carefully, you can get a rough idea of the settings the photographer used to take
the picture.

Another great way to understand portrait photography is to study the
masters:

✏ **Annie Leibovitz or Greg Gorman:** If you're into portrait photography,
study their bodies of work.

✏ **Arnold Newman:** Google him if you like to study the work of the old
portrait-photography masters. He created some wonderful environmen-
tal portraits.

✏ **Henri Cartier-Bresson:** If you like the gritty style of street photography,
Google him.

✏ **Ansel Adams or Clyde Butcher:** If you enjoy landscape photography,
study their bodies of work. Clyde Butcher is affectionately known as the
"Ansel Adams of The Everglades."

You can also find lots of examples of great photography at Photo.net (www.
photo.net). Other photography sites such as Flickr (www.flickr.com) or
500PX (www.500px.com) can be sources for inspirational photography.

Never leaving home without a camera

You can't ask a photo opportunity to wait while you go home to get your
camera. Photo opportunities happen when you least expect them. Therefore,
never leave home without a camera.

If you're nervous about taking your expensive EOS 7D Mark II with you wher-
ever you go, I don't blame you, and I actually feel the same way. That's why I
bought a relatively inexpensive point-and-shoot camera that I carry with me
everywhere I go. When I see something I want to photograph, I reach in the
glove box of my car, grab my trusty point-and-shoot camera, and snap the
picture.

Canon makes the PowerShot G16, a wonderful point-and-shoot camera with
professional features; it's a great camera to augment your EOS 7D Mark II.
The G16 won't fit in your shirt pocket, but it will fit in your pants pocket, coat
pocket, or your glove box. The Canon PowerShot S110 is another great option
for a second camera.

Some photographers think the cameras in cell phones are a joke. However,
if you have one of the new smartphones, you may have a competent camera.

The newer iPods and iPads also have good cameras. If your portable device doesn't have a great camera, you can still use it to create a digital sketch of a scene you want to photograph at a later date with your EOS 7D Mark II. As one photographer is fond of saying, "The best camera is the one that's with you."

Waiting for the light

Landscape photographers arrive at a scene they want to photograph and often patiently wait for the right light or until a cloud moves into the frame to get the perfect picture. Sometimes they'll backtrack to a spot at a time when they know conditions will be better. Good landscape photographers are very patient, which is a virtue that all photographers need to cultivate. When you arrive at a beautiful scene but the light is harsh, stick around a while or come back later when you know the lighting will be better.

Also wait when you're shooting candid pictures. Minutes may pass with nothing exciting happening, but don't put away the camera yet. If you wait patiently, something will happen that piques your interest and compels you to press the shutter button.

Defining Your Goals

Before you snap the shutter button, get a clear idea of what the final image will look like. If you don't have a goal for the picture or the photo shoot, you're wasting your time, and if you're photographing a person, you're wasting your time and your subject's time. Of course, the goal doesn't have to be a great image. You can go on a photo shoot to experiment with new ideas, master a new technique, or experiment with a new lens. After all, practice makes perfect.

When you know why you're taking the picture, you'll know what settings to use, how to light the photo, which lens to use, and so on. If you're creating an image for a friend or a client, adhere to the standard rules of composition, but also take a couple of pictures using a unique vantage point or a slightly different composition than you'd normally use; you may end up with some interesting pictures your client will like. However, if you're creating photographs for yourself, the sky's the limit and you can get as creative as you want. You can shoot from different and unique vantage points, tilt the camera, break the composition rules, use an unorthodox lens, and so on.

What's your center of interest?

When you create a picture of a person or place, decide what the main point of interest is and how you'll draw the viewer's eye there. For some photos, the point of interest may be a person's face or a landmark, such as the

Lincoln Memorial. If you're creating a portrait of a pianist, a picture of him playing the piano would be appropriate and your center of interest could be his hands on the keys.

Sometimes, you have more than one center of interest. When this occurs, you can compose the photo in such a manner that one center of interest leads the viewer's eye to the other center of interest. For example, if you're photographing a cellist on a beach near San Francisco's Golden Gate Bridge, you have two centers of interest — the musician and the bridge. Your job is to marry these two centers of interest to create a compelling image and guide your viewer's eye through the photo. You also need to compose the photo so that one center of interest doesn't dominate the other.

What's your best vantage point?

The decision you make on your best vantage point depends on what you're photographing. In most instances, you want to be eye to eye when photographing a person. If you're photographing a landscape and the sky or a mountain is the dominant feature, choose a vantage point that causes the sky or mountain to dominate the upper two-thirds of the image. If you're photographing a scene in which a lake or the ocean is the dominant feature, lie on your belly and compose the photo so that the water feature occupies the bottom two-thirds of the image. Yup. The old Rule of Thirds is at work. Figure 8-17 shows a unique vantage point for an image of a historic district in Sarasota, Florida.

Figure 8-17: Using a unique vantage point to add interest to an image.

What else is in the picture?

The only time you aren't bothered by other objects is when you shoot a portrait against a solid color background, such as a wall or a cloth backdrop. But even then, you have to notice everything in the viewfinder or LCD monitor. If your subject's too close to the background, you may notice wrinkles from a cloth backdrop or texture from a wall. If this happens, ask your subject to move forward and then shoot the picture in Aperture Priority mode with your largest available aperture. Focus on your subject, and the bothersome details in the background will be out of focus.

When you're taking pictures on location, you often have unwanted objects, such as telephone poles in the background. Sometimes you have to decide whether to include the distracting elements in the image and then delete them in an image-editing application, but that takes time. If you can move your subject slightly and make the distracting elements disappear, that's always your best option. You can also move to a different place in the same general area with a pleasing background and no distracting elements.

When you're photographing a landscape, take a careful look in the frame. Are power lines visible? Are ugly buildings or trash in the frame? If so, move slightly until the distracting elements are no longer in it.

The genius of digital photography

Immediacy is the genius of digital photography. The old days of waiting for your film to be developed and returned from the lab are gone. You know if you got the shot as soon as it appears on your camera's LCD monitor. You also never have to pay for film again. Ever.

With these advantages comes a curse: If you're not careful, the very genius of digital photography can turn you into a bad photographer. You don't pay for film, so you tend to shoot more images, which is a good thing if you take good photographs. But if you just shoot everything that pops up in front of your camera, you're going to get a lot of bad photos that end up in the trash. To take advantage of the genius of digital photography, be in the moment and do your best to make every image a keeper. Get it right in the camera and don't rely on image-editing applications to fix a bad image. Image-editing applications like Photoshop are designed to enhance a correctly exposed, well-composed image and make it better. I cringe when I hear a photographer say, "I'll Photoshop it." Photoshop is not a verb; it's a tool.

Practice also enters into the equation. When you know your camera like the back of your hand and you apply all your attention to your photography, you're well on the way to utilizing the genius of digital photography to its fullest and capturing compelling photographs.

Part III
The Part of Tens

Enjoy an additional Canon EOS 7D Mark II Part of Tens chapter online at
www.dummies.com/extras/canoneos7dmark2.

In this part . . .

- Get familiar with creating custom menus that contain your favorite commands.

- Find out how to register user settings and make them available whenever you select a user setting on the camera Mode dial.

- Learn how to add copyright information to your images.

- Utilize the GPS feature of the Canon EOS 7D Mark II as well as discover lots of additional cool features on your camera.

- Enjoy an extra Canon EOS 7D Mark II Part of Tens chapter online at www.dummies.com/extras/canoneos7dmark2.

9

Ten Tips and Tricks

In This Chapter

- Creating custom menus
- Adding copyright information
- Adding the author name to the camera
- Creating and registering picture styles
- Editing movies
- Updating your firmware
- Registering camera settings
- Restoring camera settings
- Customizing your camera
- Getting help

When the weather is dismal and you're fresh out of ideas for shooting macro or still life photography in your house, you can always photograph your pet rock or the collection of dust bunnies under your dresser. Or better yet, you can do some cool things with your camera, such as creating a custom menu or a custom picture style. In this chapter, I show you more than a handful of tips and tricks that you can do on a rainy day.

Creating a Custom Menu

Do you have a set of menu commands you use frequently? How cool would it be not to have to sift through all 4,000 commands in your camera menu? That's right: You can cut to the chase and create your own custom menu with your very own favorite commands. If I've piqued your curiosity, read on. To create a custom camera menu:

1. **Click the Menu button.**

   The last used menu displays.

2. **Use the Quick Control button to navigate to the My Menu1 tab.**

   This displays the options for creating a custom menu.

3. **Use the multi-controller button to navigate to the My Menu set-up tab and then press the Set button.**

   The Add My Menu Tab dialog box displays (see the left image in Figure 9-1).

4. **Rotate the Quick Control dial to select OK and then press Set.**

   The My Menu1 tab is added and the Configure My Menu1 option is selected by default.

5. **Press Set.**

   The Configure My Menu1 dialog box displays. The Select Items to Register option is highlighted when you first open the menu (see the right image in Figure 9-1).

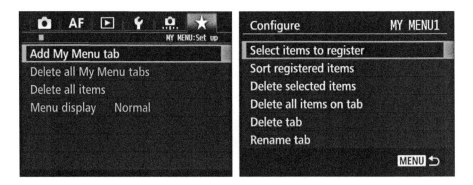

Figure 9-1: Gonna make your very own menu.

6. **Press Set again.**

   A list of menu commands you can register displays (see the left image in Figure 9-2).

7. **Rotate the Quick Control dial to highlight a command and then press Set to register it.**

   A dialog box appears asking whether you want to register the command in your custom menu (see the right image in Figure 9-2).

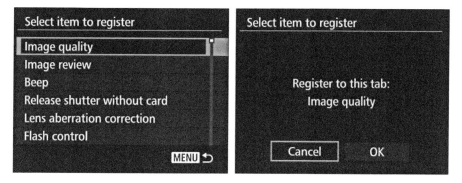

Figure 9-2: Choosing commands to register.

8. **Rotate the Quick Control dial to highlight OK and then press Set.**

   The command is grayed out on the list, which means it has been registered to your custom menu.

9. **Repeat Steps 7 and 8 to add other commands to your menu.**

10. **After registering commands to your menu, press the Menu button.**

    You're returned to the My Menu Settings dialog box (see the left image in Figure 9-3). You have the following commands at your disposal:

    - **Sort registered items:** Press Set and then your menu commands display. Select a menu command and press Set to display an up and down arrow next to the command. Use the multi-controller button to move the command up or down in the list and then press Set when the command is in the desired position. Repeat for other commands you want to move. Press the Menu button when finished.

    - **Delete selected items:** Press Set to display all commands on your menu. Rotate the Quick Control dial to highlight a command and then press Set to delete it from the list. This opens a dialog box asking you to confirm deletion. Rotate the Quick Control dial to highlight OK and then press Set. Press the Menu button to return to the My Menu Settings dialog box.

    - **Delete all items on tab:** Press Set to reveal a dialog box asking you to confirm deletion of all registered items. Rotate the Quick Control dial to highlight OK and then press Set to finish the task.

    - **Delete tab:** Press Set to delete the currently displayed custom tab.

    - **Rename tab:** Press set to open the Rename tab dialog box. You then use the camera text editor to give your custom menu a different name. I show you how to use the camera text editor in the next section.

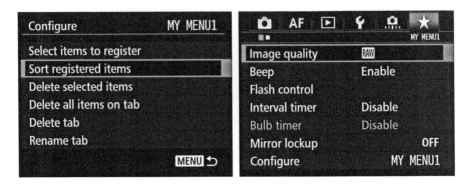

Figure 9-3: Configuring My Menu Settings options.

You can create additional custom menu tabs for different shooting options. Just make sure you give them a meaningful name. The right image in Figure 9-3 shows a custom menu tab. To access the custom menu, simply use the Quick Control button to navigate to the menu, use the Quick Control dial to select the desired command, and then press Set to access the command.

Adding Copyright Information to the Camera

You can add your copyright information to the camera. The data you enter will be added to the EXIF (Exchangeable Image File Format) metadata recorded with each image. To add copyright information to the camera:

1. **Press the Menu button.**

   The previously used menu displays.

2. **Use the Quick Control button to navigate to the Set Up tab and then use the multi-controller button to select the Set Up4 tab.**

3. **Rotate the Quick Control dial to highlight Copyright Information (see the left image in Figure 9-4) and then press the Set button.**

   The Copyright Information menu displays(see the right image in Figure 9-4).

4. **Rotate the Quick Control dial to highlight Enter Copyright Details and then press Set.**

   The Enter Copyright Details dialog box appears (see the left image in Figure 9-5).

5. **Press the Quick Control button to enter the text selection box.**

   Use the Quick Control button to navigate between the text box and the text selection box.

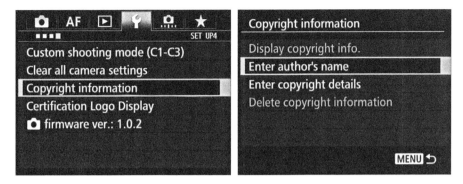

Figure 9-4: Adding your copyright to the camera.

6. **Use the multi-controller button to navigate to a letter or number.**

   You move a gold rectangle to highlight the desired character. The Quick Control dial moves the gold rectangle left or right along the current row, and the multi-controller moves the rectangle up or down to the next row.

7. **Press Set.**

   The character appears in the text box.

8. **Continue adding characters to complete your copyright information.**

   Your completed copyright information appears in the text box (see the right image in Figure 9-5).

9. **Press the Menu button.**

   A dialog box appears giving you the option to Cancel the operation or OK it.

Figure 9-5: Entering copyright information.

10. **Rotate the Quick Control dial to select OK and then press Set.**

    Your copyright information is registered with the camera and is added as EXIF data when you take your next picture.

If you select a wrong letter by mistake, you can edit the information before completing Step 9. To edit your copyright information:

1. **Press the Quick Control button to enter the text box and then use the Quick Control dial to move the cursor.**

2. **Position the cursor before a character you want to delete and then press the Erase button.**

Adding Author Name to the Camera

You can add your name as the author of each image you capture with your camera. The information is added as EXIF data to each picture you take. To register your author information with the camera:

1. **Press the Menu button.**

    The previously used menu displays.

2. **Use the Quick Control button to navigate to the Set Up tab and then use the multi-controller button to select the Set Up4 tab.**

3. **Rotate the Quick Control dial to highlight Copyright Information (see the left image in Figure 9-6) and then press the Set button.**

    The Copyright Information menu displays.

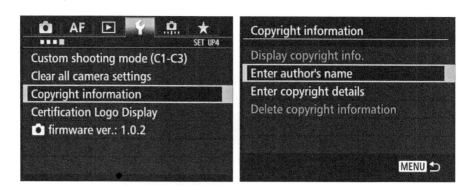

Figure 9-6: Adding your name to the camera information.

4. **Rotate the Quick Control dial to highlight Enter Author's Name (see the right image in Figure 9-6) and then press Set.**

   The Enter Author's Name dialog box appears (see the left image in Figure 9-7).

5. **Press the Quick Control button to enter the text selection box.**

   Use the Quick Control button to navigate between the text box and the text selection box.

6. **Use the multi-controller button to navigate to a letter or number.**

   You move a gold rectangle to highlight the desired character. The Quick Control dial moves the gold rectangle left or right along the current row, and the multi-controller moves the rectangle up or down to the next row.

7. **Press Set.**

   The character appears in the text box.

8. **Continue adding characters to complete your name.**

   Your completed author information appears in the text box (see the right image in Figure 9-7).

Figure 9-7: Registering your name with the camera.

9. **Press the Menu button.**

   A dialog box appears giving you the option to Cancel the operation or OK it.

10. **Rotate the Quick Control dial to select OK and then press Set.**

    Your name is registered with the camera and is added as EXIF data when you take your next picture.

You can edit your name with the techniques from the preceding section.

Creating and Registering a Picture Style

If you like to use picture styles in your photography, you'll be glad to know that you can customize your favorite picture style. After customizing the picture style, you can register it as a User Defined picture style, making it available whenever you want to use it for pictures. To customize a picture style:

1. Press the shutter button halfway.

You're in picture-taking mode.

2. Press the Creative Photo/Comparative Playback button.

The Creative Photo menu displays on the camera LCD monitor. The Picture Style option is displayed (see the left image in Figure 9-8).

3. Press Set.

The Picture Style menu displays (see the right image in Figure 9-8).

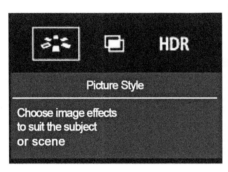
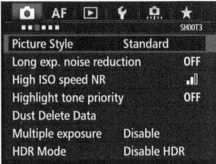

Figure 9-8: Creating a user-defined style.

4. Rotate the Quick Control dial to select one of the User Defined options and then press the Info button.

The Detail Set dialog box displays (see the left image in Figure 9-9). The Picture Style option at the top of the menu enables you to select the style that is the basis for your custom style.

5. Press the Set button.

The Picture Style option appears on the screen with up and down arrows to the right of the Standard option (see the right image in Figure 9-9).

6. Rotate the Quick Control dial to select the picture set that's the basis for your custom style and then press Set.

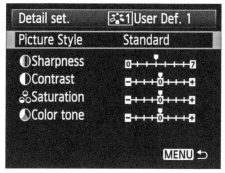 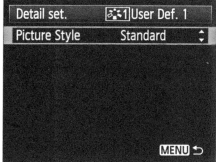

Figure 9-9: Customizing a picture style.

The details for the picture set display on the camera's LCD monitor (see Figure 9-10). You can customize the following:

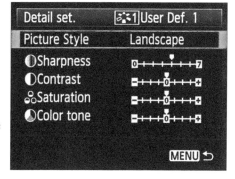

- **Sharpness:** You can increase or decrease image sharpness.

- **Contrast:** You can increase or decrease the amount of contrast in the image.

- **Saturation:** You can increase or decrease color saturation.

Figure 9-10: Customizing a picture style.

- **Color tone:** You can change the skin tone of people you photograph. You can make skin tones more yellow by moving the indicator to the left side of the scale, or more red by moving the indicator to the right side of the scale.

7. **Rotate the Quick Control dial to select Sharpness (the first on the list), or rotate the Quick Control dial to highlight another detail and then press Set.**

   The selected detail appears on the camera LCD monitor. You can now customize it (see the left image in Figure 9-11).

8. **Rotate the Quick Control dial to increase or decrease the amount of the detail.**

   Rotate the dial right to increase or left to decrease.

9. **Press Set.**

   The change is applied, and you're returned to the Detail Set menu.

10. Repeat Steps 5–9 to customize the other details in the picture style.

Customize the details that make sense to the style you're customizing. For example, you wouldn't change Color Tones when customizing the Landscape picture style. The right image in Figure 9-11 shows a customized set that's ready to be registered with the camera.

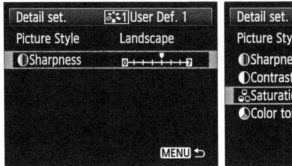 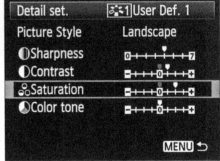

Figure 9-11: A customized set.

 11. Press the Menu button.

Your custom picture style is registered. The text above the style shows the style on which your style is based; it also shows the changes you've made to the base style in blue.

You can also customize a Standard picture style. Follow the preceding steps, but instead of selecting one of the User Defined styles, select one of the Standard styles and then press the Info button. Follow Steps 7–9 to customize the picture style to suit your taste.

Editing Movies in the Camera

When you review movies in your camera, they may need to be trimmed. Heavy editing is best done in a movie-editing application such as Adobe's Premiere Pro, but you can cut footage from the beginning or end of a movie clip in the camera by following these steps:

  1. Press the Playback button and then rotate the Quick Control dial to select the movie you want to edit.

You can press the Index/Magnify/Reduce button and then rotate the Main dial to view multiple thumbnails. Movies have a filmstrip icon around the border of the thumbnail.

2. Select the movie you want to edit and then press the Set button.

The playback controls display.

3. Rotate the Quick Control dial to select the Edit icon that looks like a pair of scissors (see the left image in Figure 9-12) and then press Set.

The editing controls display (see the right image in Figure 9-12). Cut Beginning is the first icon. This icon enables you to trim footage from the beginning of the movie clip.

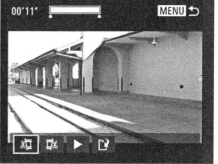

Figure 9-12: Editing a movie in camera.

4. Press Set.

The Cut Beginning edit tool is available.

5. Rotate the Quick Control dial to advance frame by frame to the spot where you want the clip to begin and then press Set.

The icon that indicates where the movie begins displays above the clip.

6. Rotate the Quick Control dial to highlight the Cut End icon and then press Set.

The tools for trimming from the end of the movie display.

7. Rotate the Quick Control dial left to rewind the movie to where you want the clip to end and then press Set.

The revised starting and ending points for the movie display above the clip (see the left image in Figure 9-13).

8. Rotate the Quick Control dial to Save and then press Set.

The Save button is the icon to the right of the Play button in the image on the left side of Figure 9-13. After pressing the icon, a dialog box appears asking you whether you want to create a new file, overwrite the existing file, or cancel (see the right image in Figure 9-13). If you still have footage on the original file you want to keep, make sure you create a new file.

Figure 9-13: Trimming the beginning and ending of a movie clip.

9. **Rotate the Quick Control dial to highlight the desired option and then press Set.**

10. **A dialog box appears asking you to confirm the option.**

    Your choices are Cancel (selected by default) or OK.

11. **Rotate the Quick Control dial to select OK and then press Set.**

    Your movie clip is on the cutting room floor.

Updating Your Camera's Firmware

Canon is constantly making changes to make its cameras better. Canon locates any potential problems based on user input and its own tests, and then takes this information and modifies the camera's firmware. *Firmware* is like the operating system for your computer. If you've registered your camera, Canon notifies you by email when a firmware update is available. You can register your camera online or mail in the card provided with the camera documents. If you mail in the card, make sure you fill in the email section of the form to be notified of any changes. When you get the notification, follow the link to the firmware. You can also find out online if your camera has a firmware update. Open your favorite web browser and navigate to:

```
http://www.usa.canon.com/cusa/consumer/products/cameras/
          slr_cameras/eos_7d_mark_ii#DriversAndSoftware
```

Look at the Firmware section and you'll see whether any updates are available for your camera. If an update is available, follow the prompts to download the information to your computer. You then transfer the firmware program to a CF (CompactFlash) or SD (Secure Digital) card to install it on your camera. Canon posts detailed instructions on how to install the firmware on one of the web pages associated with the download.

Make sure you have a fully charged battery in your camera when you update firmware. If the battery exhausts itself during the firmware upgrade, you may permanently damage your camera.

Registering Camera User Settings

Everybody has a preferred way of working. That's why you have preferences in computer programs and why you can register user settings to the Mode dial. The settings are available whenever you select a user setting on the camera Mode dial. For example, you may have custom settings that you use when you do flash photography, settings you use often but don't use every day. You can register these settings and they'll be there, even if you clear all camera settings. To register your favorite settings:

1. **Use the camera menu to choose the settings you use frequently.**

   For example, you can specify the image format and size, set up exposure compensation, or set any other settings you use frequently.

2. **Rotate the Mode dial to select your preferred shooting mode.**

   For example, you can rotate the dial to Av, if your favorite mode is Aperture Priority. After you select all your favorites, you're ready to register them.

3. **Press the Menu button.**

   The previously used menu displays.

4. **Use the Quick Control button to navigate to the Set Up tab and then use the multi-controller button to navigate to the Set Up4 Menu.**

5. **Rotate the Quick Control dial to highlight Custom Shooting Mode (C1-C3) (see the left image in Figure 9-14) and then press Set.**

   The Camera User Setting menu appears with the Register Settings option highlighted (see the right image in Figure 9-14).

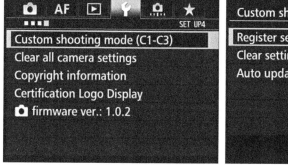
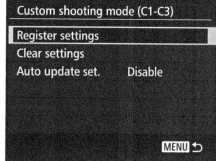

Figure 9-14: Preparing to register a setting.

6. Press Set.

The Register Settings menu appears (see Figure 9-15).

7. Rotate the Quick Control dial to highlight the desired option: Custom shooting mode C1, Custom shooting mode C2, or Custom shooting mode C3.

A dialog box appears asking whether you want to register your settings to the selected mode dial. If you have registered settings to a button previously, make sure you don't select that button or you'll override the previous settings.

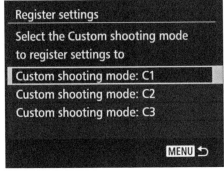

Figure 9-15: Registering user settings.

8. Rotate the Quick Control dial to highlight OK and then press Set.

Your settings are registered to the selected mode dial.

To erase user settings:

1. Follow Steps 3–5, select Clear Settings, and then press the Set button.

2. Select the mode dial you want to clear from the next menu and then press Set.

3. Rotate the Quick Control dial to select OK from the Clear Settings menu and then press Set.

A dialog appears asking you to select the custom shooting mode to clear.

4. Rotate the Quick Control dial to select the custom shooting mode you want to clear and then press Set.

The settings for the custom shooting mode are cleared.

Restoring Your Camera Settings

Sometimes you need to do some spring cleaning and wipe the slate clean. If you have more stuff on your camera than you care to deal with, or even know about, you can restore camera settings to factory defaults. This wipes out all your menu changes, your custom menu, and any picture styles you've registered or customized. So think twice before doing this. To restore your camera settings to the factory default:

1. Press the Menu button.

The previously used menu displays.

2. **Use the Quick Control button to navigate to the Set Up tab and then use the multi-controller button to navigate to the Set Up4 Menu.**

3. **Rotate the Quick Control dial to select Clear All Camera Settings (see the left image in Figure 9-16) and then press Set.**

   A dialog box appears asking you to confirm that you want to clear all settings (see the right image in Figure 9-16).

4. **Rotate the Quick Control dial to highlight OK and then press Set.**

   A dialog box appears telling you the camera is busy. When it stops, the camera settings have been cleared.

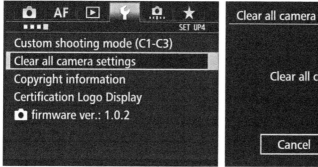 

Figure 9-16: Clearing all your camera settings.

Customizing Your Camera

Many of the buttons on your camera can be customized to perform different takes. For example, you can change the task that the shutter button performs when you press it halfway. Nine buttons on the camera are customizable. You may find it useful to customize some of these buttons. Instead of going through a long, boring Niagara-Falls-and-slowly-I-turn, step-by-step dissertation on how each button can be customized, I point you in the right direction with this short tutorial. Exploring each option for each button is another good rainy day project. If it's still rainy at night, shoot some reflections of city streets. Just make sure you're under cover when you do it so you don't damage your camera. To customize the buttons on your camera:

1. **Press the Menu button.**

   The previously used menu displays.

2. **Use the Quick Control button to navigate to the Custom Functions tab and then use the multi-controller button to navigate to the C.Fn3:Disp/ Operation menu (the left image in Figure 9-17).**

3. Rotate the Quick Control dial to highlight Custom Controls and then press Set.

The Custom Controls menu displays (see the right image in Figure 9-17). This depicts an images of the camera and the shutter button is selected by default. The default option is displayed to the right of each button. For example, the default task performed by the shutter button when pressed halfway is achieving focus automatically. The following steps show you how to customize the button. The steps are similar for the other customizable buttons.

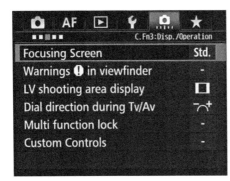
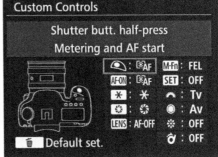

Figure 9-17: Customizing camera controls.

4. Use the Quick Control dial to highlight the button you want to customize. For this exercise, leave the shutter button highlighted.

When you highlight a customizable button, a dark orange rectangle surrounds it. As you select different buttons, the button is highlighted on the camera image. The camera view also changes when you highlight a button that's on the front or back of the camera.

5. After you highlight a button, press Set.

The options for the button display. The right image in Figure 9-18 shows the options for the shutter button when pressed halfway. The default task for the button is highlighted with an orange border.

6. Use the Quick Control dial to highlight the desired option.

The task that the button performs is listed above the option.

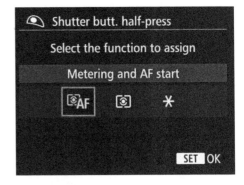

Figure 9-18: Customizing the shutter button.

7. **Press Set to finish customizing the button and then repeat Steps 4–7 to finish customizing camera buttons.**

8. **Press the Menu button when you've finished customizing buttons.**

If you're not happy with your customized buttons, you can revert to the default set by opening the Custom Controls menu as outlined above and then press the Erase button.

Getting Help

Oh my. So many menu commands, so little time, and definitely not enough pages in this book to show them all to you in their infinite geekiness and glory. But there is an option if you're out and about shooting and you've left this wonderful book at home, or you run across one of the more obtuse commands that isn't covered in this book. That option is known as *Help.* When you access a menu and have a momentary brain hiccup, look at the bottom of the menu dialog box. If you see the word Help (see the left image in Figure 9-19), press the Info button. A dialog box appears with information about that particular menu item (see the right image in Figure 9-19). If there's more text than will fit in the screen, continue to hold the Info button and rotate the Quick Control dial to scroll down through all of the text.

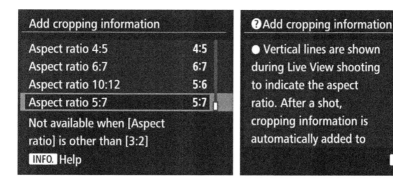

Figure 9-19: Help!

10

Ten More Tips and Tricks

In This Chapter

Adding GPS information to images

Silencing the beep

Creating HDR images

Creating multiple exposures

Using the Interval timer

Using the Bulb timer

Modifying the Rate button

Creating a makeshift tripod

Creating abstract images

Looking at Adobe Photoshop Lightroom

*W*ell, dear reader, if the last chapter of tips and tricks wasn't quite enough for you, here I present even *more* cool things you can do with your camera, in this, the final chapter of the book. Have you ever wondered how to create HDR images? Create multiple exposures or abstract images? Use the Interval and Bulb timers? How about make a makeshift tripod during those times when you see the perfect shot but don't have your tripod with you? In this chapter I show you how to do all of those things as well as introduce you to Adobe Photoshop Lightroom, the image-editing application of champions. Whew! Time to start the chapter.

Adding GPS Information to Images

Your camera is equipped with a GPS receiver. When it's enabled, you can use this option to log the GPS coordinates of each place you photograph. The GPS coordinates are stored as metadata with each image. In addition, you can store a GPS log on the camera that you can use to create a map of the places you photographed. In order to log GPS coordinates, you must first enable the GPS receiver as follows:

1. **Press the Menu button.**

   The last used menu displays.

2. **Use the Quick Control button to navigate to the Set Up tab and then use the multi-controller button to navigate to the Set Up2 menu.**

3. **Rotate the Quick Control dial to highlight GPS/Digital Compass Settings (see the left image in Figure 10-1) and press Set.**

   The GPS/Digital Compass Settings menu displays (see the right image in Figure 10-1).

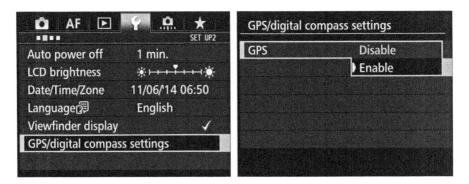

Figure 10-1: Enabling GPS.

4. **Rotate the Quick Control dial to highlight Enable and press Set.**

   You're ready to receive signals on the camera GPS from GPS satellites when you take a picture.

When you enable GPS, you see the GPS icon in your viewfinder and on your LCD panel. If the GPS icon is flashing, the camera has not acquired a GPS signal. When the GPS signal is steady, your camera is receiving signals from a GPS satellite.

When you enable GPS, the camera uses default settings to refresh the GPS signal. You can change the refresh rate and view other information about the current GPS coordinates by following these steps:

1. **Enable Internal GPS as outlined in the previous steps.**

   After you enable GPS the GPS/Digital Compass Settings menu becomes available.

2. Use the Quick Control dial to highlight Set Up (see the left image in Figure 10-2) and then press Set.

The GPS/Digital Compass Settings set up menu displays (see the right image in Figure 10-2). Most of the set up options are perfect, and a detailed explanation of each and every option is beyond the scope of this book. Your camera is all ready to add GPS data to each image. In the following steps, I show you how to change the update interval.

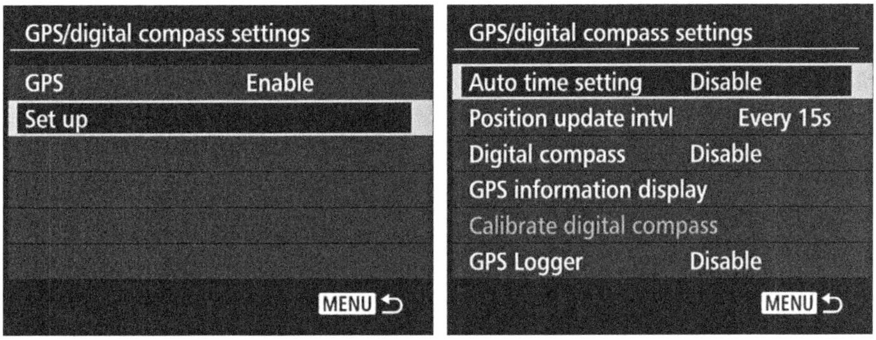

GPS/digital compass settings		GPS/digital compass settings	
GPS	Enable	Auto time setting	Disable
Set up		Position update intvl	Every 15s
		Digital compass	Disable
		GPS information display	
		Calibrate digital compass	
		GPS Logger	Disable
	MENU ↩		MENU ↩

Figure 10-2: Setting up the GPS.

3. To change the amount of time between position update intervals, use the Quick Control dial to highlight Position Update Intvl and press Set.

The Position Update Interval options display (see the left image in Figure 10-3). By default the GPS position data is updated every 15 seconds. However, if you have a tendency to spend a long time in one location, you can specify a longer interval for updates. If you specify a shorter interval for updates, GPS drains the battery quicker.

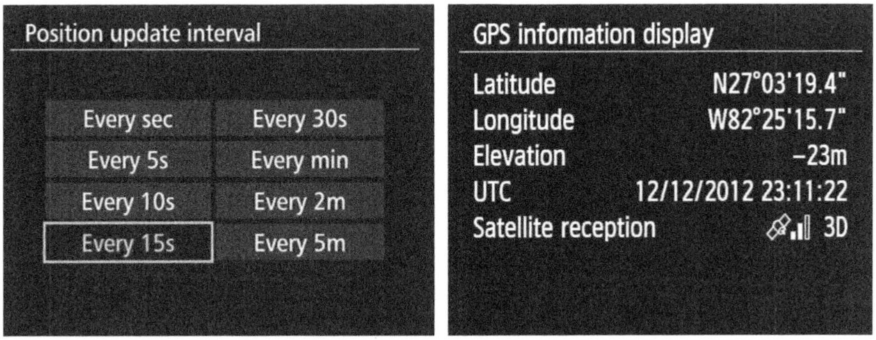

Position update interval		GPS information display	
Every sec	Every 30s	Latitude	N27°03'19.4"
Every 5s	Every min	Longitude	W82°25'15.7"
Every 10s	Every 2m	Elevation	−23m
Every 15s	Every 5m	UTC	12/12/2012 23:11:22
		Satellite reception	⚓.ıl 3D

Figure 10-3: More GPS settings.

4. **Use the Quick Control dial to highlight the desired interval and press Set.**

   The updated interval is saved and the GPS/Digital Compass Settings menu displays.

5. **Use the Quick Control dial to highlight the GPS Information Display and press Set.**

   The GPS Information Display appears (see the right image in Figure 10-3). This information is useful when you first enable GPS at a specific location. The information provided is the longitude and latitude of your current position, the date, and the time (UTC, which is essentially Greenwich Mean Time). In addition, the display shows you the relative strength of the satellite signal. If you see 3D listed next to the satellite strength, you can receive elevation information as well.

   Take the elevation information with lots of grains of salt; it's not that accurate, as you can see by the elevation listed in the display on the right image in Figure 10-3. According to this display, I'm 23 meters below sea level, and I can assure you, I was high and dry. If you see 2D listed next to the satellite strength, you can only receive longitude and latitude information.

6. **After reviewing the information, press Set.**

   You're returned to the GPS/Digital Compass Settings menu.

7. **Press the shutter button halfway and start taking pictures.**

   As long as you see the GPS signal in your viewfinder (or on the LCD panel) and it's not blinking, the camera will record GPS information with the images you photograph. When you create images with GPS enabled, the information can also be seen when you review images on your LCD monitor.

Note that you also have the option to set up and use the digital compass, which records the direction in which the camera was pointed when you took the picture. I don't see many photographers needing this feature. If you're one of the few that do, feel free to wade through the manual that comes with the camera, which is definitely not written by a friendly geek like your author. You may also be interested in logging the locations where you created the image. When you use the GPS logger, you can map your day out with the software provided by Canon. However, you can also map your locations with a much more sophisticated application known as Adobe Photoshop Lightroom, which I introduce to you later in this chapter.

The GPS feature is a wonderful option; keep in mind, however, that it does drain the battery. Many photographers will enable GPS, shoot some images, put the camera in the camera bag, stow it away in the closet, and then not use the camera for a week. This drains the battery; even though the camera's not in use, the GPS is still acquiring a signal at the specified update time interval. When you're not using the GPS feature, disable it. It would be wonderful if Canon had a switch on the camera that disabled GPS, but unfortunately they don't — which means you'll have to access the camera menu to disable GPS and stop the drain on the battery. Alternatively, you can remove the battery from the camera.

Disabling the Autofocus Beep

By default, your camera beeps at you when focus is achieved. However, when you're in a situation where silence is golden, like when you're photographing animals in the wild, or photographing a wedding complete with Bridezilla, disabling the beeper is a wonderful option. To disable the camera autofocus beep:

1. **Press the Menu button.**

   The last used menu displays.

2. **Use the Quick Control button to navigate to the Shoot tab, use the multi-controller button to navigate to the Shoot1 menu, and then press Set.**

   The Shoot 1 menu appears.

3. **Rotate the Quick Control dial to highlight Beep (see the left image in Figure 10-4) and press Set.**

   The Beep options display (see the right image in Figure 10-4).

4. **Rotate the Quick Control dial to highlight Disable and press Set.**

   The camera no longer beeps when it achieves focus.

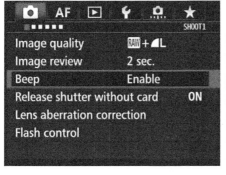
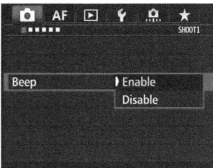

Figure 10-4: Shushing the beep.

Creating HDR Images

HDR (high dynamic range) images are all the rage. An HDR image combines multiple exposures of a scene with a wide dynamic range to create a single image that shows details in the shadow areas and bright areas of the image. Many photographers use camera-menu commands with expensive software to create HDR images, but you can create HDR images with your EOS 7D Mark II as follows:

1. **Press the Menu button.**

   The last used menu displays.

2. **Use the Quick Control button to navigate to the Shoot tab and then use the multi-controller button to navigate to the Shoot3 menu.**

   The Shoot3 menu displays.

3. **Rotate the Quick Control dial to highlight HDR Mode (see the left image in Figure 10-5) and then press Set.**

   Alternatively, you can press the Creative Photo/Comparative Display button, select the HDR icon, and then press Set to access this menu. Using either method, the HDR Mode menu is displayed (see the right image in Figure 10-5), and the HDR Mode option is selected.

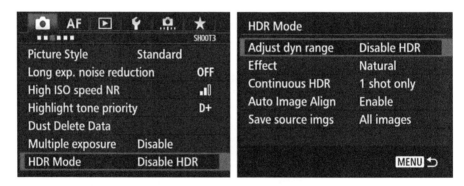

Figure 10-5: Creating HDR images starts in the camera menu.

4. **Press Set.**

   The HDR exposure options are displayed (see the left image in Figure 10-6).

5. **Use the multi-controller button or the Quick Control dial to highlight one of the following options:**

   • **Auto:** The camera sets the exposures based on the overall tonality in the scene. This is a good way to get started with HDR photography. If, after examining an HDR image, you notice that there's not enough detail in the overall image, you can choose one of the remaining options.

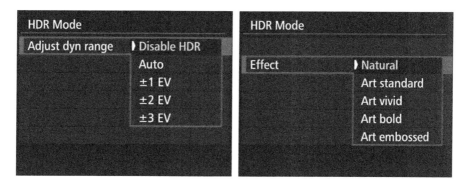

Figure 10-6: HDR, here we come.

- **+/-1 EV:** The camera captures three images: one image is underexposed by 1 EV, one image is captured with the exposure deemed correct for the scene by the camera metering device, and one image is overexposed by 1 EV.

- **+/-2 EV:** The camera captures three images: one image is underexposed by 2 EV, one image is captured with the exposure deemed correct for the scene by the camera metering device, and one image is overexposed by 2 EV. Use this option for scenes with a range of tones from shadows to bright lights.

- **+/-3 EV:** The camera captures three images: one image is underexposed by 3 EV, one image is captured with the exposure deemed correct for the scene by the camera metering device, and one image is overexposed by 3 EV. Use this option for scenes with an extreme dynamic range from very dark shadows to bright highlights.

6. **Press Set.**

   The exposure option you choose will be applied to the next HDR images you create, and you're returned to the HDR Mode menu.

7. **Use the multi-controller button or Quick Control dial to highlight Effect and press Set.**

   The Effect options are displayed (see the right image in Figure 10-6).

8. **Use the multi-controller button or the Quick Control dial to highlight one of the following options:**

   - **Natural:** This option gives you an image with high dynamic range, similar to what you see through the viewfinder.

   - **Art Standard:** This option gives you an image with a painterly look.

   - **Art Vivid:** This option produces an artistic image with colors that are more saturated than Art Standard.

- **Art Bold:** This option produces an image with highly saturated images similar to what you'd find in surrealistic paintings.

- **Art Embossed:** This option produces an image with desaturated colors with bold edges.

9. **Press Set.**

   The Effect option you choose will be applied to the next HDR images you create, and you're returned to the HDR Mode menu.

10. **Use the Quick Control dial to highlight Continuous HDR and press Set.**

    The Continuous HDR options are displayed (see the left image in Figure 10-7).

11. **Use the Quick Control dial to highlight one of the following options:**

    - **One Shot Only:** Creates an HDR image the next time you press the shutter button.

    - **Every Shot:** Creates HDR images continuously until you disable HDR shooting.

12. **Press Set.**

    The option is applied, and you're returned to the HDR Mode menu.

13. **Use the Quick Control dial to highlight Auto Image Align and then press Set.**

    The Auto Image Align options are displayed (see the right image in Figure 10-7). Images are aligned by default, which is great, especially if you shoot HDR with the camera handheld. The only time I would suggest disabling this option is when you create HDR images with the camera mounted on a tripod.

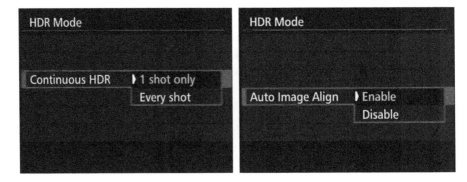

Figure 10-7: Aligning the HDR images.

14. **Choose the desired option and then press Set.**

    You're returned to the HDR Mode menu.

15. **Use the Quick Control dial to highlight Save Source Img and then press Set.**

    You have the option to save the source images along with the HDR image, which is selected by default. I suggest you keep the default option. You can then edit the source images in an HDR application such as HDR Efex Pro 2.

16. **Press the shutter button halfway to return to shooting mode and create some HDR images.**

    When you shoot HDR images, the camera captures three images as you specify through the camera menu. The camera does a good job of aligning the images, but you do need to hold the camera as steady as possible. If you're shooting in a low-light situation, and the shutter speed is too slow to create sharp images, increase the ISO until the shutter speed is fast enough to ensure a blur-free image, or mount the camera on a tripod. Figure 10-8 shows an HDR image. If this image had not been photographed with HDR, the details on the side of the boat would not be visible and the boat would be a black silhouette.

Figure 10-8: HDR increases the dynamic range of an image.

If you create HDR photographs in windy conditions, object like tree branches, leaves, and boat mooring lines will be blurred due to movement between each shot.

Creating Multiple Exposures In-Camera

Back in the days of film, photographers had to resort to trickery to expose two images on one piece of film. Your EOS 7D Mark II can create multiple exposures in camera and you don't have to resort to any kind of chicanery to get the job done. All you need to know is where to enable multiple-exposure photography in the camera menu and then have a creative eye for subjects that would look good when combined on a single image. To create multiple exposures in-camera:

1. **Press the Menu button.**

   The last used menu displays.

2. **Use the Quick Control button to navigate to the Shoot tab and then use the multi-controller button to navigate to the Shoot3 menu.**

   The Shoot3 menu displays.

3. **Rotate the Quick Control dial to highlight Multiple Exposure (see the left image in Figure 10-9) and then press Set.**

   The Multiple Exposure menu options appear (see the right image in Figure 10-9). Multiple exposures are disabled by default. Alternatively, you can press the Creative Photo/Comparative Display button, select the Multiple Exposure icon, and then press Set to access this menu.

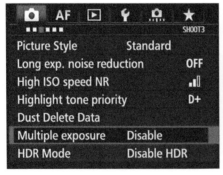

Figure 10-9: Multiple exposures in-camera. How cool!

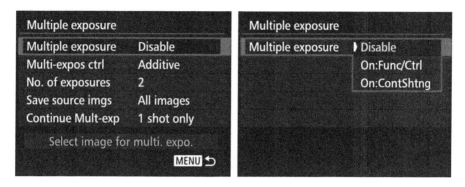

Figure 10-10: Enabling multiple exposures in-camera.

4. **With the Multiple Exposure option still selected (see the left image in Figure 10-10), press Set.**

   The option to enable Multiple Exposure appears (see the right image in Figure 10-10).

5. **Choose one of the following options:**

   - **Disable:** The default option disables multiple exposures.

   - **On:Func/Ctrl:** Choose this option to review the multiple exposure as you proceed. You'll be able to review each source image and the merged multiple exposure.

   - **On:ContShtng:** Choose this option if you are making multiple exposures of a moving subject. When you choose this option, you will not be able to view the images that will comprise the multiple exposure. Only the final image will be saved.

6. **Press Set.**

   Your choice is saved, and you're returned to the Multiple Exposure menu. You are one step closer to shooting multiple exposures.

7. **Use the multi-controller button or the Quick Control dial to highlight Multi-Expos Ctrl (see the left image in Figure 10-11) and press Set.**

   The Multi-Expos Ctrl options are displayed (see the right image in Figure 10-11).

8. **Use the multi-controller button or the Quick Control dial to highlight one of the following:**

   - **Additive:** Each exposure is added cumulatively to create the single image. You'll have to employ negative exposure compensation to decrease the exposure of each image so all of the images add up to a correctly exposed image. If you're combining two images, set exposure compensation to –1 stop; for three images, –1.5 stops; for four images, –2 stops.

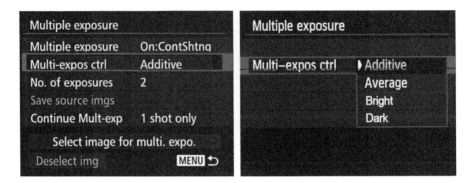

Figure 10-11: Decisions, decisions!

- **Average:** Negative exposure compensation is applied to each image. The amount of negative exposure is determined by the number of images you're combining.

- **Bright:** The brightness of the base image and the images to be added to the multiple exposure are compared at the same position, and the bright parts are added to the multiple exposure.

- **Dark:** The darkness of the base image and the images to be added to the multiple exposure are compared at the same position, and the dark parts are added to the multiple exposure.

9. **Press Set.**

   You're returned to the Multiple Exposure menu.

10. **Use the Quick Control dial to highlight No. of Exposures (see the left image in Figure 10-12) and then press Set.**

    The No. of Exposures option appears (see the right image in Figure 10-12). An arrow appears above and below the current selection.

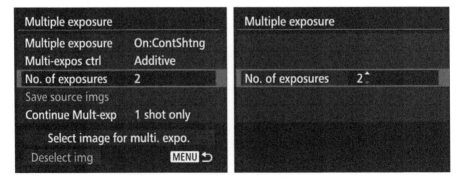

Figure 10-12: Determining how many images will be included in the final image.

11. **Use the Quick Control dial to select the number of images and then press Set.**

    You can combine from two to nine exposures to create your multiple exposure image. After you press Set, you're returned to the Multiple Exposure menu.

12. **Use the Quick Control dial to highlight Save Source Imgs and then press Set.**

    This menu gives you the option of saving all images or the result only. The default option is All Images. If you're experimenting and are only interested in the end result, choose Result Only.

13. **Make a choice and then press Set.**

    You're returned to the Multiple Exposure menu.

14. **Use the Quick Control dial to highlight Continue Multi-Exp (see the left image in Figure 10-13) and then press Set.**

    In this menu (see the right image in Figure 10-13) you choose whether to create one multiple exposure or continuous multiple exposures. If you choose the latter option, you'll have to disable multiple exposures to return to single image exposures.

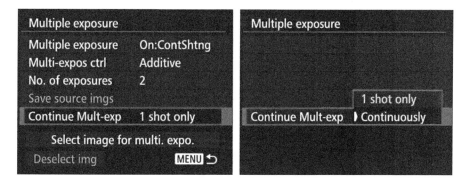

Figure 10-13: More decisions.

15. **Use the Quick Control dial to highlight the desired option and then press Set.**

    The option is applied and you're returned to the Multiple Exposure menu.

16. **Press the shutter button halfway and begin multiple-exposure photography.**

If you shoot in Live View mode, you'll see the exposures combined so far. If you use the continuous shooting mode, you only see the end result. You'll also be able to compose your multiple exposure after taking one or more shots. As you move the camera, the subjects in the frame are overlaid on the previous exposures. In the viewfinder, you'll see the Continuous Shooting icon with the number of frames remaining to be shot to complete your multiple exposure.

Choosing subjects for multiple-exposure images can be tricky. If you combine a busy subject with another busy subject, your multiple exposure will look like a surreal Salvador Dali painting. That's fine if that's the look you're after, but if you want the subjects to be recognizable, I suggest you have one subject that is the main focal point of your multiple exposure, with the other images contributing to the overall look, but not distracting from the focal point. The easiest way to grasp multiple-exposure photography is to shoot lots of multiple exposures. Figure 10-14 is an example of a multiple-exposure image using two exposures.

Figure 10-14: Creating multiple exposures for fun and profit.

Using the Interval Timer

The Interval timer makes it possible for you to capture multiple images of a scene over a time span. This gives you the raw material for combining the images in a application like Photoshop and creating a time-lapse movie, which unfortunately is beyond the scope of this book. You can, however, search for "How to create a time-lapse movie" on the Internet and find lots of useful web pages. To use the Interval timer:

1. **Set your camera on a tripod and then press the Menu button.**

   The last used menu displays.

2. **Use the Quick Control button to navigate to the Shoot tab and then use the multi-controller button to navigate to the Shoot4 menu.**

   The Shoot4 menu displays.

3. **Rotate the Quick Control dial to highlight Interval Timer (see the left image in Figure 10-15) and then press Set.**

The option to Disable or Enable the Interval timer displays (see the right image in Figure 10-15).

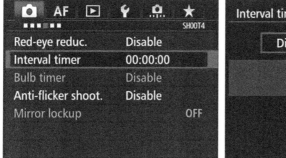 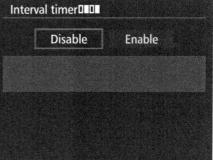

Figure 10-15: Enabling the Interval timer.

4. **Rotate the Quick Control dial to highlight Enable and then press the Info button.**

The Adjust Interval/Shots menu displays and hours is selected by default (see the left image in Figure 10-16).

5. **Press Set.**

An arrow appears above and below the current option.

6. **Use the Quick Control dial to set the desired interval and then press Set.**

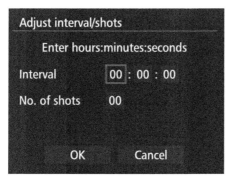 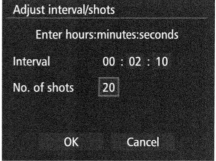

Figure 10-16: The Interval timer is ready to go.

7. **Use the multi-controller button to select the next option.**

   Continue in this manner until you've set the desired interval in hours, minutes, and seconds. The maximum interval is 99:59:59.

8. **Use the multi-controller button to highlight the No. of Shots option and then press Set.**

   An arrow appears above and below the option.

9. **Rotate the Quick Control dial to set the number of shots and then press Set (see the right image in Figure 10-16).**

   You can capture up to 99 shots with the Interval timer.

10. **Use the multi-controller button to highlight OK and then press Set.**

    Take the picture. The Interval timer icon displays on the LCD panel (see Figure 10-17).

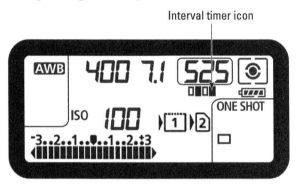

Interval timer icon

Figure 10-17: The Interval timer at work.

Shooting Time Exposures with the Bulb Timer

If you decide to explore the wild and wooly world on long exposures at night, your camera has a feature that makes it possible for you to dial in the exact exposure time, which means you don't have to attach a remote switch to the camera or an intervalometer (a device that connects to your camera and enables you to program the length of exposure). To shoot long exposures, all you need to do is set your camera on a tripod and specify the exposure duration using the Bulb timer as outlined in the following steps.

1. **Press the Menu button.**

   The last used menu displays.

2. **Use the Quick Control button to navigate to the Shoot tab and then use the multi-controller button to navigate to the Shoot4 menu.**

   The Shoot4 menu displays.

3. **Rotate the Quick Control dial to highlight Bulb Timer (see the left image in Figure 10-18) and press Set.**

   The Bulb Timer menu appears (see the right image in Figure 10-18).

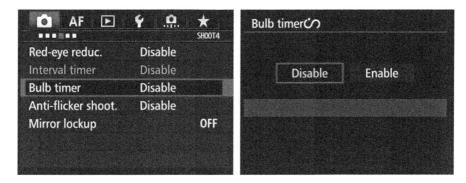

Figure 10-18: Enabling the Bulb timer.

 4. Use the Quick Control dial to highlight Enable and then press the Info button.

The Adjust Exposure Time menu appears, and the Hours option is selected by default (see the left image in Figure 10-19).

5. Press Set.

An arrow appears above and below the current selection.

6. Rotate the Quick Control dial to set the exposure duration in hours and then press Set.

Of course you may only need an exposure time that is minutes or seconds in duration. If this is the case, select the appropriate measure of time with the multi-controller button, press Set, and then set the duration.

7. Continue in this manner until you've specified the desired exposure duration.

8. Use the Quick Control dial to highlight OK (see the right image in Figure 10-19) and then press Set.

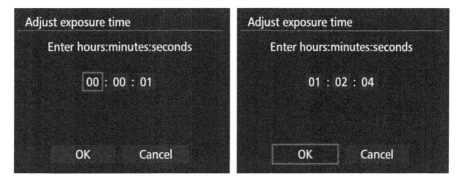

Figure 10-19: Setting the exposure duration.

9. **Press the shutter button halfway to return to shooting mode and take the picture.**

   The Bulb timer icon appears on the LCD panel (see Figure 10-20).

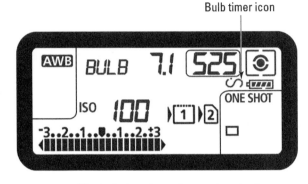

Bulb timer icon

Figure 10-20: The Bulb timer is ready to rock and roll.

To prevent the vibration of your finger pressing the shutter button from being transmitted to the tripod, I suggest you enable the 2-second timer to open the shutter two seconds after you press the shutter button. This gives the camera a chance to stabilize before the camera records the image. (See "Using the Self-Timer" in Chapter 2 for details on how to set the timer duration.)

Long exposure photography is very rewarding if you have the patience to sit and wait while the shutter is open. The image shown in Figure 10-21 is an example of the type of image you can create with a long exposure at night. Note that if you do try to photograph lightning, make sure you're in a safe place, or the storm is far away.

Figure 10-21: Nighttime photography is worth the wait.

Modifying the Rate button

Okay. I need to get on my soapbox here. The Rate button, which is on the left side of the camera, is used to rate images from 1 to 5 stars. Interrupting your photography to rate images takes time away from your creativity and focus. IMHO, to rate images, you should use an image editing application such as Photoshop Lightroom. If you agree, you'll be happy to know that you can use the Rate button to protect images, which prevents you from accidentally deleting them. This is much quicker than the menu command to protect images; therefore, I suggest you modify the Rate button to protect images as follows:

1. **Press the Menu button.**

   The last used menu displays.

2. **Use the Quick Control button to navigate to the Set Up tab and then use the multi-controller button to navigate to the Set Up3 menu.**

   The Set Up3 menu displays.

3. **Rotate the Quick Control dial to highlight Rate Btn Function (see the left image in Figure 10-22) and then press Set.**

   The Rate Btn Function menu displays (see the right image in Figure 10-22).

4. **Use the Quick Control button to highlight Protect and then press Set.**

   The Rate button can now be used to protect images.

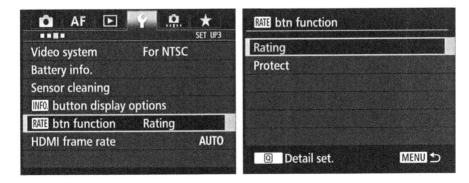

Figure 10-22: Modifying the Rate button to protect images.

To use the Rate button to protect an image after you review it on the LCD monitor, press the Rate button. Once the image is protected, a lock icon appears. To unprotect a protected image, press the Rate button again.

Creating a Makeshift Tripod

Your EOS 7D Mark II can capture images in very low-light conditions. However, at times, you absolutely can't do without a tripod. But what do you do when you've left home and didn't bring one along? Here are some ways you can steady your camera without a tripod:

- **Switch to Live View mode and place the camera near the edge of a table.** If you can see the tabletop in the viewfinder or LCD monitor, move the camera closer to the edge.

- **Hold the camera against a wall.** Use this technique when you rotate the camera 90 degrees (also known as *Portrait mode*).

- **Lean against a wall and spread your legs slightly.** This is known as the *human tripod.* Press the shutter button gently when you exhale.

- **Use a small beanbag to steady the camera.** You can just throw the beanbag in your camera bag; it doesn't take up much space. Place your camera on the beanbag and move it to achieve the desired composition. You can purchase beanbags at your local camera store.

  As an alternative to the bean bag, you can carry a baggie filled with uncooked rice (cooked rice is messy and will spoil) in your camera bag. Place your camera on the bag and move it until you achieve the desired composition.

In addition to using one of these techniques, use the 2-Second Self-Timer. This gives the camera a chance to stabilize from any vibration that occurs when you press the shutter button. These techniques are also great when you're on vacation and don't have the room to carry a tripod in your baggage.

Creating Abstract Images in the Camera

When you stretch the envelope, you can create some very cool images with your camera. I read an article about a technique where the photographer walked with the camera while taking a picture at a very slow shutter speed. I loved the technique and decided to take it to the next level. I've dubbed this technique: Drive-By Shooting. This abstract technique involves creating a photo while you're a passenger in a vehicle. To create an abstract image:

1. **Ask a friend or relative to drive you somewhere.**

   This technique works best after the sun has set. Choose a place with a lot of traffic. You're after the headlight patterns.

2. **Attach the desired lens to the camera.**

   Don't use a wide-angle lens; this would include part of the car interior in your shot. Choose a lens with a focal length that's the 35mm equivalent of 80mm or greater.

3. **Press the Mode Lock button and then rotate the Mode dial to Av (Aperture Priority).**

   You're using the aperture to control how long the shutter is open.

4. **Press the Flash Compensation/ISO button and then rotate the Main dial to set the ISO speed to 100.**

   You want the shutter to be open for a long time. The lowest ISO setting makes the camera less sensitive to light requiring a longer shutter speed.

5. **Rotate the Main dial again to specify the smallest aperture (highest f-stop value) for the lens you're using.**

   This ensures the shutter will be open for a long time.

6. **Wait until your friend drives near a lot of moving traffic.**

   You want lots of lights in the image. You can try this technique on a busy city street or a freeway. Another option is to take the picture when your friend drives away from a traffic light.

7. **Press the shutter button halfway.**

   The camera achieves focus. If the camera can't achieve focus, switch the lens to manual focus and then focus by rotating the focus ring on the lens.

8. **Press the shutter button fully.**

   The shutter opens, and the picture is taken. Depending on the ambient light, your lens may be open for several seconds.

9. **Rotate the camera.**

   This is painting with light. When you rotate the camera, or move it up and down or from side to side, you create abstract patterns. An alternative when you're not in a car is to move the camera from left to right to create an abstract image of a horizontal subject, or up and down to create an abstract image of a vertical subject (see Figure 10-23).

10. **Edit your pictures.**

   When you edit images in an application like Adobe Photoshop or Photoshop Elements, you can use filters to

Figure 10-23: Creating an abstract image in-camera.

tweak the images. Figure 10-24 shows an abstract image created using this technique and edited in Photoshop.

Working with Photoshop Lightroom

You have a camera with features that are used by professional photographers. In fact, professional photographers use the Canon EOS 7D Mark II in their daily work. If you're like professional photographers, you take a lot of pictures. If you also heed my sage advice and use your camera's RAW format to capture images, you need a program that's capable of quickly processing lots of images quickly. The program that most professional photographers use to catalog and process their images is Adobe Photoshop Lightroom. This powerhouse application makes it possible for you to keep track of, edit, and find thousands of images quickly.

Figure 10-24: A tweaked abstract image.

Lightroom is currently in its fifth iteration (Lightroom 5) and is updated on a regular basis when manufacturers introduce new cameras. I've been using the application since its first iteration. I do all of my heavy lifting in Lightroom and then fine-tune my images in Adobe Photoshop. Lightroom is divided into the following modules:

- **Library:** The Library module (see Figure 10-25) is where you organize your images. I organize all of my images into folders that are titled to reflect the date and place where the photographs were taken. I also add keywords to my photographs,

Figure 10-25: The Lightroom Library module.

which makes it easy for me to find specific images in seconds. You can easily organize your images into folders, and rename and add keywords when you import them into Lightroom. You can also delete duds, rate photos, and much more. If you use Lightroom, you can spend your time taking photographs without having to worry about renaming them in the camera, deleting duds while shooting, and rating images. When you're out and about with your camera, you should be photographing. You name and rate your images when you get home.

✓ **Develop:** The Develop module (see Figure 10-26) is where you process your images. You can easily and quickly adjust exposure, brightness, white balance, contrast, and so on. Many years ago, I was hired to photograph a professional model. I photographed her in

Figure 10-26: The Lightroom Develop module.

my studio, but I didn't have my glasses on when I set the camera white balance to match the color temperature of my studio lights. I messed up and the images had a bluish color cast to them. In the Develop module I corrected the white balance of the first image, and then synchronized that setting with the other 600-some odd images from the shoot, and fixed the white balance or each image in seconds. Whew!

You can also crop images in the Develop module, sharpen them, and add special effects to an image such as split toning, converting images to black and white, and much more. You can also create presets in Lightroom. Presets contain steps for things you do frequently. Rather than doing the same steps over and over again, you click a preset and the task is done in a flash.

✓ **Map:** Your camera can add GPS information to each image if you enable the feature as outlined earlier in this chapter. The GPS information is saved as metadata that you can use in the Map module to map out the exact location where you photographed the image.

✓ **Book:** The Book module makes it possible for you to use selected images and create a photo book. The templates are set up for Blurb (www. blurb.com), a company that does an excellent job of creating hardcover and softcover books. I've created several photo books with Blurb and have been very happy with the results.

✓ **Slideshow:** The Slideshow module is where you take selected images and create slide shows that you can view on your computer and slideshows that you can export as PDF documents.

- ✔ **Print:** The Print module is where you can print selected images. You can print single images or multiple images on a sheet.

- ✔ **Web:** The Web module is where you take selected images and convert them to web pages. There is a wide variety of templates you can use to crate beautiful web pages that can be uploaded to a web server directly from Lightroom.

The beauty of Lightroom is that when you close the application, it saves all the processing you've done on each image in the catalog. When you launch the application the next time, everything is just as you left it. Way cool. If I've piqued your curiosity, you can get Lightroom through an Adobe subscription service for as little as $9.99 per month. To find out more about Adobe Photoshop Lightroom, visit www.adobe.com/products/photoshop-lightroom.html.

Appendix A

Digital SLR Settings and Shortcuts

Many people graduate to a digital SLR and think it's the ticket for creating great photos. Well it is, but there's a bit of technique involved. Part of that is your creativity and the way you see the world around you. You translate the vision that is in your head into an image when you capture it with your digital SLR.

To fully master your digital SLR and create compelling photos, you have to venture forth into a brave new world that involves making decisions about settings that will enable you to capture the images you see in your mind's eye. This does not happen when you shoot in your camera's automatic mode. When photographers have the urge to branch out, they turn to the manual for help. And then they get more confused. Which is where this appendix comes in. My goal in writing this appendix is to demystify taking photographs with a digital SLR.

Capturing Sporting Events

Photography is a wonderful pastime. You can use your camera to capture memories of the things that interest you. If you're a sports fan, you can photograph your favorite sport. You can photograph individual athletes, but sports have more to them than just the athletes. Whether your favorite sport is football or auto racing, each one has its own rituals. And every sport includes a supporting cast. When you photograph a sporting event, you photograph each chapter of the event, from the pre-games festivities, to the opening kickoff, to the winning touchdown. Your creative mind, knowledge of the sport, and the information in this section give you all the tools you need to tell a story. You begin at the beginning, before the athletes flex their muscles or the drivers start their engines.

Setting the camera

This section gives you a couple of different shooting scenarios. When you're photographing the pre-event festivities, you shoot in Aperture Priority mode.

When your goal is to photograph an athlete preparing for the event, you want a shallow depth of field; therefore, you choose a large aperture (a small f/stop number). When you want to photograph the crowd, or a group of athletes practicing, you use a small aperture (a large f/stop number) to ensure a large depth of field. When your goal is to stop action, you shoot in Shutter Priority mode at a speed fast enough to freeze the action. For an athlete, you can freeze motion with a shutter speed as slow as 1/25 of a second. To stop a racecar dead in its tracks, you need a fast shutter speed of 1/2000 of a second. To capture the beauty of a speeding racecar with a motion blur, you pan the camera and shoot with a shutter speed of 1/125 of a second. The focal length you use varies depending on how close you can get to the action. If you're photographing a large crowd before the event, use a wide-angle focal length of 28 to 35mm. If you're photographing individual athletes, zoom in.

Taking the picture

When you photograph a sporting event, you have to be in the moment. Before the event starts, you can capture interesting pictures of the crowd, the athletes performing their pre-event rituals, and the athletes warming up. When the event starts, you can capture the frenetic action. When the event is well and truly underway, keep alert for any interesting situations that may arise and, of course, any team player who scores. If you're photographing an automobile race, be sure to include pictures of pit stops and other associated activities. And you probably want a picture or two of the winning driver spraying the champagne.

1. **Arrive at the event early and take pictures of anything that interests you.**

   You have to change settings based on what you're photographing.

2. **Photograph the pre-event activities, such as the introduction of the players, the coach meeting with her team on the sidelines, or if you're attending a race, pictures of the drivers getting ready.**

   You can get creative with your composition when you photograph the pre-race events. Don't be afraid to turn the camera diagonally or venture to an interesting vantage point. Let your inner child run amuck and capture some unusual pictures.

3. **Photograph the start of the event.**

   The action can get a little crazy. Each team is trying to gain an advantage over the other. If you're photographing a race, drivers may battle fiercely to achieve the lead by the first corner. You never know what might happen. Stay alert for any possibility. Hold the camera and be ready to compose an image when you see something interesting about to happen. Be proactive: Have the camera to your eye a split second before the crucial moment.

4. Photograph the middle of the event.

The middle of any event is a great time for photographers. If you're photographing an event such as a basketball or football game, you can get some shots of substitutions. You can also photograph the fans to capture their reactions to a winning score and so on. If you're photographing an auto race (as shown in Figure A-1), the cars are now a little battle weary, with tire marks, racer's tape, and other chinks in their armor.

Figure A-1: Photograph the middle of the event when the participants are a little battle weary.

5. Photograph the end of the event.

Be on your toes, especially if the score is close. In the final minutes or final laps, it's do or die. Athletes give their all to win the event, which gives you opportunities for some great pictures.

6. Photograph the post-event activities.

Take photographs of the winning team celebrating and capture the glum looks of the losers. Take photographs of any award ceremonies. Tell the complete story of the event.

Photograph an athlete going through his pre-event ritual. Figure A-2 shows champion driver Allan McNish with a mask of concentration at the drivers' meeting.

Troubleshooting

✓ **I don't know which mode to use.** If you're photographing athletes in motion, use Shutter Priority mode to freeze motion. If you're photographing people and things before the event, use Aperture Priority mode to control depth of field.

✓ **The picture isn't level.** This problem often happens when you're photographing people in motion, especially when you're panning the camera. Make sure that you're standing straight and that you don't lean when you pan the camera. You may also want to use the grid that's built into many cameras as a guide.

✓ **I can't get close to the action.** When you photograph a spectator event, sometimes you just need to wait for someone to move. Of course, always try to get a good seat ahead of time. If the event doesn't include assigned seating, arrive early.

Figure A-2: Photograph athletes performing their pre-event rituals.

Photographing Animals in the Wild

If you live near a state park or wilderness area, you can capture some wonderful photographs of animals such as deer, raccoons, and otters in their natural surroundings. You can easily spook these kinds of wild animals because they're relatively low in the food chain. They have a natural fear of people, which means you have to be somewhat stealthy to photograph them; patience is a virtue. If you're patient and don't do anything startling, you can capture great images of animals such as the one shown here.

If you live near a state park, go there often to find out in which areas of the park you're likely to find your subjects and to get to know the habits of those animals — including their feeding habits. After you know the habits of the animals you want to photograph, get familiar with the lay of the land, and use the settings I recommend, you can capture some wonderful wildlife images.

Setting the camera

The goal of this type of photography is to capture a photograph of an animal in the wild. You use Aperture Priority mode for this type of photography to control depth of field. The animal is the subject of your picture, therefore you use a large aperture to create a shallow depth of field and draw your viewer's attention to your subject. Continuous Auto-Focus mode enables the camera to update focus while the animal moves. You also use Continuous Drive mode to capture a sequence of images of the animal as it moves through the area. The focal length you use depends on how close you can safely approach the animal. Use image stabilization if you have to shoot at a slow shutter speed.

 The slowest shutter speed you should use when handholding your camera is the reciprocal of the 35mm-equivalent focal length. For example, if your camera has a 1.6 focal length multiplier and you're using a 50mm lens, the slowest shutter speed you should use when holding the camera by hand is 1/100 of a second (1 ÷ 50 × 1.6).

Taking the picture

When you're taking pictures of animals in their natural habitat, you have to stay out of the open so that you don't frighten the animal. I also recommend wearing clothing that helps you blend in with the surroundings.

1. **Go to a place where you've previously sighted the species you want to photograph, hide behind some natural cover, and wait.**

   Photograph during the early morning or late afternoon when the light is better and animals are out foraging for food.

2. **Switch to the camera settings mentioned earlier in this chapter.**

3. **When you see an animal, zoom in until the animal fills the frame and then zoom out slightly.**

4. **Position the autofocus point over the animal's eye, press the shutter button halfway to achieve focus, move the camera to compose the picture, and then press the shutter button fully to take the picture.**

   When you use Continuous Drive mode, the camera continues to capture images as long as you have your finger on the shutter button.

 Zoom in tight on the animal to capture an intimate portrait and compose the image according to the Rule of Thirds. This kind of photo is as close as you'll get to shooting a portrait of a wild animal (see Figure A-3).

Figure A-3: Zoom in close for an intimate animal portrait.

Troubleshooting

✔ **The image isn't sharp.** Make sure you're shooting at an ISO that's high enough to enable a relatively fast shutter speed, and use image stabilization if your lens or camera has this feature. If you don't have the image stabilization feature, mount your camera on a tripod or monopod.

Don't use image stabilization if the camera is mounted on a tripod because you may get undesirable results as the camera or lens attempts to compensate for operator motion when in fact the camera is rock steady.

✔ **The animal blends into the background.** The coloration of some animals causes those animals to blend into the background. Try shooting from a different angle. You can also use the largest aperture to blur the background as much as possible. If you use a large aperture, make sure you get the animal's eyes in focus. If you don't, the entire picture appears to be out of focus.

✔ **The animal disappears before I take the picture.** Make sure you're well hidden and not upwind from the animal.

Photographing Horse Racing

The fluid motion of a horse and her rider are all the ingredients you need for an exciting picture. There are many forms of horse racing. When you photograph an event like steeplechase or barrel racing, you can hone in on the rider and her trusty steed as they negotiate the obstacles. If you photograph an event on a 5/8-mile course, you can photograph many racers at one time. This section focuses on events where a single rider and horse are racing against time. The rider is focused on making the horse do something that is not second nature to the animal. The pictures you capture show the interaction between the rider and her horse as she guides the animal around the obstacles.

Setting the camera

When you photograph a horse race, you want to capture a slice of action, a frozen moment in time when horse and rider act in unison. To achieve this, you use Shutter Priority mode and a relatively fast shutter speed. If you're photographing a steeplechase or barrel race, you can use the slowest setting when the horse slows and navigates an obstacle. For other horse racing events, where the horse is going flat out, you need a faster shutter speed. If you want to capture a sequence of images as horse and rider negotiate obstacles, choose Continuous Drive mode. The ISO setting you choose will be dictated by the amount of light and the aperture the camera dials in. Because the horse and rider are your main subjects, you can get a good, crisp photo with an f/stop of f/5.6. Use Continuous Auto-Focus mode and the camera updates focus as the horse and rider move through the frame. Image stabilization is a plus because it ensures a sharp image if your arms get tired and your hand isn't as steady as it was at the start of the event. If you don't have image stabilization, and the light gets dim, you'll have to increase the ISO.

Taking the picture

To create a compelling photo of a horse and rider at a horse race, your focus has to be spot on. You want to set up the shot before you take it. This involves a bit of thought and anticipation on your part. It's a good idea to watch a couple of racers negotiate the course before you take a picture.

1. **Move to an unobstructed vantage point and enable the camera settings discussed previously in this chapter.**

   Choose a vantage point where there's a lot of action, such as a place where the racers are jumping a hurdle or negotiating a barrel. (See Figure A-4.)

Figure A-4: Photographing horse and rider as they approach an obstacle.

2. **Adjust the ISO setting until you have an f/stop of f/5.6 or smaller (meaning a larger f/stop number).**

   If you're shooting in overcast conditions, or at a night race, you may have to use a very high ISO setting. This adds the risk of noise to the equation, but it's better than not getting the shot.

3. **Aim the camera at the horse and rider as they race toward the place where you're going to take the picture.**

   The camera updates focus as the team moves toward or away from you. If the horse and rider are parallel to you, you'll have to pan. The alternative is to prefocus on a horse and rider that negotiate the obstacle before the subjects you want to photograph get there.

4. **Zoom to the desired focal length.**

   Leave some room in front of the racers to give viewers the impression that horse and rider are going somewhere.

5. **Press the shutter button halfway to achieve focus.**

6. Press the shutter button fully to take the picture.

If you're photographing in Continuous Drive mode, release the shutter button to stop taking pictures. Review the images on your LCD monitor to make sure the image is properly exposed and that your subjects are in focus.

If you're photographing on an overcast afternoon, or at night, switch to a slow shutter speed of 1/6 or 1/15 of a second. Pan with the horse and rider to capture an artistic impression of speed, as shown in Figure A-5.

Figure A-5: Use a slow shutter speed to capture an artistic impression of speed.

Troubleshooting

- ✔ **The largest f/stop number is blinking.** This happens when you switch to a slow shutter speed in bright light. There's too much light to properly expose the image. Switch to your lowest ISO setting. If this doesn't solve the problem, place a neutral density filter over the lens.

- ✔ **The horse and rider are not in focus.** Make sure the camera is in Continuous Auto-Focus mode. If it is, make sure the autofocus point is over the horse and rider when you press the shutter button to achieve focus.

✔ **The horse is in focus, but the rider isn't.** This happens in low light conditions. The camera chooses a large aperture to accommodate for the low light, which gives you a limited depth of field. The first cure is to increase the ISO setting until you get an f/stop of f/5.6 or larger (smaller aperture). The other alternative is to position the single autofocus point over the rider. Many cameras give you the option of moving a single autofocus point to a different part of the viewfinder other than dead center.

Capturing a City Skyline

Every city has a unique skyline composed of landmark buildings that form a shape anyone who has visited the city can readily identify. Big cities such as New York City have skylines that are indelibly etched into the memory even of people who have never been there. If you live in or visit a city that has an interesting skyline, you can capture some wonderful pictures by using the settings in this section.

Setting the camera

When you photograph a skyline, you want to capture every subtle detail. Therefore, use Aperture Priority mode and a fairly small aperture because these settings give you a large depth of field, especially when you use a wide-angle focal length. The suggested focal-length range lets you either capture a wide expanse of the skyline or zoom in to photograph a single landmark building. The suggested ISO range lets you capture photos in bright sunlight or bright overcast conditions. If you photograph a skyline at dusk or during a dark day, you have to increase the ISO setting or use a tripod.

Taking the picture

Some photographers get in too much of a hurry when they take a picture. When you want to photograph a city skyline, you may be tempted to take a photograph from the first vantage point that shows the entire skyline. But if everyone else photographs the skyline from the same vantage point, people viewing the photo may think it's nice, but they don't spend much time looking at the image. If you slow down and photograph the skyline from several different and perhaps unique vantage points, you end up with a few images that stand out as different from everybody else's.

1. **Drive to the area from which you want to photograph the skyline.**

   You can see a lot more and locate interesting points from which to photograph the skyline if you're a passenger, rather than the driver.

2. **Enable the settings discussed previously in this chapter.**

3. **Find an interesting vantage point from which to photograph the skyline and then press the shutter button halfway to achieve focus.**

4. **Compose the image and, if necessary, zoom in to crop out extraneous details.**

Figure A-6: Rotate the camera 90 degrees to photograph tall buildings from the skyline.

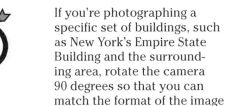

   If you're photographing a specific set of buildings, such as New York's Empire State Building and the surrounding area, rotate the camera 90 degrees so that you can match the format of the image to the shape of the building, like I've done here with the Bank of America building in Tampa, Florida (see Figure A-6). Notice how the bridge and reflections lead your eye to the building.

5. **To take the picture, fully press the shutter button.**

To create a unique photo of a landmark building in a city skyline, travel to a neighborhood that's readily identifiable to people who know the city and explore until you find a unique vantage point. Wait until one of the locals walks into the scene and take the picture (see Figure A-7).

Troubleshooting

⮕ **The buildings aren't level in the photo.** When you photograph a city skyline, you may not have a horizon for reference and therefore end up with an image that's off kilter. Take the picture again and pay attention to the vertical lines in the center of the image: Make sure they go straight up and down, and aren't slanted.

⮕ **The buildings appear distorted in the photograph.** You run into this problem if you photograph the scene with a wide-angle lens from up close. Back up a little bit and take the picture again.

⮕ **The buildings appear to be falling over in the picture.** This problem happens when you're close to the buildings and tip the camera up to get everything in the frame. Back up until you can get everything in the frame without tilting the camera.

Figure A-7: Photographing a landmark building from a unique vista.

Photographing Landscapes

*W*hen you create images with your EOS 7D Mark II, the robust features this camera offers stacks the odds in your favor. You're shooting with a camera that many pros use on a daily basis. However, professional photographers benefit from years of shooting experience, and they instinctively know which settings to use as a starting point to create great images of a specific subject matter. I've always been interested in landscape photography, and over the years, I've learned which settings to use to create compelling images of the landscapes I visit. In this appendix, I show you the camera settings I use when photographing landscapes, mountains, sunsets at the beach, and reflections in still water. I also show you a tried and true method for taking the picture, because contrary to popular belief, you can't create great images by just pointing and shooting. In addition to showing you settings and steps I use to take each picture, I also offer some troubleshooting tips in case the image you see on the LCD monitor doesn't live up to your expectations.

Even if you have no interest in photographing landscapes, this appendix will give you an insight into the thought process involved when creating any photograph. Analyze the subject matter you most love to photograph, use this appendix to guide your thought process, and you'll come up with settings that will be the basis for some wonderful images.

Photographing Grand Vistas

No matter where you live, you can find lovely landscapes, usually within a few miles of your home. Landscape photography done right is stunning. It captures the mystery and grandeur of the place where you took the picture (see Figure B-1). When you photograph a landscape, your vantage point and the way you compose the photograph go a long way toward creating something that's a work of art and not just a snapshot. You want to draw viewers into the picture so that they take more than just a casual glance.

When you photograph a vast landscape, you photograph the big picture; a wide sweeping brushstroke that captures the beauty of the area. So, you want every subtle detail to be in focus, which means you want a huge depth of field. In addition to a large depth of field, composition also plays a key role when you photograph a landscape. Notice the placement of the tree in Figure B-1. The picture would not be as interesting if the tree was in the middle of the image.

Figure B-1: Photographing a landscape.

Setting the camera

The following list shows the settings you use to photograph grand vistas in places like the Grand Canyon, Yosemite, or for that matter, a state park close to your home.

- ✔ **Metering Mode:** Evaluative
- ✔ **Drive Mode:** One Shot
- ✔ **Shooting Mode:** Aperture Priority
- ✔ **Aperture:** f/11 to f/16
- ✔ **ISO Setting:** 100 to 200
- ✔ **Focus Mode:** One Shot
- ✔ **Autofocus Point:** Single autofocus point
- ✔ **Focal Length:** 24mm to 35mm
- ✔ **Image Stabilization:** If the lens you are using has this option, enable it — especially if the shutter speed dips below 1/30 of a second.

When you photograph a beautiful landscape, you want to see every detail, which is why you use Aperture Priority shooting mode and a small aperture. A wide-angle focal length lets you capture the majesty of the landscape in your photograph, and a low ISO setting gives you a noise-free image. However, if you're photographing landscapes on overcast days, you may have to increase the ISO setting to maintain a shutter speed of 1/30 of a second. If you don't want to increase the ISO setting, use image stabilization if your camera or lens has this feature, or mount your camera on a tripod.

Being a great landscape photographer requires practice and a bit of study. Shoot landscapes whenever you have the opportunity and study the work of master landscape photographers, such as Ansel Adams, Clyde Butcher, and David Muench. Studying the work of the masters can help give you an eye for landscape photography and, after much practice, develop your own unique style. Do an Internet search for the above photographers to see samples of their eye-popping work.

Taking the picture

You can photograph a landscape whenever you see one that piques your interest. However, whether you're photographing landscapes on vacation or at home, try to set aside a block of time in which to photograph landscapes. Travel to your favorite area, or spice things up and travel to a place you've never visited before. Then, you just need to embark on your quest to capture the perfect photograph of the area you're in.

1. **Enable the camera settings outlined in "Setting the camera" earlier in this section.**

2. **When you find an area that you want to photograph, find the ideal vantage point.**

Don't place the horizon line in the middle of the picture. Place the horizon line in the upper third of the image when the most important part of the landscape you're photographing dominates the bottom of the scene, such as when you're photographing sand dunes in the desert. Place the horizon line in the lower third of the image when the most important part of the landscape dominates the upper part of the scene you're photographing, such as when you're photographing a mountain range.

3. **Press the shutter button halfway to achieve focus, and then compose the image.**

   If you're photographing with a zoom lens, zoom out until you see something you like in the viewfinder.

4. **Take the picture.**

To get the best shot possible, keep these points in mind:

✔ When you find an interesting element in the landscape, such as a photogenic rock or dead branch, move close to the object and then move around it until you see an interesting composition in your viewfinder (see Figure B-2).

Figure B-2: Use an interesting landscape element to create an interesting picture.

- ✏ Many landscape photographers have tunnel vision and look straight ahead. Notice what's both above and below you. You may find an interesting photograph hiding there.

- ✏ Some people litter everywhere. Before taking your picture, take a good look at the area you have framed in the viewfinder to make sure there isn't any litter, such as empty soda cans or candy wrappers, that can ruin an otherwise great image.

- ✏ The best time to take great landscape pictures is early in the morning, just after the sun rises, or late in the afternoon, when the light is pleasing. The first hour and the last hour of daylight are known as the *Golden Hours*, times when you have great light for photographing landscapes, because the light accentuates forms such as rocks and trees.

Barren landscapes can be saved with dramatic clouds. If you live near a place that's beautiful but stark, visit it when there are some moody clouds or thunderheads in the distance. Make this the focal point of your photograph by placing the horizon line in the lower part of the image (see Figure B-3).

Figure B-3: Barren landscape and brooding clouds equals a compelling photograph.

Troubleshooting

✓ **The foreground is too busy.** If the picture has details such as twigs, vines, or branches that detract from the overall picture, move to a slightly different vantage point to remove the offending details from the image.

✓ **The background doesn't seem sharp.** When you're photographing a huge landscape that goes on for miles and miles, atmospheric haze can cause distant details to look soft. If you encounter this problem, consider purchasing a UV filter for your lens.

If your lenses have different accessory thread sizes, purchase filters for the largest-diameter lens you own, and then purchase a step-up ring for the smaller-diameter lenses. For example, if your biggest lens accepts 77mm filters and you also own a lens that accepts 58mm filters, buy a 58–77mm step-up ring, which is much cheaper than the cost of another filter.

✓ **There are telephone lines and houses in the picture.** Sometimes, you can't avoid getting a bit of civilization in your nature photos, but at other times, you can change your vantage point slightly to remove the offending elements from the picture. Alternatively, change your vantage point until a tree or other landscape element hides the objects.

✔ **The sky is boring.** If the scene you're photographing would benefit from a few clouds, patiently wait a few minutes for some clouds to drift into the scene. Alternatively, you can come back to the area on a different day or time, when atmospheric conditions are more conducive to a picture-perfect sky.

Photographing Mountains

If you live or vacation near a mountain range, you have a rich vein to tap for incredible photographs. Mountain ranges are like humans; they have their own distinct personalities. The Smoky Mountains are gently undulating, draped in evergreens, and often shrouded in mist. The Rockies and the California High Sierras (see Figure B-4) are macho mountains with jagged granite outcroppings that have sparse vegetation sprouting from bare rock when you venture above timberline. (The fragile vegetation at these altitudes are similar to what you find in the Arctic Tundra, yet somehow survive against all odds.)

Figure B-4: Photographing majestic mountains.

Many mountains are in state parks and readily accessible from your car, yet some mountains make you work a bit harder, requiring you to hike steep terrain to get to the best vantage points. When you arrive at a great mountain vista, you need only the right settings and the right equipment to capture a great photo that will be the envy of friends and family who think they're photographers.

Setting the camera

The following list shows the settings you use when you photograph mountain ranges in places like the Rocky Mountains, the Smoky Mountains, or any mountain range you care to photograph.

- **Metering Mode:** Evaluative
- **Drive Mode:** Single Shot
- **Shooting Mode:** Aperture Priority
- **Aperture:** f/16
- **ISO Setting:** 100 or the lowest setting that yields a shutter speed of 1/30 of a second or faster
- **Focus Mode:** Single Shot
- **Autofocus Point:** Multiple autofocus points
- **Focal Length:** 28mm or wider
- **Image Stabilization (Optional):** If you're shooting in low-light conditions and the shutter speed is faster than 1/30 of a second.

When you photograph a mountain, you want to capture the wide majestic view and give your viewers a scene of the grandeur of the scene. So, you need to use a wide-angle focal length, such as 28mm or wider. This type of photography also cries for a depth of field that goes from the foreground clear into the next county. You want to see every subtle nuance of a mountain landscape, which is why you use an aperture of f/16 coupled with a wide-angle focal length to get a huge depth of field. Multiple autofocus points are ideal for this type of photography. Just make sure that no autofocus points illuminate over foreground objects, such as a twig. A low ISO setting is also ideal. However, if you're photographing in overcast conditions, you may have to increase the ISO setting. Alternatively, instead of increasing the ISO setting, you can mount the camera on a tripod.

Don't use image stabilization if you mount the camera on a tripod, because this may lead to unpredictable results when image stabilization attempts to compensate for operator movement that isn't present.

Taking the picture

If you're a seasoned mountain goat, you can hike to just about any good vantage point. If you're a city slicker vacationing in the mountains, you have the odds stacked against you and may need to rely on roadside vantage points or hikes that you're physically able to take. Ask park rangers or locals where the best vantage points are or buy a guide prior to your vacation. When you find a great vantage point, bring the viewfinder to your eye and digitally capture the magic of the majestic scene before you; just follow these steps:

1. **Enable the camera settings discussed in "Setting the camera" earlier in this section.**

   To become a better photographer of mountain landscapes, study the work of master landscape photographers, such as Ansel Adams and David Muench.

2. **Find a suitable vantage point from which to photograph the picture.**

   Look for objects to draw your viewer into the picture. You can also frame the mountain range by positioning the camera so a branch from a nearby tree appears at the edge of the image.

3. **Compose the picture, and then press the shutter button halfway to achieve focus.**

   You can take great pictures of mountains from low vantage points with the mountain range towering above you or from high vantage points to show the jagged details of the mountains that seem to go on forever (see Figure B-5).

   When you photograph a mountain from ground level, place the horizon line in the lower third of the picture. This compositional trick draws the viewers' attention to the mountains and clearly establishes the focal point of the photograph. This also gives you a much more compelling image than you'd get with the horizon line smack dab in the middle of the image.

4. **Take the picture.**

Great mountain scenes need great light. When the sun's shining, you can get your best shots when you photograph mountains early in the morning or late in the afternoon. If at all possible, try not to photograph mountains in the middle of the day, when the light is harsh and unflattering.

Figure B-5: Find an interesting vantage point.

Look for interesting objects in the mountains, such as this old Jeffrey pine that Ansel Adams photographed in the 1940s when it was still alive (see Figure B-6). Objects such as this pine provide the focal point of your scene, but you can also use them to frame other parts of the scene, such as a distant ridge of mountains.

Troubleshooting

- ✓ **The mountains look flat and uninteresting.** This problem occurs if you take a picture when the sun is directly overhead. Photograph mountains in the early morning or late afternoon, when the low angle of the sun produces shadows that add depth to and model the mountains. The light is also a wonderful golden hue.

- ✓ **The foreground is busy.** Small objects littering the foreground, such as fallen leaves or pebbles, can create distraction. Often, you can cure this problem just by moving a few feet to a similar vantage point that has subtle foreground details, such as flowing grass, that enhance the picture. Alternatively, you can do a bit of landscape maintenance and re-arrange the elements to be more aesthetically pleasing. But if you do move things around, please be mindful of the environment. And if the details you want to remove are trash, place them in a trash receptacle rather than moving them to another spot.

Figure B-6: Using objects to capture your viewer's attention.

Photographing Beach Sunsets

Sunset is a wonderful time for photographers. The hour before sunset is known as the *Golden Hour*. The sun is low and diffused by the atmosphere. Clouds are bathed in wonderful hues of orange, pink, and purple. Add a sandy beach, ocean waves, and someone walking on the sand or in the water, and you have the recipe for a wonderful photograph (see Figure B-7).

Setting the camera

To create a great photograph of a sunset at your favorite beach, use the following settings:

- **Metering Mode:** Evaluative
- **Drive Mode:** One Shot
- **Shooting Mode:** Aperture Priority
- **Aperture:** f/8 or smaller
- **ISO Setting:** The lowest ISO setting that enables you to achieve a shutter speed that's the reciprocal of the focal length you're using
- **Focus Mode:** Single Shot
- **Autofocus Point:** Single autofocus point
- **Focal Length:** 28mm to 35mm
- **Image Stabilization:** Enable this feature if your camera or lens has it.

Figure B-7: Photographing a beach at sunset.

When you photograph a beach at sunset, you want everything in focus, from the vegetation in the sand dunes to the distant clouds, which is what you get when you shoot in Aperture Priority mode with a small aperture of f/8 or smaller (a larger f/stop number). A low ISO setting ensures that you get a sharp image that has little or no digital noise. The Single Shot focus mode is perfect because landscapes don't move. When the camera achieves focus, you're ready to shoot the picture. The wide-angle focal length range provides you with a wide view that captures the clouds and landscape with a nice reflection of the sun on the water.

While the sun sinks and eventually drops below the horizon, the amount of available light changes. Therefore, you need to increase the ISO setting to keep the aperture at f/8 or smaller. The alternative is to place your camera on a tripod.

Taking the picture

The trick to getting a good sunset picture at the beach is having some interesting clouds in the sky. If you're vacationing or live near the beach, look toward the ocean 45 minutes before sunset. If you see some nice clouds, grab your camera and high tail it to the beach.

You can use a bit of science to pinpoint the direction from which the sun will rise and where it will set on any given day of the year by using a software application called the Photographer's Ephemeris (http://photoephemeris.com). As of this writing, the application is free for a PC or Macintosh desktop computer. You can also purchase the application for your iPad, iPod, iPhone or Android. With the application, you enter the day and the name of the place where you plan to shoot, or its longitude and latitude, to find out the direction from which the sun rises and the direction in which the sun sets.

After determining the precise details of where and when the sun will set, you're ready to follow these steps:

1. **Arrive at the beach about 20 minutes before sunset, find a suitable vantage point, and enable the camera settings discussed in "Setting the camera" earlier in this section.**

2. **Start taking some pictures when the sun reflects on the bottom of the clouds and bathes them with a golden hue.**

3. **Move around and compose pictures with interesting objects between you and the sun.**

   Beach vegetation and people walking on the beach add interest to your image.

If you photograph beaches in sub-tropical or tropical paradises, be careful where you step. Small rattlesnakes often hang around vegetation such as sea oats.

Many photographers pack up their gear as soon as the sun goes down. If a lot of clouds are in the sky that don't go all the way to the horizon, wait 10 or 15 minutes. While the sun sinks lower, it still casts light on the clouds, and they turn giddy shades of orange, purple, and blue (see Figure B-8).

Troubleshooting

- **The picture is brighter than the scene.** Cameras have a tendency to slightly overexpose scenes such as sunsets. Dial in enough exposure compensation until the picture you get matches the scene in front of you.

- **The sun is an orange blob.** Digital cameras can't record the brightness range in a scene like a sunset. If the sun is *blown out* (over-exposed, with no detail), use exposure compensation to reduce the exposure or compose the picture so that the sun is behind some vegetation or a tall tree.

Figure B-8: Photograph the scene 15 or 20 minutes after the sun sets.

⊯ **The ocean is too dark.** Cameras can't record the same dynamic range of brightness that our eyes can see. Therefore, the exposure is often a compromise; you get a properly exposed sky but a dark ocean. If you like to photograph sunsets, consider investing in a graduated neutral density filter, which darkens the sky without affecting the rest of the picture.

Singh-Ray makes an excellent reverse-graduated neutral density filter that's perfect for photographing sunsets (www.singh-ray.com/ reversegrads.html). The gradient is darkest at the horizon, which is where the sun will be when it sets.

Photographing Reflections in Still Water

If you live near a large body of water, you know it has a temperament, just like you. Sometimes it's turbulent, other times it's fairly calm, and sometimes (when no wind is blowing) the water is flat with absolutely no ripples. When you're near calm water, you can capture some wonderful images with the water reflecting the clouds, boats, and any objects that are nearby (see Figure B-9).

Figure B-9: Reflections of the day.

Like any other type of photography, you can find good times and bad times to take pictures of calm water. The best times to capture these types of images are early in the morning or late in the afternoon, when the sun is low on the horizon and the light has a wonderful golden hue.

Setting the camera

When you see a body of still or almost calm water with wonderful reflections, use the following camera settings:

- **Metering Mode:** Evaluative
- **Drive Mode:** Single Shot
- **Shooting Mode:** Aperture Priority
- **Aperture:** f/16 or smaller (larger f/stop number)
- **ISO Setting:** The lowest ISO setting that allows you to achieve a shutter speed of about 1/50 of a second or faster
- **Focus Mode:** One Shot

✓ **Autofocus Point:** Single autofocus point

✓ **Focal Length:** 28mm to 35mm

✓ **Image Stabilization:** Enable image stabilization if it's available on your lens or camera, unless you're using a tripod.

This type of photography begs for a huge depth of field. When you have a scene that includes wonderful reflections, you want the objects that are reflecting on the water to be in sharp focus, as well as the water itself, which is why you choose Aperture Priority mode with a small aperture. A wide-angle focal length lets you capture the big picture. If you have one with you, a tripod ensures that you can keep the camera rock steady and produce a blur-free picture. If you don't have a tripod, steady hands and a relatively fast shutter speed can yield a crystal-clear image.

The slowest shutter speed at which you can hand-hold the camera is the reciprocal of the 35mm equivalent of the focal length you're using to take the picture.

Taking the picture

When you want to capture an image that includes great reflections on still water, you have to be a little spontaneous and, at the same time, do a bit of planning. You can't get flattering light in the middle of the afternoon. Therefore, plan your photo shoot for early morning or late afternoon. Also, find out the direction from which the sun is shining. If you try to shoot directly into the sun, the reflections and the water look dark in the photo. You get the best pictures of reflections when the sun is shining at the objects casting the reflections.

1. **Find a good vantage point, compose your image, and enable the settings discussed in "Setting the camera" earlier in this section.**

   When you take this type of photograph, the reflections are the main focus of your image. Therefore, place the horizon line near the upper third of the image (see Figure B-10).

   You can wait until a gentle breeze kicks up. The breeze causes small ripples on the water, which result in painterly reflections.

2. **Press the shutter button halfway to achieve focus.**

3. **Press the shutter button fully to take the picture.**

Figure B-10: Place the horizon line in the upper third of the image.

You can get compelling images of reflections from common objects such as mirrors and store windows. When you see a reflection that you find worthy of a photo, move around until you can see part of the reflection and part of what's behind the window (see Figure B-11) and take a picture.

Troubleshooting

☞ **The reflection is dark.** This problem can occur when you photograph a scene that has a dynamic range that your camera can't capture, such as when the sun is in the image, along with deep shadows. Change your composition so that the sun is hidden behind a building or a tree. Alternatively, you can change your vantage point until the scene doesn't have a huge dynamic range from dark areas to bright areas.

☞ **The reflection doesn't have vibrant color.** You may have this problem when you're shooting in harsh light, such as mid-afternoon sun. You can also experience it when you have a lot of cloud cover in your scene. If you capture an image that has a dull reflection, you can only wait until the lighting conditions change or return at a different time.

✏ **The entire image is too bright or too dark.** Digital camera metering systems do their best to give you a properly exposed image. If the image is too bright, use exposure compensation to decrease the exposure by 1/3 or 1/2 a stop. If the image is too dark, use exposure compensation to increase the exposure by 1/3 or 1/2 a stop.

Figure B-11: Capture reflections from a store window.

Index

• Numerics •

29.97P video, 108
59.94P video, 108
500PX, 213

• A •

A+. *See* Full Auto mode
abstract images, 256–258
Access lamp, 12
accessories
  Canon, 41–42
  third-party, 42–44
  video, 44–45
action, photographing
  fast-moving objects, 188–190
  freezing motion, 190–193
  horse racing
    setting up camera, 267
    taking pictures, 267–268
    troubleshooting, 269–270
  setting up camera, 261–262
  slow-moving objects, 193–194
  sporting events, 262–263
  troubleshooting, 264
Adams, Ansel, 213
Additive multiple exposure option, 247
Adobe RGB color space, 163
Adorama, 45
AE Lock
  button for, 10
  in viewfinder, 20
AEB (automatic exposure bracketing),
    17, 136
AEB in Progress, 20
AF Area Selection switch, 11
AF Point Selection button, 10
AF Status indicator, 20
AF tab, 50

AF-On button, 10
Al Focus autofocus mode, 155, 201
Al Servo autofocus mode, 155, 191, 193, 205
ALL-1 compression, 108
Ambient Light sensor, 12
animals, photographing
  birds, 205–207
  horse racing
    setting up camera, 267
    taking pictures, 267–268
    troubleshooting, 269–270
  overview, 264
  pets, 198–199
  setting up camera, 265
  at state parks, 201–203
  troubleshooting, 266
  wild, 264–266
  at zoo, 205
aperture
  camera modes and, 56
  creativity and, 208
  defined, 55, 122
  displaying shooting information, 106
  Full Auto mode and, 105
  Handy Pad and, 112
  on LCD monitor, 16
  photographing animals, 202, 264
  photographing birds, 206
  photographing city skylines, 270
  photographing landscapes, 273
  photographing people and pets, 198
  photographing sporting events, 261
  selective focus, 200
  setting for sensor cleaning, 37
  using Quick Control Screen, 90
  in viewfinder, 21
Aperture Priority mode
  changing flash-sync speed, 175–176
  defined, 56
  depth-of-field controls, 125–126

Aperture Priority mode *(continued)*
  depth-of-field preview, 96, 126–128
  macro photography, 201
  overview, 121
  photographing animals, 205
  photographing birds, 206
  photographing landscapes, 195
  photographing people and pets, 198
  recording video, 105
  selecting Drive mode for, 138–139
  selective focus, 200
  using effectively, 124–125
  using Handy Pad, 112
Art Bold effect option, 244
Art Embossed effect option, 244
Art Standard effect option, 243
Art Vivid effect option, 243
aspect ratio, 102, 103–104
audio recording options, 110–111
author name, 224–225
Auto brightness, 82
Auto Lighting Optimizer, 18, 149–150
auto mode
  available options in, 48
  comparison of modes, 56
  defined, 56
  focus
    manual, 58
    off-center objects, 57
  Full Auto mode, 48
  Handy Pad and, 112
  image information and, 76
  metering mode for, 151
  metering overview, 121
  Programmed Auto Exposure mode, 48–49
  recording video in, 105
  red-eye reduction in, 59–61
  taking pictures, 52–54
  triggering shutter remotely, 62–63
  using built-in flash, 173–175
  using Self-Timer, 61–62
Auto picture style, 160
auto power-off time, 29–30
Auto reset file-numbering method, 74
Auto switch card recording function, 119
auto white balance (AWB), 164, 168

autofocus
  best practices, 158–159
  capturing fast-moving objects, 189
  changing mode in Quick Control menu,
    100–101
  continuous, 265
  disabling beep from, 241
  displaying shooting information, 106
  freezing action, 191
  on LCD monitor, 18
  locking focus, 137–138
  metering modes, 151–152
  modes for, 154–155
  overview, 58
  Programmed Auto Exposure mode
    and, 123
  setting, 53
  slow-moving objects, 193
  using Live View, 98–100
  in viewfinder, 19
autofocus points
  modes for, 155–156, 158–159
  overview, 53–54
  photographing animals, 202
  photographing birds, 205
  photographing people and pets, 198
  selecting single point, 156–157
  selective focus, 200
  using Live View, 97
  zone autofocus, 157–158
automatic exposure bracketing (AEB),
    17, 136
auxiliary flash, 178
Av mode. *See* Aperture Priority mode
Average multiple exposure option, 248
AWB (auto white balance), 164, 168

B&H Photo, 44
backgrounds, 198
battery
  accessories for, 41
  auto power-off time and, 30
  camera bags and, 15
  caring for, 34

charging, 34–35
displaying shooting information, 106
GPS and, 26, 240–241
Live View and, 97
status on LCD monitor, 18
in viewfinder, 20
viewing information about, 147–148
beanbags, 256
BGE 16 battery grip, 41
birds, photographing, 205–207
Black Rapid, 42
Blurb, Photoshop Lightroom, 259
body cap, 13, 24
Book module, Photoshop Lightroom, 259
bracketing exposure, 134–136
bracketing white balance, 170–171
Bright multiple exposure option, 248
brightness
    Auto Lighting Optimizer, 149–150
    displaying image information, 76
    exposure and, 122
    Highlight Tone Priority, 145
    LCD monitor, 81–83
    reading histogram, 77
buildings, photographing
    setting up camera, 270
    taking pictures, 270–271
    troubleshooting, 272
bulb blowers, 37–38
Bulb mode
    depth-of-field preview, 96
    Long Exposure Noise Reduction, 142–143
    overview, 122
    using effectively, 131–133
Bulb Timer
    on LCD monitor, 18
    time exposures using, 252–254
Butcher, Clyde, 213, 267
buttons
    AE Lock, 10
    AF Area Selection switch, 11
    AF Point Selection, 10
    AF-On, 10
    Comparative Playback, 13
    Creative Photo, 13
    customizing behavior of, 233–235

Depth-of-Field Preview, 13
Drive/AF, 9
Erase, 13
Flash, 14
Flash Exposure Compensation, 9
Index/Magnify/Reduce, 13
Info, 13
ISO Speed Setting, 9
LCD Panel Illumination button, 9
Lens-Release, 14
Live View switch, 10
Menu, 13
Metering Mode, 10
Mode Dial Lock Release, 10
Movie Shooting switch, 10
Multi-Controller, 11
Multi-Function, 8–9
Playback, 13
Power switch, 12
Quick Control, 12
Rate, 13, 255
Set, 12
Shutter, 8
Start/Stop, 10
White Balance, 10

cable protector socket, 27
camera bags, 15, 42–43
Camera menu
    accessing, 48–49
    icons in, 52
    tabs in, 50–51
car battery charger, 41
CarrySpeed, 42
Cartier-Bresson, Henri, 213
cases, 42
center of interest, 214–215
Center-Weighted Average metering mode,
        151–152
CF (CompactFlash) cards
    defined, 30
    formatting, 32–33
    updating firmware using, 230
C.FN tab, 51

chimping, 90
city skylines, photographing
  setting up camera, 270
  taking pictures, 270–271
  troubleshooting, 272
cleaning
  camera body, 45
  lenses, 44
  sensor
    equipment for, 39
    manually, 37–40
    prompting automatic, 36–37
clouds, 269, 270
Cloudy white balance mode, 164
cold climates, 34
color channels, 76
color noise, 172
color spaces, 162–163
color temperature, 165–166
colorcast, 164
CompactFlash cards. _See_ CF cards
Comparative Playback button, 13
compass, 240
compensation
  exposure, 18, 133–134
  flash, 9, 18, 179
  white balance, 168–170
composing images, 208–210
Continuous file-numbering method, 74
Continuous mode
  freezing action, 192
  HDR sets, 244
  Hi Speed Continuous Shooting mode, 138
  image formats and file sizes, 69
  Low Speed Continuous Shooting
    mode, 138
  maximum burst for, 21
  Silent Continuous Shooting mode, 139
contrast, 227
controls
  AE Lock button, 10
  AF Area Selection switch, 11
  AF Point Selection button, 10
  AF-On button, 10
  Comparative Playback button, 13

connections, 26–27
Creative Photo button, 13
Depth-of-Field Preview button, 13
Dioptric Adjustment knob, 12
Drive/AF button, 9
Erase button, 13
Flash button, 14
Flash Exposure Compensation button, 9
Handy Pad, 12
Hot shoe, 10
Index/Magnify/Reduce button, 13
Info button, 13
ISO Speed Setting button, 9
LCD Panel Illumination button, 9
Lens-Release button, 14
Live View switch, 10
Main dial, 9
Menu button, 13
Metering Mode button, 10
Mode dial, 10
Movie Shooting switch, 10
Multi-Controller button, 11
Multi-Function button, 8–9
multi-function lock, 15–16
Playback button, 13
Power switch, 12
Quick Control button, 12
Quick Control dial, 12
Quick Control Lock switch, 12
Rate button, 13
Set button, 12
Shutter button, 8
Start/Stop button, 10
White Balance button, 10
copyright information, 222–224
creative shooting modes
  Aperture Priority mode
    changing flash-sync speed, 175–176
    defined, 56
    depth-of-field controls, 125–126
    depth-of-field preview, 96, 126–128
    macro photography, 201
    overview, 121
    photographing animals, 205
    photographing birds, 206

photographing landscapes, 195
photographing people and pets, 198
recording video, 105
selecting Drive mode for, 138–139
selective focus, 200
using effectively, 124–125
using Handy Pad, 112
Bulb mode
  depth-of-field preview, 96
  Long Exposure Noise Reduction, 142–143
  overview, 122
  using effectively, 131–133
button for, 13
defined, 56
Manual mode
  depth-of-field preview, 96
  overview, 122
  recording video, 105
  selecting Drive mode for, 138–139
  using effectively, 130–131
  using Handy Pad, 112
picture styles, 160–162
Programmed Auto Exposure mode
  Camera menu in, 48–49
  depth-of-field preview, 96
  overview, 121
  selecting Drive mode for, 138–139
  using effectively, 123–124
Shutter Priority mode
  capturing fast-moving objects, 189
  defined, 56
  depth-of-field preview, 96
  freezing action, 191
  horse racing, 267
  overview, 122
  photographing animals, 202
  photographing birds, 205
  recording video, 105
  selecting Drive mode for, 138–139
  slow-moving objects, 193
  using effectively, 128–129
  using Handy Pad, 112
creativity
 abstract images, 256–258
 always carrying camera, 213–214
being in moment, 211
developing, 207–208
Interval Timer, 250–252
multiple exposures, 246–250
picture styles, 226–228
practice, 211–212
studying photography, 212–213
waiting for light, 214
cropping information, 103–104
curves, 209
Custom Controls menu, 234
custom functions
 clearing, 141–142
 overview, 140–141
custom menu, 219–222
custom white balance, 166–168

dark conditions, 149–150
Dark multiple exposure option, 248
data recovery, 31
date and time, 28–29
Daylight Savings option, 28
Daylight white balance mode, 164
DC coupler, 13
deleting images
 overview, 83–87
 protecting images from deletion, 88–89
depth-of-field
 Aperture Priority mode
  controls for, 125–126
  previewing, 126–128
 button for, 13
 overview, 55
 photographing city skylines, 270
 photographing sunsets, 196
 using Live View, 96
Develop module, Photoshop
  Lightroom, 259
digital compass, 240
Digital terminal, 27
dimensions, video, 107–109
Dioptric Adjustment knob, 12, 22
distracting elements, 216

Drive mode
  button for, 9
  on LCD monitor, 18
  selecting, 138–139
  in viewfinder, 19
dual-axis level, 7, 44
duds, 75
dust, 24

• E •

EF/EF-S Index mount, 23
elevation information, 240
EOS 7D Mark II
  author name for, 224–225
  camera bags for, 15
  copyright information in, 222–224
  customizing button behavior, 233–235
  multi-function lock, 15–16
  updating firmware, 230–231
Erase button, 13
E-TTL II option, 182
Evaluative metering mode, 151–152
EXIF (Exchangeable Image File Format), 222
exposure
  bracketing, 134–136
  compensation, 18, 133–134
  displaying shooting information, 106
  elements involved in, 122
  Highlight Tone Priority, 145
  lens flicker reduction, 150–151
  locking, 136–137
  locking flash exposure, 180
  metering overview, 121
  multiple exposures, 246–250
  overview, 54–57
  Safety Shift and, 140
  simulation of, 103
  time exposures, 252–254
  using Live View, 97–98
  in viewfinder, 19, 21

• F •

Face Plus Tracking autofocus mode, 98–99
Faithful picture style, 161

fast-moving objects, 188–190
FHD (Full HD), 108
file-numbering methods, 74
Fine quality, JPEG, 69–70
firmware, updating, 230–231
flash
  accessories from Canon, 41
  auxiliary, 178
  bouncing off large surface, 199
  built-in, 173–175
  button for, 14
  changing flash-sync speed, 175–176
  compensation, 179
  Flash Exposure Compensation, 18
  locking exposure, 180
  PC port, 27
  photographing people and pets, 199
  red-eye reduction using, 59–61
  second-curtain sync, 176–177
  Speedlites
    controlling from camera, 181–183
    defined, 10
    photographing people and pets, 199
    supported models, 178
    wireless control of slaves, 183–186
    wireless support, 8, 183–186
  in viewfinder, 20–21
Flash Exposure Bracketing, 183
Flash Exposure Compensation, 9, 182
Flash white balance mode, 165
FlexiZoneAF-Multi autofocus mode, 99
FlexiZoneAF-Single autofocus mode, 99
flicker detection, 20
Flickr, 213
fluid ball head, 44
focal length, 25, 54–57
focus
  autofocus
    best practices, 158–159
    capturing fast-moving objects, 189
    changing mode in Quick Control menu, 100–101
    continuous, 265
    disabling beep from, 241
    displaying shooting information, 106
    freezing action, 191

on LCD monitor, 18
locking focus, 137–138
metering modes, 151–152
modes for, 154–155
overview, 58
Programmed Auto Exposure mode
    and, 123
setting, 53
slow-moving objects, 193
using Live View, 98–100
in viewfinder, 19
autofocus points
modes for, 155–156, 158–159
overview, 53–54
photographing animals, 202
photographing birds, 205
photographing people and pets, 198
selecting single point, 156–157
selective focus, 200
using Live View, 97
zone autofocus, 157–158
changing mode in Quick Control menu,
    100–101
locking, 137–138
macro photography, 201
manual, 58
off-center objects, 57
photographing horse racing, 267
selective, 200
switch for, 58
using Live View, 98–100
in viewfinder, 21
folders
creating, 71–72
file-numbering method, 73–74
selecting, 72–73
format, date, 28
format, image
setting, 67–68
using Quick Control Screen, 90
using two memory cards, 30
in viewfinder, 19
formatting memory cards
CF cards, 32–33
Low Level formatting, 33
SD cards, 33

frame rate, video, 107–109
freezing action, 190–193, 205
f-stop
defined, 55, 122
on LCD monitor, 16
Full Auto mode
available options in, 48
comparison of modes, 56
defined, 56
focus
    manual, 58
    off-center objects, 57
Handy Pad and, 112
image information and, 76
metering mode for, 151
metering overview, 121
Programmed Auto Exposure mode, 48–49
recording video in, 105
red-eye reduction in, 59–61
taking pictures, 52–54
triggering shutter remotely, 62–63
using built-in flash, 173–175
using Self-Timer, 61–62
Full HD (FHD), 108
full-frame sensor, 25

● *G* ●

gamut, 163
Giottos Rocket Blaster, 37–38
Global Positioning System. *See* GPS
goals
center of interest, 214–215
defining, 214
making every image perfect, 216
other objects in picture, 215–216
vantage point, 215
Golden Hour, 195
Gorman, Greg, 213
GPS (Global Positioning System)
adding information to images, 237–241
on LCD monitor, 17
location of antenna, 10
overview, 7–8
saving battery, 240–241
uses for, 26

grid
 displaying, 152–153
 in Live View, 101–102
 in viewfinder, 19

• *H* •

Handy Pad, 12, 112
HD (high-definition), 7, 104, 108
HDMI (high-definition multimedia
  interface), 27, 93
HDR (high dynamic range)
 creating images, 242–246
 on LCD monitor, 18
 tripods and, 43
headphone port, 27
help, 235
Hi Speed Continuous Shooting mode, 138
high dynamic range. *See* HDR
High ISO Speed Reduction, 143–144
high-definition (HD), 7, 104, 108
high-definition multimedia interface
  (HDMI), 27, 93
Highlight Tone Priority feature
 enabling, 145
 on LCD monitor, 18
 in viewfinder, 21
high-speed sync mode, 21
histograms
 defined, 75
 displaying, 76
 reading, 77–78
Hoodman, 45
hoods, lens, 26
horizon, 209–210
horse racing, photographing
 setting up camera, 267
 taking pictures, 267–268
 troubleshooting, 269–270
Hot shoe
 controlling Speedlite in, 181–183
 defined, 10
 level for, 44
 supported Speedlite models, 178
HTC-100 cable, 93
human tripod, 256

• *I* •

image stabilization
 lenses for, 24
 setting, 53
 tripods and, 266
 using Live View and, 96
iMovie, 108
Index/Magnify/Reduce button, 13
Info button, 13, 76
International Organization for Standards
  (ISO), 8
Interval Timer, 250–252
IPB video, 108
iPod/iPad, 214
ISO (International Organization for
  Standards), 8
ISO speed
 button for, 9
 extending range of, 172–173
 freezing action, 191
 Full Auto mode and, 105
 Handy Pad and, 112
 High ISO Speed Reduction, 143–144
 on LCD monitor, 18
 photographing animals, 202
 photographing fast-moving objects, 189
 photographing landscapes, 195
 Programmed Auto Exposure mode and, 123
 Safety Shift and, 140
 setting, 171–172
 using Quick Control Screen, 90
 in viewfinder, 21

• *J* •

JPEG format
 Auto Lighting Optimizer, 149–150
 file sizes for, 69–70
 RAW format versus, 68
 recommended usage, 70
 resolution settings for, 68
 setting, 67–68
 setting aspect ratio, 102, 103–104
 using two memory cards with, 30, 118–121

• K •

K white balance mode, 165–166

• L •

landmarks, photographing
  setting up camera, 270
  taking pictures, 270–271
  troubleshooting, 272
landscape format, 161, 209
landscapes, photographing
  composing images of, 209
  overview, 194–196, 273
  tripods and, 43
  vantage point for, 215
large depth-of-field, 55
LC-5 wireless controller, 41
LCD monitor
  brightness for, 81–83
  display information on, 16–18
  displaying grid, 101–102, 152–153
  histograms
    displaying, 76
    reading, 77–78
  Illumination button for, 9
  image information on, 76
  image review time, 81
  overview, 12–13
  previewing images
    magnifying images, 79–80
    overview, 78–79
    rotating images, 87–88
    selecting multiple images, 84–86
    viewing as slide show, 90–93
    viewing images side by side, 80
  previewing videos, 111–112
  protector for, 44
  using viewfinder versus, 21
Leibovitz, Annie, 213
lens flicker, reducing, 150–151
lenses
  attaching, 22–23
  cleaning, 44
  hoods for, 26

image stabilization, 24
  removing, 23–24
  sensor cleanliness and, 40
  zoom, 25–26
Lens-Release button, 14
level, dual-axis, 7, 44
Library module, Photoshop Lightroom, 258–259
lighting
  exposure and, 122
  flash
    accessories from Canon, 41
    auxiliary, 178
    bouncing off large surface, 199
    built-in, 173–175
    button for, 14
    changing flash-sync speed, 175–176
    compensation, 179
    Flash Exposure Compensation, 18
    locking exposure, 180
    PC port, 27
    photographing people and pets, 199
    red-eye reduction using, 59–61
    second-curtain sync, 176–177
    Speedlites, 181–186
    in viewfinder, 20–21
  reading histogram, 77
  waiting for, 214
Live View
  aspect ratio, 102, 103–104
  continuous shooting using, 103
  displaying grid, 101–102
  displaying shooting information, 97–98
  exposure simulation, 103
  focusing using, 98–100
  metering timer, 103
  overview, 96–97
  photographing people and pets, 199
  Quick Control menu in, 100–101
  switch for, 10
location
  adding GPS information, 237–241
  image metadata for, 7–8
locking exposure, 136–137
locking flash exposure, 180

locking focus, 137–138
Long Exposure Noise Reduction, 142–143
Low Level formatting, 33
Low Speed Continuous Shooting
    mode, 138
LowePro, 43
luminance noise, 172
LumiQuest, 199

● *M* ●

M mode. *See* Manual mode
macro photography, 201
Magnify button, 13
magnifying images, 79–80
Main dial, 9
Manual mode
    depth-of-field preview, 96
    overview, 122
    recording video, 105
    selecting Drive mode for, 138–139
    using effectively, 130–131
    using Handy Pad, 112
Manual reset file-numbering method, 74
Map module, Photoshop Lightroom, 259
maximum burst
    image formats and file sizes, 69
    in viewfinder, 21
memory cards
    camera bags and, 15
    data access light and, 34
    data recovery from, 31
    deleting images, 83–87
    folders
        creating, 71–72
        file-numbering method, 73–74
        selecting, 72–73
    formatting
        CF cards, 32–33
        overview, 31
        SD cards, 33
    image formats and file sizes, 69
    inserting, 30–31
    protecting images, 88–89
    for recording video, 45

    removing, 33
    rotating images, 87–88
    selecting multiple images, 84–86
    shots remaining on, 16
    slots being used, 18
    UDMA, 109, 113
    using two, 118–121
menu, custom, 219–222
Menu button, 13
metadata
    adding GPS information, 237–241
    copyright information in, 222–224
    location in, 7–8
metering
    button for, 10
    displayed in viewfinder, 19
    displayed on LCD monitor, 17
    overview, 121
    selecting mode for, 151–152
metering timer, 103
microphone, 14, 27
Mirror Lockup, 204–205
Mode dial, 10, 48
Monochrome picture style, 161
motion, freezing, 143–144
MOV format, 104
Movie Shooting switch, 10
movies. *See* videos
MP4 format, 104, 108
MRAW format
    image formats and file sizes, 69
    recommended usage, 70
Muench, David, 275
Multi-Controller button, 11
Multi-Function button, 8–9
multi-function lock, 15–16
multiple exposures, 18, 246–250
multiple images, selecting, 84–86
My Menu tab, 51

● *N* ●

Nanuk, 42
Natural effect option, 243
Neutral picture style, 161

Newman, Arnold, 213
noise reduction
  High ISO Speed Reduction, 143–144
  Long Exposure Noise Reduction,
    142–143
Normal quality, JPEG, 69–70

● *0* ●

off-center objects, 57
One-Shot autofocus mode, 154
outdoor photography, 198

● *p* ●

P mode. *See* Programmed Auto Exposure
  mode
panning video, 113
Partial metering mode, 151–152
patience, 214
patterns, 208
PC port, 27
Pelican, 42
people/pets, photographing, 198–199
photography
  of action
    fast-moving objects, 188–190
    freezing motion, 190–193
    setting up camera, 261–262
    slow-moving objects, 193–194
    sporting events, 261–263
    troubleshooting, 264
  always carrying camera, 213–214
  of animals
    overview, 264
    pets, 198–199
    setting up camera, 265
    at state parks, 201–203
    troubleshooting, 266
    wild, 264–266
    at zoo, 205
  being in moment, 211
  of birds, 205–207
  center of interest, 214–215
  of city skylines
    setting up camera, 270
    taking pictures, 270–271
    troubleshooting, 272
  composing images, 208–210
  digital, 216
  of horse racing
    setting up camera, 267
    taking pictures, 267–268
    troubleshooting, 269–270
  of landmarks
    setting up camera, 270
    taking pictures, 270–271
    troubleshooting, 272
  of landscapes
    composing images of, 209
    overview, 194–196
    tripods and, 43
    troubleshooting, 270
    vantage point for, 215
  multiple exposures, 246–250
  other objects in picture, 215–216
  of people/pets, 198–199
  practice, 211–212
  studying, 212–213
  vantage point, 215
  visualizing images, 211
  waiting for light, 214
Photo.net, 208, 213
Photoshop, 162, 216
Photoshop Lightroom, 240, 258–260
picture styles
  creating, 226–228
  selecting, 160–162
Pixel Protection Program, 89
pixels per inch (ppi), 66
Play tab, 51
Playback button, 13
portrait format, 161, 209, 256
portraits, 126
Power switch, 12
powering on/off, 29–30
PowerShot G16, 213
PowerShot S110, 213
ppi (pixels per inch), 66
practice, 211–212
Premiere Pro, 108

previewing images
  deleting images, 83–87
  depth-of-field preview, 126–128
  image review time, 81
  LCD monitor brightness, 81–83
  magnifying images, 79–80
  overview, 78–79
  protecting images, 88–89
  rotating images, 87–88
  viewing as slide show, 90–93
  viewing images side by side, 80
  viewing on TV, 93
previewing videos, 111–112
Print module, Photoshop Lightroom, 260
printing pictures, 66
Programmed Auto Exposure mode
  Camera menu in, 48–49
  depth-of-field preview, 96
  overview, 121
  selecting Drive mode for, 138–139
  using effectively, 123–124
protecting images
  overview, 88–89
  using Rate button, 255

• Q •

Quick Control button, 12
Quick Control dial, 12
Quick Control Lock switch, 12
Quick Control menu
  in Live View, 100–101
  using while recording video, 109–110
Quick Control Screen
  custom menu, 219–222
  overview, 89–90
QuickTime, 104

• R •

Rate button, 13, 255
RAW format
  aspect ratio and, 102
  file sizes for, 69–70
  JPEG format versus, 68

Photoshop Lightroom and, 258
picture styles and, 161
recommended usage, 70
setting, 67–68
uses for, 65
using two memory cards with, 30,
    118–121
recharge performance of battery, 148
recording functions using two memory
    cards, 119
recording video
  audio recording options, 110–111
  best practices, 112–113
  displaying shooting information, 106–107
  editing, 228–230
  frame rate, 107–109
  Handy Pad, 112
  overview, 105–106
  previewing videos, 111–112
  setting dimensions, 107–109
  taking picture while recording, 109
  using Quick Control menu, 109–110
red-eye reduction
  options for, 59–60
  taking pictures, 60–61
Reduce button, 13
remote control
  port for, 27
  sensor, 13
  triggering shutter, 62–63
remote switch, 41, 132, 203
resolution, image
  image size and, 66
  setting, 67–68
restoring settings, 232–233
Review Time menu, 81
rotating images, 87–88
RS-80N remote switch, 41, 203
Rule of Thirds, 210, 215

• S •

Safety Shift, 140–141
Sandisk, 45
saturation, 227

SD (Secure Digital) cards
  defined, 30
  formatting, 33
  updating firmware using, 230
second-curtain sync, 176–177
security, image, 88–89
selecting multiple images, 84–86
selective focus, 200
Self-Timer
  Interval Timer, 250–252
  on LCD monitor, 16
  stabilizing camera using, 203
  taking pictures using, 61–62
  tripods and, 256
  using Quick Control Screen, 90
sensors
  Ambient Light, 12
  cleaning camera sensor
    equipment for, 39
    maintenance, 40
    manually, 37–40
    prompting automatic, 36–37
  remote control, 13
Set button, 12
Set Up tab, 51
settings
  audio recording options, 110–111
  author name, 224–225
  auto power-off time, 29–30
  copyright information, 222–224
  creating picture styles, 226–228
  custom functions
    clearing, 141–142
    overview, 140–141
  custom menu, 219–222
  customizing button behavior, 233–235
  date and time, 28–29
  disabling autofocus beep, 241
  Drive mode, 138–139
  flash, 181–183
  format, 67–68
  grid, 152–153
  High ISO Speed Reduction, 143–144
  Highlight Tone Priority, 145
  image review time, 81
  image size and quality, 67–68

ISO speed
  extending range of, 172–173
  setting, 171–172
level, 153–154
Live View, 102–104
Long Exposure Noise Reduction, 142–143
for macro photography, 201
metering mode, 151–152
for photographing action
  fast-moving objects, 188–190
  freezing action, 190–193
  horse racing, 267–268
  photographing sporting events, 261–262
  slow-moving objects, 193–194
for photographing animals
  at state parks, 201–203
  in wild, 264
  at zoo, 205
for photographing birds, 205–207
for photographing landscapes,
    194–196
for photographing people and pets,
    198–199
Quick Control Screen, 89–90
Rate button customization, 255
registering, 231–232
restoring, 232–233
restoring default, 30
for selective focus, 200
for sunsets, 196–197
video
  dimensions, 107–109
  frame rate, 107–109
Shade white balance mode, 164
shallow depth-of-field, 126
sharpness
  for picture styles, 227
  shutter speed and, 56
Shoot tab, 50
shooting mode, 19
shoulder rigs, 44–45
Shutter button
  customizing behavior of, 233–235
  defined, 8
  focusing, 100
  taking pictures, 53–54

Shutter Priority mode
  defined, 56
  depth-of-field preview, 96
  freezing action, 191
  horse racing, 267
  overview, 122
  photographing animals, 202
  photographing birds, 205
  photographing fast-moving objects, 189
  recording video, 105
  selecting Drive mode for, 138–139
  slow-moving objects, 193
  using effectively, 128–129
  using Handy Pad, 112
shutter speed
  camera modes and, 56
  capturing fast-moving objects, 189
  defined, 54–55, 122
  displaying shooting information, 106
  Full Auto mode and, 105
  Handy Pad and, 112
  horse racing, 267
  image sharpness and, 56
  on LCD monitor, 16
  photographing animals, 202, 265
  photographing birds, 205
  photographing landscapes, 273
  photographing sporting events, 262
  in viewfinder, 21
Shutter Sync option, 182
Silent Continuous Shooting mode, 139
Silent Single Shooting mode, 139
Single Shot mode, 138
single-lens reflex (SLR), 1
size, image
  overview, 66
  recommended format usage, 70
  setting, 67–68
skin tones, 227
skylines, photographing
  setting up camera, 270
  taking pictures, 270–271
  troubleshooting, 272
slaves, Speedlites as, 183–186
slide shows
  using Photoshop Lightroom, 259

  viewing images as, 90–93
  viewing on TV, 93
slow-moving objects, 193–194
SLR (single-lens reflex), 1
small depth-of-field, 55
smartphone cameras, 213–214
sound attenuator, 111
sounds, disabling, 241
speaker, 12
Speed Freak Version 2 camera bag, 43
Speedlites
  controlling from camera, 181–183
  defined, 10
  photographing people and pets, 199
  supported models, 178
  wireless support, 8, 183–186
sporting events, photographing
  horse racing, 267–268
  overview, 261–263
  setting up camera, 261–262
  troubleshooting, 264
Spot metering mode, 152
SRAW format
  image formats and file sizes, 69
  recommended usage, 70
sRGB color space, 162, 163
stabilizing camera
  using Mirror Lockup, 204–205
  using Self-Timer, 203
Standard picture style, 160
Standard recording function, 119
Start/Stop button, 10
state parks, 201–203
straps, 42
sun exposure, 97
sunsets, 196–197

taking pictures
  abstract images, 256–258
  of action
    fast-moving objects, 188–190
    freezing, 190–193
    photographing sporting events, 261–263

setting up camera, 261–262
slow-moving objects, 193–194
troubleshooting, 264
of animals
  birds, 205–207
  overview, 264
  photographing in wild, 265–266
  setting up camera, 265
  at state parks, 201–203
  troubleshooting, 266
  at zoo, 205
Aperture Priority mode
  depth-of-field controls, 125–126
  depth-of-field preview, 126–128
  using effectively, 124–125
Auto Lighting Optimizer, 149–150
auto mode
  available options in, 48
  comparison of modes, 56
  defined, 56
  focus, 57, 58
  Full Auto mode, 48
  Handy Pad and, 112
  image information and, 76
  metering mode for, 151
  metering overview, 121
  Programmed Auto Exposure mode,
    48–49
  recording video in, 105
  red-eye reduction in, 59–61
  taking pictures, 52–54
  triggering shutter remotely, 62–63
  using built-in flash, 173–175
  using Self-Timer, 61–62
autofocus
  best practices, 158–159
  capturing fast-moving objects, 189
  changing mode in Quick Control menu,
    100–101
  continuous, 265
  disabling beep from, 241
  displaying shooting information, 106
  freezing action, 191
  on LCD monitor, 18
  locking focus, 137–138

metering modes, 151–152
modes for, 154–155
overview, 58
Programmed Auto Exposure mode and,
  123
setting, 53
slow-moving objects, 193
using Live View, 98–100
in viewfinder, 19
autofocus points
  modes for, 155–156, 158–159
  overview, 53–54
  photographing animals, 202
  photographing birds, 205
  photographing people and pets, 198
  selecting single point, 156–157
  selective focus, 200
  using Live View, 97
  zone autofocus, 157–158
best practices
  always carrying camera, 213–214
  being in moment, 211
  center of interest, 214–215
  making every image perfect, 216
  other objects in picture, 215–216
  practice, 211–212
  studying photography, 212–213
  vantage point, 215
  waiting for light, 214
of city skylines
  overview, 270
  setting up camera, 270
color spaces, 162–163
color temperature, 165–166
composing images, 208–210
creativity, 207–208
depth-of-field, 125–128
developing style, 197
Drive mode, 138–139
exposure
  bracketing, 134–136
  compensation, 18, 133–134
  displaying shooting information, 106
  elements involved in, 122
  Highlight Tone Priority, 145

taking pictures *(continued)*
  lens flicker reduction, 150–151
  locking, 136–137
  locking flash exposure, 180
  metering overview, 121
  multiple exposures, 246–250
  overview, 54–57
  Safety Shift and, 140
  simulation of, 103
  time exposures, 252–254
  using Live View, 97–98
  in viewfinder, 19, 21
flash
  auxiliary, 178
  built-in, 173–175
  changing flash-sync speed, 175–176
  compensation, 179
  controlling Speedlite from camera,
    181–183
  locking exposure, 180
  second-curtain sync, 176–177
  wireless control of slaves, 183–186
focus
  changing mode in Quick Control menu,
    100–101
  locking, 137–138
  macro photography, 201
  manual, 58
  off-center objects, 57
  photographing horse racing, 267
  selective, 200
  switch for, 58
  using Live View, 98–100
  in viewfinder, 21
folders
  creating, 71–72
  file-numbering method, 73–74
  selecting, 72–73
grid display, 152–153
HDR, 242–246
of horse racing
  overview, 267
  setting up camera, 267
  troubleshooting, 269–270

image size and, 66
ISO speed
  button for, 9
  extending range of, 172–173
  freezing action, 191
  Full Auto mode and, 105
  Handy Pad and, 112
  High ISO Speed Reduction, 143–144
  on LCD monitor, 18
  photographing animals, 202
  photographing fast-moving objects, 189
  photographing landscapes, 195
  Programmed Auto Exposure mode
    and, 123
  Safety Shift and, 140
  setting, 171–172
  using Quick Control Screen, 90
  in viewfinder, 21
of landscapes
  overview, 194–196, 273
lens flicker reduction, 150–151
locking focus, 137–138
macro photography, 201
making tripod, 256
Manual mode, 130–131
metering overview, 121
multiple exposures, 246–250
of people/pets, 198–199
picture styles, 160–162, 226–228
previewing images
  deleting images, 83–87
  image review time, 81
  LCD monitor brightness, 81–83
  magnifying images, 79–80
  overview, 78–79
  rotating images, 87–88
  viewing as slide show, 90–93
  viewing images side by side, 80
  viewing on TV, 93
protecting images, 88–89
Quick Control Screen, 89–90
reading histogram, 77–78
red-eye reduction, 60–61
Shutter Priority mode, 128–129

shutter speed
  camera modes and, 56
  capturing fast-moving objects, 189
  defined, 54–55, 122
  displaying shooting information, 106
  Full Auto mode and, 105
  Handy Pad and, 112
  horse racing, 270
  image sharpness and, 56
  on LCD monitor, 16
  photographing animals, 202, 265
  photographing birds, 205
  photographing sporting events, 262
  in viewfinder, 21
of sunsets, 196–197
triggering shutter remotely, 62–63
using level, 153–154
using Live View
  aspect ratio, 102, 103–104
  continuous shooting using, 103
  displaying grid, 101–102
  displaying shooting information,
    97–98
  exposure simulation, 103
  focusing using, 98–100
  metering timer, 103
  overview, 96–97
  photographing people and pets, 199
  Quick Control menu in, 100–101
  switch for, 10
using Self-Timer, 61–62
using two memory cards, 118–121
using viewfinder
  adjusting clarity of, 22
  defined, 12
  display information on, 19–21
  for shooting video, 45
  using LCD monitor versus, 21
visualizing images, 211
while recording video, 109
white balance, 164–165
Tamron, 201
TC-80N3 timer remote controller, 42
telephoto lenses
  apertures of, 55

defined, 25
freezing action, 191
photographing birds, 206
photographing fast-moving objects, 188
photographing people and pets, 198
stabilizing camera
  using Mirror Lockup, 204–205
  using Self-Timer, 203
temperature, camera, 97
Think Tank Photo, 43
third-party batteries, 34
time exposures
  defined, 122
  photographing, 131–133, 252–254
time zone, 29
time-lapse videos, 250–252
timer remote controller, 42
timers
  Bulb Timer
    on LCD monitor, 18
    time exposures using, 252–254
  Interval Timer, 250–252
  metering timer, 103
  Self-Timer
    in auto mode, 61–62
    Interval Timer, 250–252
    on LCD monitor, 16
    stabilizing camera using, 203
    taking pictures using, 61–62
    tripods and, 256
    using Quick Control Screen, 90
  timer remote controller, 42
tripods
  choosing, 43–44
  image stabilization and, 24
  level, dual-axis, 153–154
  macro photography, 201
  making, 256
  for shooting video, 44, 113
  using Mirror Lockup, 204–205
  using Self-Timer, 203
troubleshooting
  animals, 266
  city skylines, 272
  horse racing, 269–270

troubleshooting *(continued)*
  sporting events, 264
Tungsten white balance mode, 164
TV, viewing images on, 93
Tv mode. *See* Shutter Priority mode

• U •

UDMA (Ultra Direct Memory Access),
    109, 113
USB port, 27

• V •

vantage point, 215, 270
VGA (Video Graphics Array), 108
videos
  accessories for shooting, 44–45
  audio recording options, 110–111
  best practices, 112–113
  dimensions for, 107–109
  displaying shooting information,
    106–107
  editing, 228–230
  frame rate, 107–109
  Handy Pad, 112
  recording, 105–106
  taking picture while recording, 109
  time-lapse, 250–252
  using Quick Control menu, 109–110
  viewfinder for, 45
viewfinder
  adjusting clarity of, 22
  defined, 12
  display information on, 19–21
  for shooting video, 45
  using LCD monitor versus, 21
VisibleDust, 39
visualizing images, 211

• W •

Warning icon
  on LCD monitor, 18
  in viewfinder, 19
web-quality pictures
  from Photoshop Lightroom, 260
  resolution for, 66
white balance
  bracketing, 17, 170–171
  button for, 10
  color temperature, 165–166
  compensation, 168–170
  custom, 166–168
  on LCD monitor, 16
  setting, 164–165
  using Live View, 97
  using Quick Control Screen, 90
  in viewfinder, 19
White Fluorescent white balance
    mode, 165
wide open shooting, 126, 198
wide-angle lenses, 25, 55, 196
wild animals, 265
wind filter, 110, 111
windy conditions, 246
winnowing, 88
wireless controller, 41
wireless Speedlite control, 182, 183–186

• Z •

Zagg, 44
zone autofocus, 157–158
zoo animals, 205
zooming
  lenses for, 25–26
  option for Speedlites, 182
  viewing photos, 13, 79–80

About the Author

Doug Sahlin is an author and photographer living in Venice, Florida. He's written books about computer applications such as Adobe Flash and Adobe Acrobat. He's also written books about digital photography and co-authored 13 books about such topics as Adobe Photoshop and Adobe Photoshop Elements. Recent titles include *Digital Landscape and Nature Photography For Dummies*, *Digital SLR Shortcuts and Settings For Dummies*, *Canon EOS 7D For Dummies*, *Canon EOS 6D For Dummies*, and *Canon EOS Rebel SL1/100D For Dummies*. Many of his books have been bestsellers on Amazon.

Doug is president of Doug Plus Rox Photography, a wedding, event, and fine-art photography company. Doug teaches Adobe Acrobat to local businesses and government institutions. He also teaches Adobe Photoshop and Adobe Photoshop Lightroom at local photography stores.

Dedication

Dedicated to my wife, Roxanne, the love of my life and one of the most creative photographers on the planet.

Author's Acknowledgments

Thanks to Acquisitions Editor Steve Hayes for making this book a possibility. Special thanks to Project Editor Katharine Dvorak for making sure my text is squeaky clean with no grammatical errors. Thanks to Technical Editor Scott Proctor for making sure the book is technically accurate. Many thanks to the other members of the Wiley team for taking the book from concept to fruition.

Thanks to agent extraordinaire Margot Hutchison for ironing out the contractual details. Many thanks to Canon for creating some of the greatest cameras on the planet. Special thanks to my friends and family. Kudos to my wife, Roxanne, for putting up with my late nights and occasional mood swings when I'd written one more page than I should have for the day. And thanks to our furry kids, Niki and Micah, for their love, affection, and comic relief.

Publisher's Acknowledgments

Acquisitions Editor: Steve Hayes

Project Editor: Katharine Dvorak

Technical Editor: Scott Proctor

Editorial Assistant: Claire Brock

Sr. Editorial Assistant: Cherie Case

Project Coordinator: Patrick Redmond

Cover Image: ©iStock.com/Jeremy Edwards